D0930584

THE
PSYCHOTHERAPIST'S
INTERVENTIONS

Diane J Antman MD

THE PSYCHOTHERAPIST'S INTERVENTIONS

Integrating Psychodynamic Perspectives in Clinical Practice

T. Byram Karasu, M.D.

JASON ARONSON INC.
Northvale, New Jersey
London

The author gratefully acknowledges the permission of the Association for the Advancement of Psychotherapy to reprint material from the following sources:

"A Developmental Metatheory of Psychopathology," by T. B. Karasu, *American Journal of Psychotherapy* 48:581–599, 1994.

"Transtheoretical Practice of Psychotherapy," by T. B. Karasu, *American Journal of Psychotherapy* 49:484–503, 1995.

This book was set in 11 pt. Berkeley by Alpha Graphics of Pittsfield, New Hampshire.

Library of Congress Cataloging-in-Publication Data

Karasu, Toksoz B.
  The psychotherapist's interventions : integrating psychodynamic perspectives in clinical practice / T. Byram Karasu.
      p.   cm.
  Includes bibliographical references and index.
  ISBN 1-56821-689-0 (alk. paper)
  1. Psychotherapy. 2. Personality development. 3. Psychotherapist and patient. I. Title.
  [DNLM: 1. Psychotherapy. 2. Psychological Theory. 3. Personality Development.   WM 420 K178p 1998]
  RC480.5.K359 1998
  616.89'14—dc21
  for Library of Congress   97-42382

Printed in the United States of America on acid-free paper. Jason Aronson Inc. offers books and cassettes. For information and catalog write to Jason Aronson Inc., 230 Livingston Street, Northvale, New Jersey 07647-1731. Or visit our website: http://www.aronson.com

Contents

Acknowledgments

For this book as well as my prior book, *Deconstruction of Psychotherapy*, I have received enormous help from many individuals. I owe much to the conscientious and congenial staff of Jason Aronson: Norma Pomerantz, administrative assistant, Judith Cohen, senior production editor, and Lee Kassan, copyeditor, during the various stages of production. I also want to express here my belated gratitude to Lee for his careful copyediting of *Deconstruction of Psychotherapy*.

For her invaluable assistance in the long, arduous, and meticulous task of bringing my raw material into an eminently readable format, I am most grateful to Ms. Betty Meltzer. Without her enduring dedication, steady attention to even the most minute details, and sustained intellectual engagement, this book could not have become a reality.

To Josephine Costa and Hilda Cuesta, I am indebted for all their hard work, which involves and exceeds typing, retyping, xeroxing, corresponding with good humor, their unsurpassed competence, and genuine affectionate presence.

T. Byram Karasu, M.D.

Introduction

The theme of this book, the psychotherapist's *interventions*, represents my preferred term for the critical activities of therapists vis-à-vis their patients; it is deliberately distinguished here from the application of other familiar descriptors, such as techniques, strategies, procedures, or maneuvers. Whereas all of these words broadly refer to a specific set of skilled steps or operations performed by the clinician, the latter terms tend either to imply a form of impersonal manipulation that may be more artifice than artistry or, in the service of science, can connote an operational and objective but static situation, as if the methods themselves were independently devised and divorced from their recipients. A significant aspect seems to be missing, to wit, that the clinician does not simply employ certain technical postures and practices, but selectively enters the psyche of the patient as a significant presence within a highly complex human relationship.

Rather, the use of the word *interventions* better addresses my view of psychotherapy as, first and foremost, a mutual interaction. It is both an interpersonal dialogue and an intersubjective phenomenon in which the two participants always act in counterpoint. As a recent paradigm, an intersubjective view "seeks to illuminate phenomena that emerge within a specific psychological field constituted by the intersection of two subjectivities" (Atwood and Stolorow 1984, p. 41). This means that, unlike other methods of inquiry that rely upon internal intrapsychic mental events per se or that are expressly concerned with external behavioral events, this psychotherapeutic interplay reflects a continual convergence of the reciprocal worlds of helper and recipient, observer and observed. Thus the practice of psychotherapy constitutes a *dual developmental* process that is constantly constructed and changed by both parties in tandem.

More specifically, in its grammatical form as an active verb, the term of the title expressly pertains to the clinician's crucial function within the therapeutic endeavor—to *intervene*—defined as "to occur, fall, or come between points of time or events" (Webster 1989, p. 633). What is most pertinent here is that it aims at the critical crossroads at which therapist and patient are meant to meet. In great brief, it highlights the careful clinician's particular portals of entry into the therapeutic process, while exploring the recipient's responses to these salient moments. The issue of temporality is also tapped, which captures my concerns not only with what the psychotherapist does or says vis-à-vis the patient, but *when* he chooses to say (or not say) it. This is critically connected, of course, with the meaning and *timing* of the patient's specific communications in light of the dyadic encounter as an ongoing bidirectional phenomenon.

On the basis of the above, this book contains clinical material on the practice of psychotherapy with a large range of persons and problems, along with detailed descriptions of verbal exchanges during selected sessions, which are the heart of the text. Excerpts of verbatim dialogue are offered to articulate the course of psychotherapeutic interaction as a successive series of co-created communications. At the same time, not only the patient's reactions, but *explanations* of the therapist's responses—precisely why he said what he said at the particular time that he said it—have been included to provide the critical line of clinical thinking as it was actually occurring. These explicit explanatory commentaries, which are interwoven throughout the course of the text, openly inform the reader of the practitioner's rationale for the particular stand taken (for better or for worse) at each moment of the therapeutic process. They provide an intimate vehicle through which to listen to, and understand, the clinician's inner voice during real-life psychotherapy practice. Such clinical recognition can effectively be used in the future—like the developmental process itself—to mend the mistakes of the past.

Simultaneously, the book addresses the need to bridge clinical theory with the practice of psychotherapy by using an "experience-near" conceptualization of patients that is close to the practitioner's actual work. It transcends traditional diagnostic classifications, while addressing the entire spectrum of standardized entities from the neuroses to borderline personality and self disorders. It also reflects different and complementary theoretical viewpoints by drawing upon several major contributions to psychodynamic psychotherapy—drive, ego, object relations, and self theories—and by focusing upon the developmental orientation that undergirds all of these psychotherapeutic conceptualizations.

As such, a fourfold matrix of developmental descriptors—*dyadic deficit, dyadic conflict, triadic deficit,* and *triadic conflict*—is presented as the fundamental foundation for understanding patient interaction and for implementing respective regimens. More specifically, this means that individuals in treatment (in parallel to the therapeutic process that ensues) are viewed in maturational terms, based upon early needs, wishes, and fears, and on relationship patterns at various phases of development. These in turn serve as a template of adult behavior and psychopathology both outside and within the psychotherapy situation. This developmental model represents an integration of two predominant paradigms of dynamic therapy today—conflict and deficit—interfaced with a synthesis of significant preoedipal and oedipal influences in contemporary thinking—triadic (father–mother–child) and dyadic (mother–child) interactions in the complex making of the self.

Such a perspective sets the stage for a wide assortment of interventions and types of interpersonal bond with the therapist. As the clinician continually searches for the best balance between frustrating the fantasied desires and meeting the real needs of each patient, or between providing "optimal restraint" (Lichtenberg 1989) and offering "optimal responsiveness" (Bacal 1985), he can call upon a virtual panoply of options that may be as diverse as the individuals themselves. This encompasses a spectrum of expressive (uncovering) and supportive (strengthening), cognitive and affective approaches; these may also combine major mutative agents that are intrapsychic (i.e., insight) and/or intersubjective (i.e., empathy). At bottom, however, the therapeutic thrust is always toward establishing contact based on the patient's pattern of relatedness and on sustaining thereafter a resonant relationship. In the totality of treatment, complex and diverse dialogues are explored as they arise, and corresponding responses to each successive interaction are introduced selectively and integratively—toward the psychotherapist's intricate design of individually tailored interventions.

The case excerpts in this book are based, in whole or in part, on actual dialogues from my psychotherapy practice. Any deliberate departures from the original have been made only in the interests of patient privacy.

Part I

A Developmental Perspective

1

The Developmental Model

A developmental model is the fundamental framework used here for integration of the prevailing psychodynamic schools that have attempted to explore and explain human psychopathology. It holds as its pivotal premise that major maturational changes, which have their critical precursors in childhood, successively occur throughout the life cycle. These thenceforth serve as significant stimuli in establishing and sustaining necessary inner structures along the course of psychic organization (or disorganization) and adaptation (or maladaptation). This also includes the notion of development as a phasic phenomenon, which means that maturational markers make their particular appearance across a stage-related spectrum; this refers to a relatively regular, but by no means intractile, timetable. Moreover, the frequently used concept of *developmental lines* (A. Freud 1963), which suggested a series of predictably linked psychic units, may warrant modification both visually and conceptually. A linear picture may be better replaced by a more irregular graphic trajectory—a complexity of intersecting contours, and detours, in the shaping and reshaping of the psyche.

Reflecting different vantage points and levels of abstraction on the ladder between clinical observation and ideological formulation, this particular perspective serves as a tool in the creation of an orienting and systematizing model for theory as well as treatment. Whereas such collective constructs may sometimes be seen as far removed from direct data, this work addresses the need for an integrative model on two counts: to both transcend unduly disparate theories and to bridge the gap between the theoretical and the technical by positing an experience-near conceptualization. It thus serves as an initial step towards rapprochement of eclectic approaches to conceptual and clinical phenomena. As an integrative orientation it veers away from monolithic viewpoints and their polarization and, instead, towards unity that embraces diversity in theory (and practice). It proffers the prospective synthesis of separate schools and their most salient contributions by conceptualizing simultaneously in multiple perspectives, and by shifting and sharing, in whole or in part, from one to another frame of reference.

As a developmental framework, it proposes that complex clinical phenomena are reflective of a range of different significant events and stages in the evolution of the individual, which denotes what has transpired in the intrapsychic and interpersonal life of the individual—and what hasn't happened—for subsequent selfhood. This refers to what may be missing or lacking (based on deficiencies from the early inner and outer environments) and later arrests (regressions and fixations to prior periods), as well as unresolved or unexpressed urges (derived from infantile drives and desires) and the protective or adaptive mechanisms utilized in their behalf (defenses and compromise formations erected against them). It has as its central foci the ways in which crucial developmental tasks have been negotiated on the complex passage, and ofttimes wayward path, to adult psychopathology. As Tyson and Tyson (1990) succinctly state:

> the developmental perspective includes not only an investigation of internal conflict and the infantile neuroses but also takes into account the origin and development of the psychic structures that contribute to adaptation. . . . the developmental perspective looks forward with a focus on the process of psychic structure formation; that is, it con-

siders how psychic structures and functions come about from the combined influence of innate givens, maturational sequences, and individual experiences to contribute to the ever more complicated labyrinth of intrapsychic life. [pp. 21–22]

Developmental Models of Psychopathology: The Conflict/Deficit Duality

Competing crosscurrents of developmental thinking have simultaneously given rise to two predominant psychodynamic paradigms of theory and therapy today. An unresolved debate over conflict and deficit models represents the culmination of nearly a century of internecine conceptual controversy over the etiology and evolution of individual development. In encapsulated form, the original *conflict model* primarily pivots upon intrapsychic drives and ego defenses based on repressed memories and distortions of the past, whereas the *deficit model* places its crucial focus on the creation and destruction of the self structure based on real experiences and traumas in primary relationships. The former theorizes intrapsychic clashes among unconscious forces of the mind, especially repressed sexual drives and the defensive and adaptive mechanisms that guard against them (i. e., formation of the neuroses) (Freud 1933) or, in more recent theoretical expansion to earlier, archaic beginnings, proposes a primitive splitting between object love and hate in order to deal with unconscious aggression, oral envy, and rage (i. e., formation of borderline personality disorder) (Kernberg 1975).

The extension to severe character pathology embodies the broadened view that unconscious intrapsychic conflicts are not simply struggles between impulses and defenses, but denote two opposing units or sets of internalized object relations. Such psychopathology is thus composed of a defensive constellation of self and object representions directed against an opposite (and often dreaded) repressed self and object representation (Kernberg 1984). These conflict-based conceptualizations have been contrasted to a deficit model, which postulates early environmental events of interpersonal insufficiency, especially lack of affective attunement between the original caregiver and the infant, in the defective development of the self (Kohut 1971). With the arrival of the latter thesis, the new psychopathological onus is no longer placed on frustrated libidinal fantasies of oedipal origin within a triangular struggle, as the *repressed* patient desires—or rivals—the paternal parent; rather, it is attributed to traumatic failures of empathic responsiveness within the preoedipal mother–child ambience, as the *deprived* patient yearns for unmet maternal mirroring and merger (Kohut 1977).

These pivotal positions, which encompass a complexity of significant developmental influences on the psyche, have also been viewed as a chronology of separate psychologies for depicting basic human motivation and the resultant ills that befall man. Two preeminent types have been posed, each evolving out of a different historical period within the temper of the respective times. An earlier prototype, termed *guilty man,* embodies the search for gratification of hidden and forbidden sexual longings, whereas a later prototype, termed *tragic man,* expresses the basic striving for cohesion of a fragmented or missing self (Kohut 1977). Put more pragmatically in clinical practice terms, it has been noted that "The patient of today suffers most under the problem of what he might . . . be or become, while the patient of earlier [days] suffered most under inhibitions which prevented him from being . . . who he thought he knew he was" (Erikson 1963, p. 279).

In addition, this dichotomous theme has been applied to an overriding diagnostic duality: *neuroses* (pertaining to less disturbed patients) versus *personality and characterological disorders* (pertaining to more disturbed patients). Thus the traditional understanding of the etiology of psychological ailments in terms of the unfulfillment of yesterday's yearnings (i. e., the competing consequences of intrapsychic drives along with their protective ego defenses) is being compounded or replaced by the repercussions of today's traumas (i. e., interpersonal/ environmental failures and flaws of object relations and self structure). At the same time, the historical source of psychopathology long attributed to *oedipal* events (i. e., rivalrous wishes and castration fears that have their height at age 2 to 5 years) (Freud 1905) has been similarly supplanted by the salience of *preoedipal* ones (i. e., yearning for infantile bliss

through union, but beset by deficits in the primary object bond beginning at birth) (Fairbairn 1952, Guntrip 1961).

The conflict–deficit dichotomy has been framed in yet other terms,
representing a pervasive shift from an *intrapsychic* to an *intersubjective*
perspective in theory and treatment. The former is defined and bounded
by the limits of the individual psyche, as classically examined by the
objective psychotherapist. In comparison, the latter orientation focuses
on the interplay between the different inner worlds of the two participants of the psychotherapy endeavor. It takes a position within, rather
than outside of, the dyadic unit of study. The more recent observational
focus is thus a deliberate departure from a strictly scientific stance, based
instead on the psychological field constituted by the combined context
of separately organized subjectivities of patient and therapist. What is
more, this orientation is presumed to mirror the earlier intersubjectivity
between child and caretaker. Stolorow, Atwood, and Brandchaft (1994)
have recently contrasted these past and present therapeutic paradigms
as follows:

> The central metaphor of the traditional . . . paradigm is the isolated
> mental apparatus achieving compromises between conflicting inter-
> nal forces. Its vocabulary is one of endogenous drive and instinctually
> determined unconscious fantasy—words referring to intrapsychic
> processes presumed to originate within the mind of the patient. The
> central metaphor of the new . . . paradigm is the larger relational
> system or field in which psychological phenomena crystallize and in
> which experience is continually and mutually shaped. [The latter
> vocabulary] is one of interacting subjectivities, reciprocal mutual
> influence, . . . attunements and malattunements—a lexicon attempt-
> ing to capture the endlessly shifting . . . intersubjective context of . . .
> experience, both in the course of the [therapeutic] situation and in
> the course of psychological development. [pp. ix–x]

The evolution of such ostensible dualism has also wrought a related phenomenon: a marked change in the relative significance of classic *father–mother–child* impact versus core *mother–child* influences on
infant and adult development. In examining the evolution of psycho-

therapy, Wright (1991) has recently observed that psychoanalytic work has made

> a major distinction between two-person and three-person relation-
> ships. . . . It started with three-person relationships and the discov-
> ery by Freud of the Oedipus Complex. . . . Only after this situation
> had been thoroughly worked through did psychoanalysis push back
> into the area of two-person relationships and all that had to do with
> the founding and development of the self and the beginnings of psy-
> chic life. [p. 112]

In this regard, laboratory-based and naturalistic home-observational research studies of infant–caregiver bonds have found that both forma-tive configurations of infant–mother and infant–father are crucial; they are considered qualitatively distinct and independent, the former cen-trally concerned with attachment needs (i. e., felt security), the latter with affiliative ones (i. e., social stimulation and socialization) (Bridges et al. 1988). Contemporary experimental and clinical investigation of the infant further affirms that early developmental structuring becomes the fundamental foundation for two-person versus three-person rela-tionships (and even, two- and three-person patients in psychotherapy) (Wright 1991). The integration of childhood precursors of psychopa-thology here likewise encompasses the basic notion that the maturational templates upon which significant relationships are patterned are differ-entially determined by early maternal and/or paternal influences on the infant and the implicit interactions amongst them.

Moreover, these diagnostic and developmental distinctions have had direct implications for the nature of psychotherapy practices. They broadly coincide with significant therapeutic changes in the parameters of psychodynamic treatment since its classic analytic beginnings—from expressive to supportive strategies (Karasu 1995); from the pivotal vehicle of insight (Schonbar 1964) to that of empathy (Basch 1983) as a critical agent of change or cure; and, in terms of major techniques, from a dispassionate therapist's interpretation and confrontation of a pri-marily advanced (i. e., erotic) transference (Greenson 1967), to a respon-sive therapist's replacement of sustaining self-objects within a largely primitive (i. e., narcissistic) transference (Kohut 1977) (see also Chapter 3). In sum, all of the above divisions have served to sharpen the schism between the deficit (defect or deficiency)* versus conflict camps.

TOWARD AN INTEGRATIVE DEVELOPMENTAL MODEL

In keeping with the above bifurcations but implying their coexistence, Dorpat (1976) has delineated two models of the mind: a "higher" tripartite model of id, ego, and superego, and a "lower" object relations model that occurs prior to it. While Kohut's (1977) global proposal of separate psychologies represented the irreconcilable impact on man of a sociocultural succession of events (which in turn led to discernible differences in the etiology and clinical characteristics between an inhibited versus alienated self), Dorpat's model relates to a compatible progression of two successive stages of individual development (which together comprise the psyche's internal architecture).

A dualistic but potentially integrative stance also has been occurring with regard to the patient's presenting profile. It has been emphasized that looking at sheer symptomatology does not suffice. "At a minimum, it remains to be established whether intrapsychic conflict (neurosis) or developmental arrest (selfobject relationship disorder) is responsible for the symptom picture" (Basch 1980, p. 169). In a similar vein, Stolorow and Lachmann (1980), who started with the conflict/ deficit dual line of thinking, have elaborated upon a complex confluence of their subtle and often masked manifestations. Their clinical examination of developmental arrests has elucidated a crucial distinction between two types of mental activity: defenses that primarily function protectively to ward off conflicts (within a well-established psychic struc-

---

*The terms *defect* and *deficit* (or deficiency) are often used synonymously in the literature. However, I prefer to distinguish them as follows: the former term is applied here to mean that an innate structure or function is faulty (comparable to the hardware of a computer), the latter to mean that an extrinsic part is not sufficient or is missing (comparable to the software of a computer). Pine (1990) makes a similar distinction by suggesting that a defect refers to something that is not working well (usually within the person) whereas a deficit involves an insufficiency of input (from the surround) (p. 200).

ture) as compared to those manifestations that predate them (at a prestage of defensive development), which are vestiges of structural voids and defects.

These authors especially emphasize the importance of the clinician's capacity to distinguish between those phenomena that principally serve to guard against contents of intrapsychic struggles, and seemingly similar phenomena that are more accurately understood as remnants of an arrest occurring prior to the establishment of defensive foundations, that is, characterized by deficiencies in the structuralization of the representational world. They suggest that this fundamental discernment is relevant to a host of duplicitous symptoms and syndromes, from grandiosity to grief, whose origins in deficit (defect) *or* defense are frequently deceptive to the therapist. For example, detachment (as well as its presumed polar opposite, promiscuity) can be the result of either an early developmental failure of attachment or a later instance of defensive avoidance of interpersonal contact (Pine 1990). Similarly, grandiosity may reflect an early defect in the ability to affirm the real qualities of the self or, with the subsequent establishment of an unimpaired self, can constitute a defensive denial of one's vulnerability (Stolorow and Lachmann 1980).

Along with the importance of the clinical differentiations and deceptions between deficit and conflict phenomena, others have emphasized their inevitable coexistence. Pine (1990) has demonstrated their natural overlap or interface. He suggests that both can occur simultaneously in actual psychic life; they need not, indeed do not, preclude one another. Trauma due to empathic failure by the parental figure does not exempt the child from the simultaneous experience of conflict-based ambivalence toward that significant other. Eagle (1984) emphasizes that these two sources of psychopathology are intertwined and not incompatible, insofar as developmental deficiencies may influence the capacity to deal with conflict, while unresolved conflicts may in turn be precursors that trigger developmental regressions or arrests.

Working with patients having impediments to success, for example, Fogel (1994) has shown how this particular problem can involve conflicts that compound deficit phenomena, or the reverse. Fear and guilt over sexual and aggressive wishes may impose incompatible goals that result in the patient's sense of failure. Alternatively, libidinal desires and rivalrous feelings may be secondary to an already existing developmental defect, and are thus byproducts of or attempts to repair an empty or shattered self. It is thereby suggested that either combined clinical scenario is possible: competitive striving can camouflage an insecure or deficient self, while feelings of emptiness and inadequacy may also serve to ward off dangerous and conflictual aggressive or erotic affect. In short, conflicts and deficits may not only augment one another but, taken together, necessarily constitute a form of double jeopardy. As Eagle (1984) has deftly depicted it, "We are most conflicted in the areas in which we are deprived. . . . It is precisely the person deprived of love who is most conflicted about giving and receiving love" (p. 130).

In a related vein, it has been proposed that the intersubjective perspective itself is integrative, by closing the gap between those theorists who emphasize the social determinants of personality development and those who place priority upon the private world of fantasy and feelings (Atwood and Stolorow 1984). Moreover, the two paradigms are most recently merged in combined terms, suggesting that

> the specific intersubjective contexts in which conflict takes form are those in which central affect states of the child cannot be integrated because they fail to evoke the requisite attuned responsiveness from the caregiving surround. Such unintegrated affect states become the source of lifelong conflict, because they are experienced as threats both to the person's established psychological organization and to the maintenance of vitally needed ties. [Stolorow et al. 1994, p. 6]

Given their separable as well as inseparable qualities, this book will explore the respective roles of conflict and deficit along a diagnostic spectrum that extends from neurotic to personality and character pathology of varying types. Within the developmental framework of the two presumably competing models are four broad theoretical orientations (i. e., drive, ego, object, and self). This foursome, which has formed the multifaceted foundation of psychodynamic thought since Freud, is also grist for the integrative mill. Viewed individually, their vantage points, as well as the substantive phenomena they address, differ. Taken together, they are said to encompass "urges (in the drive psychology); modes of adaptation and defense (in the ego psychology); relationships and their internalization, distortion, and repetition (in the object relations psychology); and phenomena of differentiation and boundary formation, of personal agency and authenticity, and of self-esteem (in the self psychology)" (Pine 1990, p. 4). As such, each of these models emphasizes differing—but potentially complementary—developmental precursors to psychopathology, and respectively refers to a particular attempt to understand the complex structure, function, and maturational processes of the human psyche in sickness and in health.

Every age also has brought with it favored schools or ideologies that have explicitly or implicitly challenged and competed with their predecessors and peers. In fact, my prior investigation of this subject, which viewed these major theories of psychopathology in historical sequence, revealed that their chronological order was parallel to a changing focus upon successive developmental phases and problems of patients. Specifically, an inverse relationship (i. e., developmentally reverse) prevailed: the earlier the theoretical formulation, the later the stage of child development that was addressed. Drive theory focused on the most mature developmental themes of sexuality and intimacy; ego theory dwelt on preceding maturational tasks of socialization and mastery; object relations theory harkened back to earlier themes of separation and individuation; and self theory turned its attention to the makings of the earliest infant attachment and dependency (Karasu 1994).

Furthermore, each theory of phase-related psychopathology has proffered particular scenarios that underlie respective developmentally derived disturbances. For example, drive theory is concerned with the source of patients' sexual anxiety, guilt, frustration, and inhibition; ego theory, with the malformation of ideals, moral standards, and prosocial values; object relations theory, with primitive, turbulent, and often aggressive relatedness to others; and self theory, with the most fundamental lack of cohesion, identity, and sense of worth. Taken together through maturational time, however, the four basic contributors to this conceptual quartet all nonetheless share scientific anchoring points in developmental psychology (Cooper 1987). In the final analysis, they can be considered simultaneous perspectives on the phenomena of mental life, not separate ones (Pine 1990).

In elaboration of the above, a fourfold matrix of developmentally based descriptors—*dyadic deficit, dyadic conflict, triadic deficit,* and *triadic conflict*—is presented as the basis for understanding psychopathology and adaptation across a broad clinical spectrum. These are viewed as spectrum phenomena insofar as they encompass not only different diagnostic types but degrees of disorder. They are based on major maturational issues and their respective origins and reappearances at different phases of development. A distinction is made between a *dyadic* (mother–child) or a *triadic* (father–mother–child) configuration, which is utilized to characterize the particular base of difficulties in early relationships and their mental representations for the patient during his or her formative years. The resultant failures further manifest as either *deficits* or *conflicts* vis-à-vis one or another set of significant figures. Finally, when viewed as a whole, the point must be made that these dyadic and triadic deficits and conflicts are not categorical distinctions, nor could they possibly be completely separate in real life. Rather, they comprise complex patterns that inevitably overlap and change with time—as does the developmental process itself, by definition.

2

Four Developmental
and Clinical Configurations

In attempting to understand formative developmental pathways, the notion of *attachment* emerges as a pivotal concept with both positive and negative connotations. In Bowlby's three-volume treatise on the subject, his attachment theory addressed the propensity of human beings to develop strong emotional bonds to significant others, and revealed how disruptions of these ties result in various forms of disturbance. In expressly exploring the interrelated phenomena of attachment (1969), separation (1973), and loss (1980), Bowlby saw this crucial chronology as a progressive developmental process towards intimacy. He also delineated three successive stages that occurred in infancy at the prospect of the primary figure's impending absence: a phase of *protest*, in which the infant loudly expresses his frustration and pain at threatened separation (see also Chapter 5); a phase of *despair*, in which the infant has begun to realize the reality of the loss; and a final phase of *detachment*, in which he has, albeit unwillingly, emotionally disconnected from the mothering figure as a way of fending off any resurgence of his earlier symbiotic feelings (see also Chapter 4). The emphasis here was on the significance of attachment for the infant and its effects forevermore, in Walant's (1995) contemporary term, the *indissoluble bond* (p. 1).

Moreover, Bowlby called into question the idea, proffered by prior theoretical thinking, that because the vicissitudes of attachment and dependency have been so closely linked with early infant behaviors, subsequent expressions of their return in later childhood, adolescence, and especially adulthood are thenceforth necessarily infantile or immature in nature. Rather, variations of these stages continue to reverberate throughout one's lifespan, and can be both enhancing and defensive. In fact, as Bowlby (1969) pointed out, "To dub attachment behavior in adult life regressive is indeed to overlook the vital role that it plays in the life of man from the cradle to the grave" (p. 208).

In a recent look at the psychopathology around creating the capacity for attachment, Walant (1995) suggests that there is an overvaluation on autonomy and separateness at the expense of the natural need for merger with mother; the latter does not stop beyond 2–3 years—nor should it; rather, it may normally last a lifetime. She has placed such a viewpoint in bold relief when she writes:

> Merger has been seen as a fusion state normal only to the early mother–infant dyad. The neonate cannot separate himself from his mother and therefore remains in a state of symbiotic bliss, comforted by her self-state, which protects his own. From this viewpoint, merger is seen as a dangerous threat to the burgeoning self of the infant; it encourages the child to remain fused and to seek only more moments of oneness. The child has no wish for self-actualization or self-mobilization because the symbiotic state is seen as heavenly. . . . [The] long-standing denial and devaluation of merger phenomena throughout the life cycle have actually increased the likelihood of [psychopathology] *at the expense* of attachment needs. [pp. 1–2]

Similarly, the point must be made that every developmental passage, however incremental, is always two-pronged. Indeed, each successive stage or step in the complex progression from infancy to adulthood can be construed as both gain and loss. As each person proceeds along the difficult road towards growth, one of the forks in the road forges forward to the future, by reinforcing the gratification from accomplishments that befit the overall developmental timetable; the other bends backward, reminding the person of the past and giving rise to his or her reluctant renunciation of prior pleasures. Depending upon the nature and extent of psychopathology, these maturational events can be accompanied by a relatively benign nostalgic wish, or more malignant regressive need, to recapture those satisfying experiences and objects of desire that are associated, in fantasy or in fact, with a preceding phase or prior point in time.

Taken further, different attachment and affectional bonds, in all their multifaceted variety and subtlety, are the initiating events linked to the ongoing goals of separation and individuation, security and intimacy vis-à-vis major caretaking figures. They are expressed here in the following developmental prototypes as well as enduring relationship patterns (see Chapter 3), as they make their repeated appearance across the diverse spectrum of maladaptation and healthy adaptation. Perhaps more important, the ways in which one negotiates these fundamental ties are reiterated and revisited as lifelong struggles to master the maturational tasks of life, outside of the therapeutic situation as well as within it.

DYADIC DEFICIT

Developmental Precursors

Maternal deprivation, marked by the failure, insufficiency, or loss of attachment of the mothering object, as experienced by the infant, is the critical maturational precursor to dyadic deficit. Here a physically or psychologically absent, unloving, or insecurely or inconsistently bonded maternal figure or its mental representation is associated with disturbances, disruptions, and/or distortions in the early mother–child relationship (Bowlby 1969, 1973, 1980, Fairbairn 1952, Mahler et al. 1975, Spitz 1946, Stern 1985, 1990, Winnicott 1958, Wright 1991). In this regard Ainsworth's (1979) infant–caregiver research has discerned significantly different patterns of bonding (secure vs. ambivalent or avoidant) based on an array of observed and self-reported characteristics of mother–baby interaction. This type of analysis has led to longitudinal studies documenting the temporal continuity of attachment-related processes and even the intergenerational transmission of attachment styles (Bretherton 1985, Main et al. 1985). In particular, the inability to be alone with another is attributed to insufficient infantile experiences alone with mother at the earliest phases of development (Winnicott 1965).

However, it is not the lack of the maternal object itself nor the infant's pressing need for soothing contact and engagement per se, but the *reciprocal* nature of their interaction that sets the stage for the sequence of events and behaviors that ensue. The predisposed baby not only reacts to the lack of expected stimulation, but identifies with the mother's emotional deficits; in turn, she may impute negative meaning to the vulnerable infant's insufficient or unsatisfactory responses and react in kind. This suggests that within the context of a highly sensitive mutual feedback process they share an "affect attunement" (Stern 1985, p. 137) and "intersubjective mindscape" (Stern 1990, p. 83), which reflect the synchronicity of their inner worlds.

These clinical and empirical findings relate to the earliest lines of development in the course of the infant's psychological birth as it continues to negotiate the perinatal tie: from a primary narcissistic state or an undifferentiated fusion to a series of subsequent substages of separation–individuation that have had their beginnings in the first year of life (A. Freud 1965, Mahler et al. 1975). Here oral drives and tensions can serve as an overriding organizing principle upon which the infant orders his or her earliest nurturing experiences in interface with the autonomous arena of "contact comfort" (Harlow 1958); these unconsciously create the pivotal need—and wish—to sustain their inseparability, to forevermore merge with mother.

Thus any interference with both regulatory and calming functions of satisfaction and support that encompass the formative offerings of drive reduction and oral need gratification (Freud 1905) as well as an "empathic-responsive" human milieu (Kohut 1977)—holding, loving, caring, soothing, comforting, feeding, admiring, and/or confirming—constitute environmental deficiencies that may produce developmental deficits and arrests in the child. In current validation of the above observations and studies, Stern's (1983) intricate examination of the interpersonal world of the infant, particularly the early development of schemas of self and other, has asserted that "powerful relations are not forged by feeding in comparison to experience sharing and complementing. . . . the experience of being hungry, getting fed, and going to sleep, even when associated with a particular person, does not lead to subjective intimacy with the feeding person unless accompanied by subject–object complementing and state sharing" (p. 79).

More specifically, it has been suggested that when the facilitating environment of the preoedipal dyad is not "good enough" (Winnicott 1965), a common constellation of symptoms or syndrome develops, including basic problems in abstracting, language, impulse control, and relating to others; and that from a phylogenetic point of view, these areas are the most recent evolutionary acquisitions and therefore the ones most vulnerable in human adaptation (Hansen 1985). Psychological consequences, which have been viewed as the end-product of mother's unsuccessful attempts to meet the infant's normal grandiose and idealizing needs to maintain a sense of security and protective union with a powerful "self-object" (Kohut 1971), can include deep feelings and fears of desertion and annihilation through abandonment, and difficulties or delays in the establishment of such fundamental requisites as self-esteem, a consistent and cohesive internal mental representation, tolerance of intense affect, and stability of object relationships—in short, elements in the origins of one's core identity and worth. This overall deficient self, representing the absence or breakdown of intrapsychic structure building and internalization, inevitably leaves such infants highly susceptible to later rejection and devaluation.

Clinical Characteristics

Clinical features of persons with dyadic deficit are related to the above underendowments and include such complaints and symptoms as clinging dependency, lack of stability in relations, lack of a sense of self, lack of hopeful expectations, yearning for affection, and profound feelings of unworthiness. Moreover, the aggression of such persons is either suppressed, accompanied by fear of retaliative abandonment, or self-directed and self-berating.

Persons with dyadic deficit have failed to develop an appropriate affective interest in the human world (Hansen 1985), as well as the ability to regulate their affective inner state. They are both emotionally needy of others in the external environment in order to feel safe, loved, and ultimately whole, and inaccessible to those outside themselves on whom the insufficient self relies. Across a range of behaviors, these self-deficient individuals often alternate between an aloof distancing and a discernible display of their contact-making and bonding difficulties (Adler 1986); in the therapeutic setting, they may cling to others, seeking safety in symbiosis, or behave in an unduly removed fashion, finding refuge in isolation (Stolorow and Lachmann 1980). Without the early foundations for a nuclear self, they are particularly prone to feelings of inner deadness and depression (Kohut 1977).

DYADIC CONFLICT

Developmental Precursors

Dyadic conflicts are reflective of separation–individuation and autonomy-related struggles toward the development of object constancy and consolidation of self-identity (Mahler et al. 1975). Due to the infant's utter reliance on the maternal object for survival and sustenance, destructive impulses or fantasies that threaten their relationship may be repressed; such repression of aggression itself can be pathogenic and result in intrapsychic conflict as well as contribute to a bad sense of self (Settlage 1990). Consistent with a view of preoedipal infantile dependency as a predominant potential agent around which later pathology revolves (Fairbairn 1952), these object relations struggles of dependence versus independence, or having control versus being controlled by another, occur during early miscarried interactions with the primary caretaker. More specifically, such dyadic experiences are frequently associated with the child's reciprocal relationship to an intrusive, demanding, and controlling mother with whom the infant may be in danger of being pathologically enmeshed; this in turn results in major fears of engulfment or rejection, as well as defenses erected against them, particularly "splitting" of the basic affects of love and hate, or of good and bad representations of self and others (Kernberg 1975). Such psychopathology often involves the use of primitive defenses to keep apart contradictory images of self and others and to fend against conflictual affects; similarly, a major intrapsychic thrust of the dyadic conflict person is to protect positive introjects from being overwhelmed by hostile ones (Waldinger and Gunderson 1984). Indeed, their predominant interpersonal responses are depicted as rageful reactions to an unrewarding object world (Glassman 1988).

In contrast to dyadic deficits primarily associated with the earliest oral or symbiotic phases of psychological maturation, these particular conflicts are thought to most closely correspond with the anal stage of psychosexual development (Freud 1905). Dyadic conflicts during this period are also associated with the child's efforts at "rapprochement" (Mahler et al. 1975) as he or she tries to bridge the gap between self and mother, in part wanting to be soothed by her and yet at the same time not able to accept her help (Karasu and Oberfeld 1989).

As a regulatory structure, the ego ideal is concomitant with the infant's earliest conscious awareness of separateness about the mother figure (Freud 1914, Jacobson 1964). This has been contrasted to the development of the superego, which has its rudiments later in the disciplinary experiences of the child and gains greater structural definition in the oedipal phase, from 3 to 5 or 6 years (Settlage 1990). Nunberg's (1955) comparison of the formation of the intrapsychic agencies of the ego-ideal versus the superego sheds light on the dynamics of dyadic conflict (compared to its triadic conflict counterparts): the crucial role of maternal expectations (vs. paternal prohibitions); the child being motivated by the need for love (vs. fear of punishment); having their respective origins on the basis of desired (vs. dreaded) figures; and in terms of implications for later manifestations of psychopathology, resultant bad feelings of inferiority (vs. guilt); (see also Chapter 7 on the triadic conflict patient). Here the crucial role of excessive maternal expectations and demands, coupled with the infant's need for love, lay the conflictual groundwork for unrealistic ego ideals that the growing child nonetheless strives to meet (Nunberg 1955).

Clinical Characteristics

Clinical features of persons with dyadic conflict are characteristically related to problems of dependence/independence, early intrusion/control frustrations, and unachievable ego ideals. Such patients have grandiose and unrealistic aspirations of self and others, and easily feel that they themselves are failing or that others are failing them. They regard themselves as disappointments to, or disappointed with, significant love objects about whom they feel a sense of intrusiveness, rejection, or betrayal. Based on a predominance of pregenital aggressive impulses, these patients' symptoms and complaints manifest in anger, rage, irritability, demanding dependency, and defiance, and have an accusation quality of projected hostility (e. g., litanies against others, including the therapist).

Although those with dyadic conflict psychopathology tend to have an arrogant exterior, they can also have a biting charm—their aggression is directed outwards, but only with limited success. At times their aggressiveness is temporarily self-directed to appease the perceived hostile parties, but most commonly it is used as a way of engaging others through confrontation or provocation. Real or fantasied failures compound such patients' sense of loss of control or of being controlled or, paradoxically, the feeling of having too much freedom. Since these persons are particularly prone to covert feelings as well as overt outbursts of negativity and hostility, they invariably experience profound problems in interpersonal relationships.

TRIADIC DEFICIT

Developmental Precursors

The physical or psychological inadequacy or actual absence of fathering from a primary paternal object who is either unavailable or unreliable (Abelin 1975, Earls and Yogman 1979, Forrest 1967, Jenkins and Boyer 1969/1970, Prall 1978, Siegman 1966) or, at the other end of the spectrum, chronic exposure or overstimulation by antisocial parents, especially a father who is abusive to the child and/or mother (Reid 1983, Shengold 1989, Stone 1989), generate triadic deficits in the child. Indeed, ample research evidence suggests that children who are quantitatively or qualitatively deprived of good fathering are significantly damaged by that deficiency (Henderson 1982). More specifically, whereas the father-absent child is bereft of opportunities for socialization, personal mastery, and power (Henderson 1982), the present but unrelating father becomes the prototype of a cold, alien, and unmanageable world (Forrest 1967); and the child with an antisocial or abusive father misidealizes a "negative hero" (Svravik et al. 1991). In particular, such insufficiency is regarded as a major developmental precursor to arrested or defective superego formation and faulty role model identification (Crumley and Blumenthal 1973); it is also considered contributory to disturbances in separation-individuation as well as in the establishment of core sexual identity and gender differentiation (Henderson 1982, Spieler 1984).

In consequence of such early paternal privation, this type of person as an adult tends not to believe in authority or societal values at large (e. g., religion, marriage and family, legal proscriptions) nor, during treatment, in the "rules" of the therapist (Ronningstam and Gunderson 1989). He or she often lacks the formation of prosocial ideals, which manifests as "global ethical poverty" (Svravik et al. 1991). Instead such individuals tend to hold only those minimal standards required for attaining the external rewards of life, however defined (e. g., financial success, material possessions, job status, power), which are then made the focus of one's life. In more severe psychopathology, the person may develop not simply an antisocial personality style of moral impoverishment and manipulation, with lack of emotional depth or sincerity and irresponsibility for one's actions (Harpur et al. 1989), but be morally deviant by identifying with and idealizing an antisocial father or other destructive significant person as an internalized "negative hero" (Svravik et al. 1991). Destructiveness thus can become a dominant self-concept that resides behind overt aggressive and antisocial acts. In this regard, the person with triadic deficit covers a narcissistic and antisocial spectrum of varying psychopathology and severity (Vaillant 1985), in which such patients may not only try to manipulatively seduce their environment but, more pathologically, actively attempt to destroy it (Svravik et al. 1991).

Individuals with triadic deficit will sometimes behave as if obeying the basic dicta of society, but this is primarily out of fear of being punished by external forces, not the manifestation of internalized guilt or its precursor, shame (Campbell 1989); this may occur despite their characteristic inability to learn from punishment (Svravik et al. 1991). Some may at least go through the motions of being committed to causes merely because of the desirability of such traits; in reality, they lack genuine commitment and do not engage honestly with others. This constitutes a form of "mock ethics," which, according to Svravik and colleagues (1991), is not seen in those antisocial patients at the most pathological side of the personality disorder spectrum.

Gender issues can also be problematic. If those persons with triadic deficit were fortunate enough to have had a "good enough" dyadic relationship with their mothers, they may manage to look for and get attached to one or more women (maternal objects). They will typically establish highly dependent relationships with females to supply their narcissistic needs, as well as to bolster their sense of self-worth. At the same time, identification with a negative hero as role model tends to significantly support and increase their self-esteem (Svravik et al. 1991). In this regard, the fathers of such patients are frequently exploitative, non-self-respecting men who also do not respect women and who devalue their wives. In return, the insecure wives cannot present themselves to their children as desirable sex objects (for boys) or as objects for identification (for girls). Thus, neither parent emerges from this scenario as an object of desire or as a model for healthy identification. The children end up not believing in the father as a good object or role model (and henceforth other father figures and representations), or glorifying the bad father and devaluing the mother (as well as other women and maternal substitutes). Of course, not just boys but "pre-oedipal girls need fathers" (Spieler 1984). It has been suggested that if the female's first significant relationship with a man (father) is one in which he is reliable, available, attuned, and nurturant, she is most apt to acquire a mental representation of him that is whole, realistic, and essentially good (Jacobson 1964); on the other hand, Spieler (1984) has observed that

> If her view of her father is fragmented or dichotomized (i. e., good or bad) because of deficits arising in her early relationship with him . . . she may fear entering the oedipal phase. As a result, she may remain in a preoedipal attachment to him and to her mother, or she may enter the oedipal phase both loving and hating or fearing him. . . . Unless these distortions in her view of him are corrected, she is likely to enter adulthood with both unrealistic expectations and deprecating and overidealizing views of men which will interfere with true intimacy. [p. 64]

(See also Chapter 7 on triadic conflict.)

Sexual identity may also be implicated. Here father's absence is crucial for boys in the preoedipal period with regard to core gender identity, and for girls in the oedipal period with regard to sex-appropriate masculine and feminine role differentiation (Henderson 1982).

Clinical Characteristics

Clinical features of persons with triadic deficit range from various typical sociopathic behaviors (e. g., destructiveness to others' property or person, truancy, lying, stealing, abandonment of job or family, pursuit of illegal occupations, sexual crimes) to milder forms of superego deficiency (i. e., manipulative, exploitative, unethical acts). More important, they tend to see prosocial behavior as an expression of weakness (Svravik et al. 1991). In the outside world, the less disturbed triadic deficit patients appear to function well, albeit deceptively; they adroitly exploit others sexually and financially, and maneuver whomever they can in obtaining esteem and power. They may establish a semblance of traditional respectability, while neglecting or abusing their families and children. Such patients express their aggression manipulatively to maintain the upper hand and for other secondary gains. They are superficially seductive with facile pseudo-intimacy, but in reality maintain no loyalty to family, friends, business associates, or acquaintances. Their acting-out disposition frequently gets them into difficulties with others and with the law.

TRIADIC CONFLICT

Developmental Precursors

Triadic conflicts are predominantly expressions of sexual (parental and sibling) rivalries, libidinal struggles, and gender anxieties, toward the attainment of mature sexuality. As a normal developmental phenomenon and potential precursor to psychopathology, this erotic, competitive, and often aggressive scenario has its origins during a characteristic constellation of intrapsychic events in both sexes, primarily manifest at the height of the phallic-oedipal phase of maturation (Freud 1905), or in Eriksonian terms, during a stage of "initiative vs. guilt" regarding locomotor and genital activities and goals (Erikson 1963). This generally refers to a period marked by an awakening sexual focus of interest, stimulation, and excitement, and, as a crucial phenomenon of unprecedented power, the Oedipus complex, whereby the child simultaneously strives for sexual union with the opposite-sex parental figure while wishing for the disappearance or death of the parent of the same sex. For Freud (1905), this constituted the nuclear conflict, "the culminating point of infantile sexuality, which through its after-effects decisively influences the sexuality of the adult" (p. 226). It generally applies to the young child from approximately age 2½ to 6 years, although it probably persists as a major unconscious organizer throughout life (Moore and Fine 1990). Within a crosscultural context, which encompasses certain civilizations where there is no onus on the father to exercise a repressive function (thus perhaps less fear of paternal retaliation), the oedipal paradigm still holds (Laplanche and Pontalis 1973); but here it is presumably the prohibition against incest itself that gives the oedipal situation its universality (Levi-Strauss 1969).

Conflict-laden wishes, longings, and other affective reactions, defenses, and compromise formations, having centered upon themes of merging and symbiotic union vs. separation and individuation within the dyadic situation (see Chapter 5 on dyadic conflict), as a triadic phenomenon pivot upon this classic theme of the child's longing for the opposite sex and jealousy of the same sex, accompanied by fear of retaliation (based on law of talion) due to forbidden incestuous wishes and parricidal urges or fantasies (Freud 1905). In addition, because of the need for maternal comfort or paternal protection that can coincide with oedipal desires, ambivalence inevitably occurs for fear of object loss and love. For both, this may at the same time include the noncompetitive need to surrender to the same-sex parent rather than compete against him or her. Triadic conflicts are thus predominantly expressions of sexual rivalries, libidinal struggles, and gender anxieties that are linked to the complex (and often ambivalent) connections of the father–mother–child triangle; these in turn influence sexual identification and internalization, choice of love object, and the overall nature of object relations between the sexes. Disguised substitutive expressions of forbidden desires and the defenses against ungratified wishes may accompany or be the consequence of sexual anxiety and guilt, which form the symptomatic signature of triadic conflict.

Disorders of the triadic relationship and its mental representations become conflict proper when both unacceptable wishes and internalized inhibitions are repressed. These sexual, assertive, and aggressive/submissive expressions, distortions, and disturbances of the triadic configuration—the parent preferring the spouse to the child or the child to the spouse, along with the other's retaliative anger and threats; the tendency to be seductive or to be seduced by the child, or alternatively, dismissal of the child's sexual interests; either discouraging initiative, assertion, and competition, or actively promoting aggression and rivalry —all lead to various underlying conflicts and their manifestations (or defenses against them). These may include problems of sexual gratification and adequacy, gender identity and role concerns, or reactive behaviors: excessive aggressiveness or submissiveness; fear of competition or its counterpart, fierce competitiveness; confusion or delay regarding an internal sense of masculinity/femininity; and an unresolved affective replay of excessive anxiety or guilt regarding the oedipal triangle with its contradictory urges, fears, and prohibitions.

Clinical Characteristics

Clinical features of the person with triadic conflict are related to phallic losses and aspirations or superego transgressions. Here wish/fear conflicts get played out in various scenarios of aggression/submission, competition/inhibition, and masculinity/femininity. The frustration engendered by phallic failures may generate feelings of gender inferiority and ineffectiveness, as the patient nonetheless wishes to be desirable, strong, and superior. Self-aggrandizing attitudes or aggressive activities can function as defense against, or overcompensation for, anxiety, while fear or disdain may serve to camouflage latent homosexual desires and gender confusion.

Rivalrous feelings juxtaposed with fears of competition, or invitations to intimacy in conjunction with sexual inhibition, may reiterate the earlier phallic scenario in which oedipal wishes and castration fears converge. At the same time, superego transgressions can cause anxiety, guilt, self-blame, and, consequently, an assortment of self-punishing behaviors. The morbid fear of failure in its manifold forms can also be accompanied by countervailing varieties of conflictual feelings, the impediments to potential achievement that signal an ambivalent or irrational fear of success (Fogel 1994). Indeed it has become almost classic for some patients with triadic conflict to come to treatment when (if not especially when) everything is going objectively well and their prospects for the future are expressly those of impending promise (Jong 1973).

3

Primary Relationship Patterns

It has long been suggested that neither the use of symptoms and syndromes nor adherence to specific schools of psychotherapy may be sufficient in designing psychotherapeutic strategies for a wide range of patients (Frances and Cooper 1981, Kohut and Wolf 1982, Pulver 1993). Kohut and Wolf (1982) have made the intriguing observation that "it was not the scrutiny of the symptomatology but the *process of treatment* [italics mine] that illuminated the nature of disturbance of . . . patients" (p. 44). Clinical and experimental studies of agents of change in psychotherapy throughout the ages have revealed that the relationship between therapist and patient is the supraordinate influence that transcends particular techniques (Frank and Frank 1991, Strupp and Hadley 1979). More specifically, it is the establishment of transference, or rather, the fundamental type of transference that is formed—classical (i. e., advanced) versus narcissistic or selfobject (i. e., primitive)—which has remained as perhaps the most telling dimension of patient evaluation and of the kind of therapy that ensues (Kohut and Wolf 1982, Kernberg 1982). These two expressions of patient relatedness, when viewed as maturational markers, continue to comprise critical transferential axes upon which all psychotherapeutic practice is pivoted (Stolorow and Lachmann 1984/1985, Lachmann and Beebe 1992).

Transcending Classical versus Self-object Transferences[1]

Historically, although the formation of a transference neurosis has generally been used to describe the unconscious constellation of events that projects the therapist into a position of unsurpassed regard and displaced desire in the patient's conflictual psychic life, Freud (1914) initially applied the term diagnostically to separate those patients who could, from those who could not, develop such an ardent and ambivalent attachment without further decompensation; he did not believe that the latter group (narcissistic neurosis) was treatable. Today, the increasing identification of severe character pathology has indicated that the intrapsychic structural organization of these patients may well be very different from their psychoneurotic counterparts.

However, instead of simply excluding these individuals from traditional treatment, current theory as well as therapy is represented by new techniques to accommodate such underlying differences, particularly ego disturbances of self-image, faulty self-esteem, and partial object relations, as well as primitive defense mechanisms of splitting and dissociation that often characterize their clinical picture (Kernberg 1982, Kohut 1977). For Kohut (1977), it denotes that two kinds of narcissistic (self-object) transference considered pathognomonic for self disorders are direct repetitions within therapy of very early infant–parent interactions—mirror transference, in which a faultily responded to need for acceptance and confirmation is revived; and idealizing transference, which recreates the patient's need to merge with a source of idealized strength. For Kernberg (1982) it means that atypical transference mani-

---

1. The term *narcissistic transference* (Kohut 1971) was later revised to *self-object transference* (Kohut 1977).

festations prevail, distinguished from more typical ones by being chaotic, contradictory, turbulent, and impulsive.

Stolorow and Lachmann (1980) have emphasized the critical importance of differentiating transferential disposition, not only initially but during the clinician's ongoing psychotherapy practice:

> The crucial diagnostic distinction [the therapist] must make at any given point in treatment is between a classical transference phenomenon in which he is primarily experienced as a separate, more or less differentiated and integrated whole object . . . and a primitive representational configuration in which he is predominantly experienced as an archaic, prestructural selfobject. [pp. 173–174]

More recently, it has been proposed that self-object and object-related transferences occupy a "figure and ground" position as dual dimensions of the therapist–patient relationship throughout treatment (Stolorow and Lachmann 1984/1985).

This in turn has been determined by early significant relationships throughout the course of the child's development. Wright's (1991) investigation of infant interaction (noted earlier), which suggested a chronological link between the history of psychoanalytic thought and the respective importance of parental dyadic (mother–child) and triadic (father–mother–child) influences, likewise has implications for treatment. He observed that one's early developmental structuring becomes the fundamental foundation for "two-person" versus "three-person" patients. Moreover, it has also been suggested that therapists themselves, due to their own earlier experiences and personality needs, may be prone towards a "maternal" (e.g., Winnicott, Kohut) or "paternal" (e.g., Freud, Kernberg) mode of relating (Adler 1986).

This chapter proposes that all patients have both dyadic and triadic stage-related psychopathology and corresponding relationship-oriented predispositions. Therefore the therapist has to be able to switch paradigms to flexibly accommodate different types of relatability (Karasu 1992a).

PATIENTS WITH DYADIC DEFICIT

Primary Relationship Pattern

Patients with dyadic deficit characteristically demonstrate an inability to make contact or establish and consolidate a stable relationship with the therapist. In reiteration of the earliest unavailability or inconsistency in infancy of a nurturing object, this deficiency is especially expressed in a highly ambivalent or, more often, avoidant bonding pattern (Ainsworth 1979). Such patients present to the clinician a sense of "absence," whereby one barely exists, easily disappears, or remains hidden or remote (Havens 1986). This inability to relate may also result in an overdependent dyadic deficit patient, who likewise defends against feelings of emptiness and abandonment; whereas the former reflects dread of annihilation from utter failure of union, the latter represents a "wish for reunion by clinging" (Masterson 1976, p. 42).

During treatment the patient invariably reexperiences the earlier complex of abandonment feelings, including depression, passivity and helplessness, and sense of void (Karasu 1992b, Masterson 1976). Although the patient may speak about past and present events, it is virtually without acknowledging the therapist's presence or showing natural curiosity about who he is or what he says. In fact, details about the particular therapist and specific verbalizations made are less relevant than the sense that something is being supplied. As Chessick (1977) has observed in the treatment of such patients, "The patient is not interested in words at all, any more than when the mother picks up the baby, the baby cares which lullaby the mother is singing" (p. 179).

Therapist's Stance

In order to merely make contact here, an empathic, unconditionally accepting therapist provides a reassuring presence, "a safe place" (Havens 1989), in which the clinician must maintain credibility as an extremely reliable person. Interventions are primarily geared to facilitate bonding to the therapist; they are not necessarily intended to generate insight. Moreover, insofar as the patient's low self-regard is mostly a matter of deficiency, not conflict, it will not change through interpretations of it. Rather, at the early attachment-inducing phase, interpretations purposely need to remain "inexact" (Glover 1955). These can be either partially incomplete by avoiding certain transferential dimensions, such as a need for merger, or partially incorrect by omitting certain threatening content areas, such as lack of a sense of self.

Once a rudimentary psychological attachment does occur, explorations may begin to focus on the feeling of not deserving more from the world and from the therapist, as well as on the patient's secondary gains in having deficits (e. g., perpetuating worthlessness and self-defeat in order to secure the therapist's love) (Beck et al. 1979). Subsequently, greater focus can be placed on the relationship with the mother (i. e., as unloving or unreliable in contrast to the patient's unlovability). Eventually, at the deepest level, he or she may be able to actually "experience the absence" (Kohut 1977, p. 123). Only then can the therapist make empathic interpretations[2] of the patient's primary gains associated with deficiencies (e. g., insecurity as a secure base, and helplessness as an anti-anxiety device, a tie to mother, a self-defining necessity, or merely to remain intact).

Common Countertherapeutic Responses

Exposing the patient's inability to connect, or confronting the feeling that he or she does not deserve to have a relationship, is especially disruptive to the therapeutic bond. Thus any attempts by the clinician to interpret the deficit beneath the disengagement would not only be denied or otherwise defended against, but can unnecessarily add insult to an already profound injury to the self (Pine 1990). Thus Pine has warned against interpreting defects in ego function or deficiencies in parental input that produce faulty self-experience, because "interpretations that make the patient see . . . defects in the subjective self (low esteem, shaky boundaries, discontinuity) pose the danger of rubbing salt

---

2. Empathic interpretations are generated from the emotional self of the therapist; they are not objectively understood and cognitively formulated as much as "felt." With this type of interpretation, the affective experience of the therapist resonates with that of the patient, and insight is transmitted through empathy.

in wounds or of eliminating hope or of merely causing pain" (p. 250); such interpretive interventions may themselves result in patient help-lessness, depression, or narcissistic mortification.

A very difficult matter is often these patients' tendency to deny the clinician's existence as a person. Havens (1986) has pointed out the deleterious impact on psychotherapists who cannot function "if the patient's mind is outside the room" (p. 84). A common nontherapeutic reaction of such therapists is to psychologically remove themselves from the therapy (i. e., not listening), thus compounding their own increas-ing sense of alienation or need to escape. These clinicians can find them-selves unwittingly responding to the patient as the patient does to them—leaving the other emotionally deserted and unengaged.

PATIENTS WITH DYADIC CONFLICT

Primary Relationship Pattern

The dyadic conflict patient's engagement usually takes the form of re-jecting and demanding dependency, which may be regarded as a defense against earlier feelings and fears of engulfment (Masterson 1976). Due to the overriding influence of preoedipal aggression, particularly from a dangerous pregenital mother (Kernberg 1975), this type of patient is chronically angry and appears to be refueled by his or her own rage. Sometimes a thin layer of sharp wit can cover biting sarcasm and con-descension, or the patient may even present a compliant surface whose deceptive cover temporarily seals over the underlying anger. With strong resentment harbored beneath a facade of pseudo-submission to the thera-pist, however, repression of aggression still results in a bad sense of self (Settlage 1990).

In general, these patients tend to act out feelings rather than ver-balizing them (Kernberg 1975), angrily submitting to others—includ-ing the therapist—despite deep distrust, and continually manipulating them for their affection and approval (Masterson 1976). Despite the fact that the patient tends to mistrust and devalue the therapist (Kernberg 1975), he or she nonetheless expects to receive love. Although afraid of being rejected, such a patient will repeatedly precipitate the very rejection he fears. While making demands and displaying dependency, he or she will be critical of the therapist (Kernberg 1975), with personal or professional qualifications of the clinician frequently the target of direct or indirect challenge. The therapist's interpretive comments or queries, for example, are frequently received as criticism and, in turn, the patient feels betrayed, becomes argumentative, complains about not being understood, or accuses the therapist of taking someone else's side. Expressions of flattery or praise are usually short-lived, to be followed by more typical testiness, demands, and devaluation.

Therapist's Stance

The therapist strives to survive the negative scenario, a therapeutic no-win situation wherein the patient will get upset with empathy, will reject interpretation, and will not cooperate with content focusing. The therapist primarily maintains an unintrusive presence and supplies only what is necessary to meet the patient's dependency needs, without interpreting its demanding quality or challenging the dyadic conflict patient's sensitivity to rejection. In Ornstein's (1992) terms, this orientation means "to accept the patient's psychic reality, namely, that what the therapist . . . could not recognize as an 'offense' was experienced as such by the patient" (p. 24). A vigilant seriousness is required so as not to miss minimum cues to the dyadic conflict patient's anger, disappointment, or manipulation.

The therapist lets the patient complain and express anger and rage, but only centripetally[3]; it is not advisable to assuage the aggression by kindness. This is concordant with Kernberg's (1982) treatment of borderline patients, which emphasizes the need to encourage expressions of anger, because ignoring such suppressed affect will only heighten these patients' fear of their own impulses and elicit acting out, and the disad-

---

3. *Centripetal interpretation*: the patient's feelings, thoughts, and behaviors, as expressed to others in the present and past, are redirected toward the therapist. *Centrifugal interpretation*: The patient's feelings, thoughts, and behaviors, as expressed toward the therapist, are redirected to others in the patient's present and past.

vantage of too much empathy, because gratification of transference needs significantly distorts these patients' perception of the therapeutic situation (i. e., they identify with an overly idealized figure whom they feel incapable of living up to).

Since the specific content of the sessions will largely relate to the patient's fear of being intruded upon or stifled while yearning to be accepted, the stance of the therapist must mesh with Winnicott's (1965) observation that the child not only needs mother's support, but her presence without making demands. The clinician needs to provide that noninvasive experience of letting the child qua patient alone. According to Havens (1986), "he must distance himself from any actual invasiveness of the patient; [and] he must refrain from reinforcing any expectation the patient has of invasiveness" (p. 84).

The patient's devaluation of the therapist is interpreted ad hoc as a kind of shotgun request for empathy (forcing the therapist to experience how he or she feels). When rage surfaces, the therapist deintensifies negative transference by systematically interpreting the anger and hostility (e. g., as self-protection against anticipated rejection, as a way of engaging for fear of engulfment while yearning to be loved, or as projection of badness in order to preserve one's sense of self). However, the therapist does not interpret projections onto others, because the patient would feel accused and perceive it as the therapist's alliance with them. This is a tightrope walk between a narcissistic alliance and paranoid collusion. As Ornstein (1992) points out, interpreting projected hostility of the patient will only confirm the patient's worst fear—that he or she is a fundamentally evil person.

The dyadic conflict patient's negativity constitutes his or her pattern of relating; the aggression is not discharge- or damage-seeking, but object-seeking (as in Fairbairn's understanding of libido). Thus, first, the therapist must recover from being diminished in order to assure that the patient's aggression can be expressed without fear of retaliation. Second, through *projective interpretation*[4] the therapist conveys to the

---

4. *Projective interpretation*: The therapist is forced to experience certain emotions from the patient's projections; he then cognitively formulates the patient's intentions for generating such feelings in him and offers this back to the patient. Therapist and

patient that he or she is understood, that the patient's attacks on or devaluation of the therapist are intended to make him feel just how the patient feels all the time.

Common Countertherapeutic Responses

Clinicians usually feel uneasy in the patient's presence and find themselves apprehensive or actually fearful of harm; countertransferentially, they may experience dislike of these patients and even rage or wish to destroy them (Strasburger 1986). As a result, they can easily become critical of their own performance as therapists or, worse, indignant and self-justifying in order to ease their own hurt and anger. A sense of invincibility or invulnerability can be another counterreaction to more realistic feelings of helplessness (Strasburger 1986). In a discussion of transference and countertransference with such patients, Kernberg (1975) has noted that

> The patient's aggressive behavior . . . tends to provoke from the therapist counteraggressive feelings and attitudes. It is as if the patient were pushing the aggressive part of his self onto the therapist and as if the countertransference represented the emergence of this part of the patient from within the therapist. [p. 80]

Indeed, it has been suggested that the most difficult skill for the therapist is the ability to recognize and control his or her own identification with these patients' projections (Masterson 1976). Moreover, devaluation, including feelings of invalidity and loss of identity, often occurs from acceptance of projected badness (Strasburger 1986).

The chronic narcissistic injury that the therapist has to sustain may tax professional and personal limits, lower self-esteem, and evoke irrita-

---

patient are not yet in emotional or cognitive synchrony, but in projective reciprocation, which is the base for process interpretation. (This is in contrast to *empathic interpretation*, wherein patient and therapist are in emotional synchrony, which is the base for content interpretation.)

bility and anger. In counterresponse to the patient's aggressiveness—by (aggressively) getting into arguments or (passive-aggressively) suggesting alternative therapy or increasing fees—the therapist may unwittingly encourage these patients to leave treatment. When these patients finally do drop out, however, their therapists often feel even worse.

PATIENTS WITH TRIADIC DEFICIT

Primary Relationship Pattern

The triadic deficit patient is "not in conscious conflict" (Tarachow 1963, p. 241) with his or her symptoms (e. g., acting out behaviors), in fact is often comfortable with them. Thus such patients characteristically resist, or only minimally tolerate, the patient role, regarding it as an expression of weakness. Because these patients have failed to achieve normal idealization of objects, they do not easily form a positive transference. Indeed they see themselves as self-sufficient and are contemptuous of the constructive efforts of others (Svravik et al. 1991). Although they may demonstrate temporary or token appreciation of the clinician, particularly in response to specific usefulness, such patients will at best consider the therapist a dispensable expert. Moreover, they have little difficulty asking for favors, such as changes in procedures to suit their own personal needs and outside priorities—a way of getting something from you that you hadn't intended to give (Tarachow 1963). With this high need for defensive maneuverability (Person 1986), those who are treatable often arrive with a premeditated agenda (e. g., to regain a former love object), are very guarded in what they disclose, and will manipulate the therapist primarily for secondary gains.

More specifically, triadic deficit individuals typically show lack of interest in focusing on the patient–therapist relationship. Any insistence on making therapeutic interaction the focus of treatment (e. g., interpretations of these patients' disengagement as a fear of intimacy) will only alienate them, without having any productive result.

Therapist's Stance

In light of the predominant tendency of the triadic deficit patient to distrust, dismiss, and disengage from treatment, special determination and ingenuity by the therapist is necessary. As this type of patient is prone to identify with and aggrandize an antisocial father (Ronningstam and Gunderson 1989, Svravik et al. 1991), the clinician needs to reverse this by maintaining the presence of a strong and steady paternal self-object[5] who sets reasonable external controls. In essence, these clinicians have to establish structure, command compliance, and reject manipulation—without rejecting the patient; they have to respond to the triadic deficit patient's underlying dependency and fragility behind the compensatory show of strength (Person 1986).

All interventions are geared toward establishing and maintaining the patient's belief in the therapist, as he or she is being repeatedly tested. This means that the clinician has to live through a great deal with the patient before any attempts at interpretation are made (Tarachow 1963). By providing him- or herself as corrective evidence to counter the patient's belief that no one has anything worthwhile to offer, the patient can begin to respect the therapist and identify with some of the latter's values and characteristics. Only then will the therapist be able to make connections, albeit nontransferential, between the present and past (e. g., feelings of emotional isolation and aloneness, experiences of a psychologically absent or discredited father and devalued mother).

Common Countertherapeutic Responses

Because of their antisocial manipulations and mistrust, triadic deficit patients often produce strong countertransferential reactions (Vaillant and Perry 1985). One major countertherapeutic response is to fall vic-

---

5. *Maternal selfobject*: the patient experiences the therapist as the *emotional* extension of his/herself, with affectional functions. *Paternal selfobject*: the patient experiences the therapist as the *cognitive/behavioral* extension of his/herself, with affiliative functions.

tim to "the seduction to become an accomplice of the patient" (Vaillant and Perry 1985, p. 248), for example, to impulsively act in the patient's behalf when he or she gets into trouble. In reaction to constant evaluation (with the implicit demand to perform), the clinician may also feel impelled to excessively exhibit knowhow or wit or, alternatively, to hide behind a transference-inducing attitude, only to fail to keep the patient engaged in treatment. Thus psychotherapy with this type of patient either loses therapeutic leverage because the clinician has accepted the patient's conditions (Tarachow 1963), or remains at the initial stages of discussing only the patient's presenting issues; it does not progress to remedying deficit, partly because the patient tends to dismiss, if not actively discourage, discussion of historical material and related transferential interpretations. As a result, the sessions gradually become too present- or content-oriented and quickly get repetitive, while the therapist has been rendered impotent in failing to overcome the patient's disengagement. This often leads to premature termination—to the disappointment of both therapist and patient.

PATIENTS WITH TRIADIC CONFLICT

Primary Relationship Pattern

The triadic conflict patient easily engages with the therapist, albeit at times with irrational intimacy and dependency; he or she tends to be jealous, seductive, playfully aggressive and competitive, or, at the other end of the spectrum, shy and submissive. Despite some expected ambivalent feelings and resistance (Brenner 1976), this type of patient will typically regard treatment as a helpful process and is highly motivated; such patients easily accept the patient role in an effort to be liked and respected by the therapist and will compliantly supply whatever will earn attention and interest—self-searching elaborations, dreams, early childhood material, or the like. In wishful reciprocation, they may also continually venture to equalize or sexualize the therapeutic relationship in fantasy or fact (Gabbard 1991).

Therapist's Stance

The therapist maintains a dispassionate attitude (Freud 1912) that requires suspending judgment and responding to the patient with neutral interest and inquiry; any reciprocation of the patient's attempts toward more personal engagement would hinder treatment, forcing appropriate, problematic topics underground. On the other hand, fear of intimacy, whereby the patient may not want to be known, even at the risk of being found undesirable or losing the therapist's regard, requires vigorous interpretations. These are designed to intensify transference, focus on seduction (e. g., invitation to intimacy) and aggression (e. g., the patient's attempts at undoing treatment or personalizing it), or to related affects of fear and guilt.

Every interaction (including procedural ones) is examined as a way of making the relationship central to treatment. The therapist relatively deprives and frustrates the patient's wishes, bringing all present life conflicts into the patient–therapist context, then relating them to the past. Strategies include encouraging free association, inducing regression through recollection of dreams, fantasies, and early memories, and repeated interpretation and clarification of the patient's conflicts in vivo as well as within their natural context (Greenson 1967).

The contents of interpretations, including transferential ones, are not as important as the aim of the interpretation: cognitive synchrony. Whereas through empathy the therapist seeks emotional synchrony with the patient, he tries to reach its cognitive equivalent through interpretation. Yet both activities, empathy and interpretation, are utilized for building and maintaining a therapeutic relationship with the patient.

Common Countertherapeutic Responses

Typically these patients drop out in transferential panic, if not interpreted early enough to prevent it. Yet, at the same time, most therapists would find it very difficult to deprive and frustrate such "good patients," thus diluting the transference and bringing the sessions to a positive impasse or undoing the whole process. The dilution or destruction of transference may take various forms, ranging from very obvious unethical behaviors to subtle transferential mistakes disguised as technical errors. The latter can include attributing the patient's feelings toward the therapist to the patient's relationship with others; providing self-identifying information, thus differentiating one's self from the transferential object; or bypassing the transference by attributing the patient's present life behaviors and feelings to his or her relationship with past objects.

However, the major danger here is the clinician's being seduced by, or seductive with, patients, submitting to their wishes or receiving personal gratification or gain from them (Brenner 1976). The most common temptation is to compromise treatment with modifications that are inappropriate (i. e., yielding to a special request that is not warranted by the therapeutic structure). Sexual boundary violations (e. g., meeting outside of the office or otherwise inviting intimacy) (Person 1986) are more complex and nontherapeutic, despite often mutual beliefs to the contrary. Here, confusion of the clinician's needs with those of the patient is epitomized in the "lovesick therapist" who is no longer able to maintain professional objectivity and control over the therapeutic relationship (Gabbard 1991).

Towards an Integrative Developmental Approach to Psychotherapy Practice

An integrative developmental approach to psychotherapy practice is presented that utilizes diverse clinical contributions. It does so primarily by providing both a safe, accepting and neutral place within which to reiterate old conflicts and to experience a caring therapeutic relationship that serves to remedy some of the deficiencies of the past. Such a perspective in practice, as in theory, incorporates the conflict model's emphasis on sexual and aggressive drive gratification and tension regulation as well as the deficit model's focus on the need for significant others as selfobjects, objects, and introjects for internalization and identification. It has direct implications for the therapist's dual roles as transference figure who becomes the displaced source of drive frustration or pleasure, as well as a real object as a temporary auxiliary ego for soothing, security, and, ultimately, sense of self. It places in bold relief the multifaceted functions of early caretakers and, as an extension of them, the therapist in the professional role of substitute primary object. Most important, the developmental perspective in practice firmly places the therapeutic relationship in center stage, as the harkening back to both symbolic and real parental ties within the therapist's office becomes, in today's term, a form of "virtual reality."

More specifically, it means that the therapist's combined roles as a listening and empathic healer are titrated and tailored to the patient's prototypic pattern of relatedness, which in turn reflects earlier attachment bonds (erotic and/or narcissistic) with significant figures. By shifting and sharing specific interactions and techniques, they can be geared to respective defects and voids, drives and defenses at various stages of development. This integrative concept expresses the need for a cultivated flexibility of the clinician's relationship pattern with the patient. Although this may be accomplished intuitively by the seasoned clinician, Section Two that follows, which presents case excerpts with the therapist's commentary, offers a systematic articulation of the subject.

Part II

The Psychotherapist's Interventions

4

The Dyadic Deficit Patient
and the Empathic Self-Object

PSYCHOTHERAPY SCENARIO

Treatment of *dyadic deficit* patients entails working with—and being affectively attuned to—severely traumatized and threatened persons with fragile or fragmented selves, who are unable to make contact, feel or express authentic emotion, or engage in an interpersonal dialogue. So profound have been their developmental deficiencies that the clinician cannot afford to further frustrate their conflictual fantasies and repressed desires (see Chapter 7); rather, he must replenish and replace real losses as well as symbolic ones, especially with regard to missing maternal mirroring and an unsated yearning for union.

However, being the therapeutic target of the patient's inordinate need for—or fear of—fusion, as well as a compromised capacity to care, takes a particular toll. As these patients present along a pathological spectrum from primitive merger to grandiose self-sufficiency, it may mean, reciprocally, a discomfited and defended therapist who counter-transferentially continues to struggle between two comparable (albeit less extreme) poles of tenacious and tenuous attachment. Parallel to the patient's problems can be the clinician's own narcissistic need to heroically rescue their relationship rather than surrender to a progressive sense of estrangement.

In order to redress these patients' deficits, the cornerstone of treatment is supplying an empathic self-object to repair, if not reconstruct, the damaged and deficient self. Yet the pivotal mutative element of empathy, which encourages emotional resonance with the dyadic deficit patient, has its own by-products that may undermine the psychotherapy endeavor. These can include the potential perils of overidentification with another's feelings and increasing loss of intersubjective boundaries. Thus the therapist is vulnerable to taking on the patient's depersonalized qualities and himself becoming detached and defeated (e. g., feelings of boredom, loneliness, depression, and eventually despair).

Somewhat less devastating to both parties is managing to maintain one's own professional identity and personal sense of worth, but succumbing to defensive behaviors in countertransferential compensation (e. g., reaching beyond the patient with statements and interpretations that do not match his or her capacity, trying to get a rise out of the unresponsive patient through undue pressure or playfulness) or, worse, resorting to resentful interactions in countertransferential reciprocation (e. g., covertly hostile banter, overtly aggressive offense). Both types are countertherapeutic: the former actions, which usually occur for relatively benign purposes of prodding or provocation, are frequently ineffective; the latter, which often occur for more malignant reasons of retaliation or reprisal, are invariably inappropriate. To varying degrees they each reflect, perhaps paradoxically, those very empathic failures that the dyadic deficit patient has repeatedly experienced earlier in his relationships to others—which the psychotherapist's interventions and critical role as surrogate maternal self-object are expressly designed to undo.

OUTLINE OF INTERVENTIONS
FOR DYADIC DEFICIT PATIENTS

CASE EXCERPTS WITH THERAPIST COMMENTARY

In the characteristic psychotherapy situation with a dyadic deficit patient, the therapist is presented with an extraordinary challenge: an unreachable other, a markedly detached and depersonalized patient whose major modus operandi is that of interpersonal distance or its common counterpart, primitive merger. In treatment, as in larger life, these individuals have lost touch with—if indeed they were ever able to embrace—feelings for self and others. They cannot care or truly bond with another, because they simply do not have the developmental capacity. So deep may be the injury to the inner structures of their selfhood that they are often thought to be split, severed, or even dead at the core.

It has been suggested that the most crucial cause of such impaired attachment resides in the inability of the individual to master the lack (Kohut 1971) or loss (West and Keller 1994) of an empathic relationship with the primary maternal figure of earliest childhood. The psychological process that subsequently ensues—which has been likened to a form of pathological mourning (Bowlby 1980) or abandonment depression (Masterson 1981)—is marked by repression of feelings and denial of loss. Its cumulative course has been succinctly depicted as follows:

> Chronic experiences of caregiver insensitivity or rebuff summate and become for the individual mini-experiences of loss. These experiences create relational distance and perpetual feelings of not being understood, the results of which are loneliness and the despair of alienation. The typical response to loss is an amalgam of sorrowful yearning, anger, guilt, and partial or complete withdrawal from meaningful relationships. [West and Keller 1994, p. 326].

More recently, such severe psychopathology has been emotionally encapsulated as "psychic deadness" (Eigen 1996), a numbing and repudiation of life in which a living death can become less toxic, threatening, and painful than the risk of allowing themselves to experience their aliveness in vital relationships. As Cooper and Maxwell (1995) have put it, "As they cannot internalize anything—nothing can feed, be digested or metabolised—their lives feel permanently empty" (p. 118). Viewed along this spectrum of desolation and inner death, these mortified individuals all have in common an invisible and inaccessible self that is accompanied by a sense of utter unworthiness and dread of coming apart. Since the capacity itself, or the conditions needed to support aliveness were unable to develop, or could only develop in deformed or deficient ways, the effects are devastating. It has been posited that in such cases, "deadness substituted for aliveness, not as a defense so much as a *default* [italics mine]. The gap left by failure of aliveness to develop is filled by a sense of deadness, as if deadness rushes in to fill the void that deficient aliveness leaves" (Eigen 1996, p. 8).

Thereafter, as patients face their therapists within the treatment setting, their extreme developmental deficiencies—not having had the earliest experiences of love, comfort, and confirmation of self, or having been otherwise hurt or humiliated by those from whom nurture was more than denied—can manifest as affectless and self-sufficient detachment or, alternatively, clinging and helpless dependency; here the sheer terror of attachment and its constant companion, utter fear of abandonment and annihilation, underlie profound failures to feel or to connect. Thus the therapist must attempt to sustain an interpersonal relationship with these patients despite (or because of) being indiscriminately met with apparent indifference or chameleonlike merger—the hallmarks of an absent or faulty self.

As a consequence of such scenarios, dyadic deficit patients in psychotherapy exemplify varieties of psychological "absence" (Havens 1986). Out of its remote array three inaccessible types have been identified: those who hide (i. e., isolated individuals who need to protect themselves from invasive others and take on an existence on an outside model in order to replace their own undeveloped individuality); those who keep disappearing (i. e., submissive and elusive individuals who totally lose themselves in others and are only knowable through their projections and compliance); and those who barely exist (i. e., supine individuals who have virtually no independent life due to inordinate criticism from self and others). Deriving from Kohut's self psychology, Baker and Baker (1987) have comparably portrayed three fundamental forms of relatedness (or their lack) that result from particular shortcomings in early self-object relationships: those with *contact-shunning* characteristics, who avoid social interaction and become isolated because they fear that they will be swallowed up or that further nonempathic mirroring will destroy the remnants of their already vulnerable nuclear self; those with *merger-hungry* characteristics, who must continuously attach themselves to self-objects in such an entangled way that they are often unable to distinguish their own thoughts, wishes, and intentions from others; and those with *mirror-hungry* characteristics, who need to display themselves in ways that can obtain continuous confirming and admiring responses, without which they feel worthless.

In the psychotherapist's interventions across the entire diverse range of developmental disorder from dyadic deficit to triadic conflict, it is no doubt most difficult for the clinician to make contact and create a connection with those who are virtually dead, invisible, hidden, or fused, or to sustain an affective tie with those who are affectless. Indeed, the symbiotic bond of undifferentiated dependence is deceptive, itself a message that bespeaks their ardent avoidance of attachment and morbid fear of feeling, while signaling the desperate attempt to fill the void of an empty self. Moreover, moving in the direction of real contact and the accompanying feelings toward others can result in the reiteration of those very early, extreme experiences of loss, reverberations of intense abandonment trauma suffered in their preoedipal past. Viewing psychotherapy as an emotional microcosm of the interpersonal world, the critical therapeutic question thus becomes: If these patients cannot form an unthreatened connection with others or tolerate having authentic affective relationships outside of therapy, how are they going to be able to answer their attachment needs *within* treatment? And how does the clinician accommodate their unresolved desire, in the novelist E. M. Forster's (1954) famous yearning words, to ". . . only connect"?

MAKING CONTACT WITH A NONRELATING PATIENT: FINDING THE OTHER BY EMPATHICALLY SPEAKING TO ABSENCE

In psychotherapy with dyadic deficit patients, the major thrust of treatment is also its primary peril: utilizing the therapeutic relationship as the critical connection for reconstructing the self. The basic tasks of the therapist are therefore manifold, each formidable in itself: first, to search for, next, to confirm or strengthen, and ultimately, to rebuild a sustained self. The clinician has a special charge: to try to locate the person in order to gain entrance into another's world, attempting to reach and make contact with the patient. This means initially "finding the other" by empathically "speaking to absence" (Havens 1986).

Integrally related to the above, the therapist's work continually entails "creating the capacity for attachment" (Walant 1995) (see Intervention 2). The latter purpose means to remain engaged in order to progressively develop the patient's ability to bond, however unformed or deformed the original tie to mother. Together these therapeutic tasks in turn serve as basic requirements for erecting or resurrecting the structure of the self through maternal mirroring and affirmation. Therefore the totality of treatment becomes a matter of helping dyadic deficit patients to establish and sustain, replace or revivify a cohesive sense of self. During seemingly insurmountable obstacles, what becomes apparent throughout therapy is that although the therapist can help dyadic deficit patients to create some semblance of self-esteem and selfhood to augment their missing or arrested inner structures, their newly formed self continues to elude them, especially in stressful situations.

Intricate studies of infant and mother interaction suggest the salience of *affective attunement* as an intersubjective phenomenon that composes their early emotional resonance (Stern 1985). It is also the basis for the more globally applied term of *empathy* (Kohut 1971, 1977), which has been increasingly extrapolated from the earliest childhood environment to the therapeutic ambience as a primary requisite of treatment. In fact, the notion of empathy as the fundamental mode of human relatedness (along with the avoidance of its antithesis, *empathic failure*) is currently considered to be the centerpiece of psychotherapy in reaching toward and repairing the injured self. It is regarded as pivotal in the making—or, breaking—of the formative structures of selfhood.

Empathy, however, is a complex and controversial concept with a long history (Basch 1983, Chessick 1993, Starcevic and Piontek 1997). It was initially viewed solely as a mode of perception or observation, a way of listening in order to get to know another. In particular, empathic listening reflects the intuitive manner through which the therapist learns about the patient. It has subsequently been endowed with the power to heal, or cure, by making the other *feel* understood. Comparable concepts, such as empathic understanding or empathic attunement, similarly serve the functions of an interpersonal sharing and a confirming "human echo" (Kohut 1971, 1977).

What is significant here is that the therapeutic applications of these concepts have become a critical bridge from the past to the present, from mother and baby to therapist and patient. Daniel Stern's (1985) contemporary exploration of the interpersonal world of the infant has expressly examined the earliest nuances of mutuality of affective states. He refers to *affective attunement* as "the most pervasive and clinical germaine [sic] feature of intersubjective relatedness" (p. 138). More specifically, a crucial consideration is that affective attunement constitutes only one initial aspect of empathy. Whereas both begin with emotional resonance, empathy is said to consist of four distinct and largely consecutive processes: "(1) the resonance of feeling state; (2) the abstraction of empathic knowledge from the experience of emotional resonance; (3) the integration of abstracted empathic knowledge into an empathic response; and (4) a transient role identification" (p. 145). It is believed that cognitive processes involved in the abstraction and integration of another's experience are what specially distinguish the empathic response (Demos 1984, Schafer 1968). The therapist, like the early maternal figure, must cognitively "read," translate, and return the inner subjective state back to the other (i. e., infant/patient).

At bottom, empathy denotes a way of entering and comprehending the patient's experiential world from that person's point of view and, like affective attunement, can vary in its degree of authenticity and degree of match between the feeling state and the recipient's response, that is, the fine translation of one to the other. To the extent that the therapist's empathically derived perceptions provide for the possibility of explanations and interpretations that are not only insightful (the primary aim with triadic conflict patients; see Chapter 7), but make the receiver *feel* understood (the primary aim with dyadic deficit patients), such affective affirmation and validation offers sustenance for a frail sense of self. Thus empathy has become more than an assist to the *therapist* in getting to know the patient, it has an additional mutative asset for the *patient.*

Such cognitive and affective attunement—the empathic capacity to reciprocally participate in or experience another's thoughts and feelings—may be regarded as the sine qua non of clinicians who treat dyadic deficit patients. However, it is not simply a therapeutic technique, strategy, or imposed stance. As Kohut (1977) has pointed out,

> Empathy is not a tool in the sense in which the patient's reclining position [or] the use of free associations . . . are tools. . . . Empathy is not just a useful way by which we have access to the inner life of man—the idea itself of an inner life of man, and thus of a psychology of complex mental states, is unthinkable without our ability to know via vicarious introspection—my definition of empathy—what the inner life of man is, what we ourselves and what others think and feel. [p. 306]

As such, empathy is a human developmental necessity that is transmitted between caregiver and infant and thenceforth has corrective value in treatment to rectify the empathic failures of the past. As the clinician communicates an emotional understanding of the patient's problems and psychic pain, a resonance enters the inner world of the patient to meet unmet needs; it may also facilitate insight. Clinical observation increasingly suggests that even the most accurate and well-timed interpretation will not be effective in the absence of an accepting, empathic atmosphere (Basch 1980, Karasu 1992a). Havens (1986) has in fact posited that "the most certain way of knowing when a person is present—of finding the other—lies in the ability to empathize with that person" (p. 16). One of the foremost principles of treatment of the dyadic deficit patient is thus that of "expressing empathy, affectively and verbally" (Settlage 1994).

In his examination of the uses of language in psychotherapy for the primary purpose of making contact through the communication of empathy, Havens (1986) has expressly explored the therapeutic application of different linguistic forms for gaining entrance into the inner experiences of unrelating patients; he calls it "speaking to absence." In particular, empathic speech addresses isolation by reaching something unexpressed by the patient. Depending upon the depth of inaccessibility, such utterances can require something akin to mindreading or the most subtle translation of a foreign language. These verbalizations can range from the utilization of the most rudimentary imitative statements in query form, in which the therapist silently completes the patient's unspoken thoughts and verbalizes them back to him or her in the form of a single sentence (e. g., "What is one to do?" said to an indecisive patient, or "What hope is there?" said to a depressed patient). Beyond these, simple empathic statements in exclamatory form can be offered, which are short emotional utterances whereby the patient's feeling state is affectively acknowledged and shared by the therapist (e. g., "How awful!"). More complex empathic statements go further both by confirming, and even consensually celebrating, the naturalness of privately held feelings (e. g., "No wonder you were frightened"). These serve to secure and validate the patient's sense of self by articulating what has remained unarticulated. What these interventions all have in common is the makings of a gradually accepted advance into the inner life of the patient.

In light of the special needs and vulnerabilities of dyadic deficit patients, as well as of their therapists, an implication for intervention is that typical insight-oriented, exploratory methods, which deliberately delve beneath the surface and reach beyond fragile interpersonal boundaries, are not appropriate; indeed, they are doomed to fail. Rather, the clinician must proceed with the greatest caution—he dares not try to force entry, extend into, question, or challenge what is as yet unknown, secret, private, or desperately defended by the patient. This refers to the inadvisability of the therapist's expressly pointing out unacknowledged or unacceptable, repressed, or repudiated aspects of the deficient self, such as an apparent absence of affect and obvious defective attachment. Interventions that aim at direct confrontation or interpretation of deficits and defenses before the fractured self has been repaired and strengthened will invariably be ineffective, or even damaging. This is exemplified by the following familiar scenarios, which may greet the unsuspecting, though not necessarily inexperienced clinician.

The Uselessness, If Not Harmfulness, of Pointing Out the Patient's Inability to Feel or Relate to Another

When beginning therapy, what the clinician frequently finds is that he may be met with a hollow silence or shallow response. Beyond this, the patient with dyadic deficits is not necessarily mute. Such a patient may start to talk about minute events in everyday life, including personal details about self and others, but without speaking *to* the therapist. In short, there is no genuine and reciprocal interpersonal connection. These patients, who are still at a primitive phase of development, may feel like nothing yet grandiosely see themselves as the center of the universe and everyone else as existing simply to serve their unsated needs. An archaic *merger transference* (Kohut 1971) may maintain their fragile and undifferentiated sense of self and others, by which they view the therapist not as a separate and independent human being, but as an inanimate object over whom they can ostensibly gain some semblance of control, however fleeting. Such patients, like automatons, will present current or historic material as if reading from a script to an anonymous audience, without emotional expression or appropriate affect.

Having to be the recipient of such an impersonal presentation by the patient may naturally prompt the overanxious, rigidly traditional, or even merely earnest therapist into clinically commenting upon an obvious observation: what is *not* happening between them. With the dyadic deficit patient, however, such an approach is invariably not only unproductive but countertherapeutic. It can be especially damaging by adding to the very alienation that resides at the core of this severe self disorder.

More specifically, despite the fact that the therapist may be tempted to talk about the patient's inability to relate or to express feelings, these efforts would most likely to be responded to by the patient with puzzlement, if not with a sense of hurt, because the dyadic deficit patient does not have any other model of being or interacting. Such a patient is reacting to the therapist in the same indiscriminate and impersonal way that this individual has always related to everyone else. Identification by the therapist of that person's lack of connection (e. g., "I feel like you are not with me" or "You seem emotionally absent") will only serve to salt the patient's wounds, not unlike blaming a blind person for not seeing.

In return, the characteristic reaction is apparent oblivion to these statements, as if the patient is either not totally listening or is unconsciously dismissing what is heard. For the most part, such patients will give no special attention to any of the therapist's comments, so that in effect it may seem as if neither the most salient statements nor the most blatant blunders are likely to be differentially discerned. Ivey (1996), for example, confessed to a significant slip of the tongue (referring to a self-destructive patient's suicidal fast as a "suicidal farce"), which horrified the therapist and made him take a second look at his own countertransferential reactions, but which the very compromised patient never noticed!

However, such oversights by the dyadic deficit patient do not mean that the therapist can relax. Indeed, like Orwell's (1945) last, lone commandment that "Not all animals are equal; some animals are more equal than others" (p. 88), not all of the therapist's verbalizations are equal in impact—some are not merely unheard; they can be harmful. The latter is most likely to occur when the clinician tries to delve into the major deficiencies of the patient, such as an inability to feel, to make contact, or to interpersonally relate and care about another.[1]

The potential problems that dealing with deficits present can be particularly perplexing, because the inexperienced therapist may have little precedent for, and the experienced therapist little patience for, the interactions that arise. For example, the frustration from trying to

---

1. There is one major exception: the therapist's words are of no apparent moment to the patient, *unless* they generate anxiety with regard to the therapist's stability and availability (see Offering Object Constancy: Exquisite Attention to Reliability and Dependability, p. 76).

repeatedly reach toward an absent response can easily evoke an unsettling temptation on the part of the clinician to speak directly to the heart of the matter—to confront the chasm between them. In such instances, resorting to the use of more familiar exploratory and confrontative psychodynamic techniques may be a natural, albeit defensive, consequence of the therapist's sense of increasing pressure and impending failure. More covertly, however, it can carry with it a message of retaliatory hostility, that of punishing the patient for repudiating the therapist and in effect rendering him impotent. In either event, the delicacy of such efforts, especially at the onset of treatment, is noteworthy, as the following two prototypical instances of initial intervention attest.

Early in the course of the psychotherapy process, this ineffectual interchange transpired after an alienated patient had described, in a very bleak and emotionally bland, matter-of-fact manner, his lack of contact with family, absence of friends and acquaintances, and even not liking to have animals or other "living creatures" around him.

Therapist: Yours must be a very lonely experience.

The therapist attempts to identify—and thereby merely begin to touch—what the patient is feeling. It has as its purpose to enter the other person's world, to not only see but share what the patient is presumably experiencing. It also serves to convey such a message back to him or her in order to articulate the therapist's empathic acceptance of that individual's sense of isolation.

Patient: If you say so.

Since the patient's conditional reply has neither explicitly confirmed nor completely denied the therapist's initial statement above, the therapist has proceeded to pursue the same content, but with a different, hopefully less threatening format, a query.

Therapist: Painful to recognize it?
Patient: Not sure what you mean, but I guess so.

The patient, albeit still reluctant, seems to have come a tiny bit further in acknowledging his feelings, so the therapist has utilized this small opening to gently urge him to elaborate.

Therapist: Tell me about this pain a little bit.
Patient: [frightened-looking and querulous] Which pain?
Therapist: The pain of loneliness.

The therapist patiently repeats himself, recognizing that the recipient's question and apparent denial reveal the potency of the renewed threat. Even this modicum of emotional entry has apparently been too much for this patient, who retreats rather than move forward to face his feelings. He seems to remain virtually frozen by his fear of affect.

Patient: The pain of loneliness?
Therapist: Yes, how you must feel, that emotional loneliness, not really having family or friends you can talk to. . . .

As the therapist persists in his elaboration, the patient becomes more and more quiet.

Patient: [long silence]

Unsuccessful in the earlier attempts to tap the actual affect, the therapist has turned to a more tangible matter—the immediate silence between the two of them.

Therapist: So silent?
Patient: I have nothing to say.
Therapist: You feel that you also want to remove *me* from the interaction with you.

To address the new stalemate, the therapist has moved the focus of attention from the outside world to their relationship—perhaps in part out of his own escalating sense of alienation and abandonment.

Patient: Remove you?
Therapist: With your silences?
Patient: It's that I really have nothing to say. Nothing comes to my
    mind.

The patient has become progressively more remote, which confirms that the therapist has moved away from, rather than toward, a place of contact or attunement.

There is no direct challenge or expression of emotion on the patient's part, just withdrawal and apparent emptiness. Havens (1986) has warned that under such circumstances, "Empathic statements, if insufficiently tested for the accuracy of empathy, can easily be used to force patients to feel what the therapist believes they feel or should feel. Many patients, like poorly protected children, do not indicate their displeasure or may not even feel it" (p. 29). The successive silences and paucity of response represent the kind of barren reactions that the therapist is likely to receive when bringing up the subject to the dyadic deficit patient of the latter's lack of affect or failure to make contact.

At these times, the therapist should not necessarily be surprised at the temptation he may feel to tap a sensitive subject (both because of the pervasive nature of these self deficiency characteristics, as well as the greater appropriateness of such an approach when working with other types of patients). However, in attempting to identify and validate the feelings of the dyadic deficit patient here, the therapist has gone beyond the patient's degree of awareness, thus ascribing qualities (i. e., feelings of loneliness) that were not explicitly expressed. They were *attributed* to the patient, so nowhere near consciousness. At best such attempts are always translations, which are renderings of what is presumably happening within the patient, at times inaccurately or prematurely put into words by an impatient or insensitive therapist—or it can occur with a seasoned therapist who is presumably both patient and sensitive.

In this regard, Wolf (1994) has pointed out that potential errors on the practitioner's part, which are invariably *received* by the dyadic deficit patient as empathic failures, are not necessarily the therapist's fault, or the patient's for that matter. Instead they are "due to a *discrep-*

ancy between the experiences of reality" (p. 94, italics mine) of the two participants. These potential disruptions of the therapeutic process, which often occur when the patient feels that he or she is not being understood, are hallmarks of dyadic deficit interaction. Under the circumstances, Adler (1986) reassures the therapist that expressing empathy "does not mean that the therapist has to be perfect but that everyday failures to understand the patient can have profound meanings and be perceived as empathic failures" (p. 432). Pine (1990) has gone further to place the onus of these distorted perceptions not on the therapist, but back on the patient because of the particular psychopathology. The easily wounded dyadic deficit patient is, in effect, preprogrammed for empathic failure by others; the therapist is thus less of a perpetrator than a partner. In such cases he or she is, rather, an unerring recipient.

Nonetheless, even when the therapist's translations may be on target—and empathic—there is always the alternative prospect that such presentations are still too painful and as yet too buried for the patient to acknowledge; they would be better placed on a back burner. Since such a scenario is a fundamental and anticipated aspect of treatment with dyadic deficit patients, one of the major tasks of the therapist is "to know when the patient is stuck" (Cooper and Maxwell 1995, p. 122). More important, it should signal to the clinician that further collaborative inquiry is needed in order for the two realities to better mesh (see Co-authorship of the Therapeutic Discourse: Formation of a Narrative Alliance, p. 81).

In addition, in the above excerpt the language used by the therapist may have had untold impact. Although these patients often appear oblivious to the therapist, the other side of this picture is their exquisite sensitivity to perceived slights. In this regard, it has been observed clinically that declarative sentences that have the *least* subject–object differentiation are most effective in dealing with those who are very alienated. This is because such statements serve to satisfy the patient's wish for the comfort of closeness while posing minimal threat to his or her sense of estrangement (Havens 1986). Conversely, by having said, "*Yours* is a very lonely experience," the therapist may have unsuspectingly separated the patient from himself. Paradoxically, this presumably empathic statement tended to trigger the same distancing response that the therapist had hoped to repair.

In the infant–mother interaction, Stern (1985) refers to such phenomena as *unauthentic attunements* (p. 217).While attuning behavior on the part of the maternal parent can potentially be quite good, it can suffer from the effects of fatigue, competing agendas, or external preoccupations, and thus can fluctuate from hour to hour or even minute to minute. Likewise, there may be fluctuations of attunement by the therapist, with effects that may bode well or ill for the patient. Having carefully explored the nuances of attunement and malattunement, Stern's (1985) conclusions have both positive and negative implications for the mother–child and therapist–patient relationships:

> When viewing the ways attunement can be used, for good or for ill, one might get the impression that dangers lurk everywhere. . . . After all, parents, at best, are only "good enough." That leaves room on both sides of the optimal, for the infant to learn the necessary realities about attunement—that it is a key that unlocks the intersubjective doors between people; and that it can be used both *to enrich* one's mental life, by a partial union with an other, and *to impoverish* one's mental life, by bending or appropriating some part of one's inner experience. [p. 214, italics mine]

(For the latter effects on one's mental life, see also Chapter 6 on the triadic deficit patient.)

Since this is early in their relationship, the therapist is at high risk for empathic failure, for it came at a time when the patient was still too insecure to believe that it is possible for one to connect with the clinician, as well as survive separation (see also Consolidation of Connection through "Illusion of Fusion," p. 87).

The Uselessness, if not Harmfulness, of Interpretation of the Patient's Lack of Relatedness and Inaccessibility of Affect

When the treatment is farther along, attempts at interpretation of the patient's inaccessibility still rarely, if ever, produce a fruitful outcome. Even if these efforts do not continue to isolate the patient from the therapist, the patient may slowly begin to express some feelings, but they are not as yet authentic. It should be borne in mind that "*all* interpretations are *always* deprivations" (Karasu 1992, p. 243). This is because the therapist is to some extent depriving the patient of childhood illusions and idealizations, which act as armor against harsh adult reality. As Tarachow (1963) put it,

> The patient wants to keep all his infantile wishes. There is a perpetual battle between patient and therapist, the patient guarding his defenses and his infantile wishes and the therapist attempting to rob the patient. More often than not the patient is unwilling to make the effort of renunciation which you are demanding of him. [p. 101]

In the case of the dyadic deficit patient, interpretations qua deprivations do not merely bring disappointment and object loss, they bring *disengagement* and *self loss*. While other types of patients with an established ego and cohesive self structure may be able to eventually tolerate, however ambivalently, therapeutic attempts toward enlightenment by making careful connections between lack of engagement within therapy and similar behavior outside of therapy or by linking current to prior events, such observations may never produce insight or true affect in dyadic deficit patients.

As the next example portrays, the deeper or more complete the interpretation (i. e., referring to its genetic and/or transferential components), the more invasive the impact. This invariably means a greater need to protect the fragile self and to fend off what has been presented. Occasionally, like the mother who physically hovers over her child, the therapist may express a form of psychic hovering, or "overattunement" (Stern 1985, p. 218). Here the clinician, like the early maternal figure, is so overidentified with the patient or so earnest in the need for entry that he or she appears to penetrate every experience. Stern believes that such overattunement can be the psychic counterpart of physical intrusiveness (see also Chapter 5).

Moreover, even if affect is beginning to be tapped, the earliest responses expressed by the patient are rarely real feelings. Instead, he may compliantly adopt the emotions the therapist assumes he has as temporary camouflage to cover the false or insufficient self. In the following excerpt, unlike the earlier example, the retreating patient does not become silent. Rather, he verbally disavows or falsifies feelings of the past as well as current feelings within the therapy situation.

> *Therapist:* I wonder whether your remaining aloof to me is related to your not being able to get close to another person, because that person ultimately betrays you by leaving—like your mother did by getting sick when you were about 2 years old.

With these patients in particular, such statements can represent transferential as well as countertransferential "overkill" by a too conscientious clinician, who is strenuously trying to connect.

This type of double-barreled interpretation, however compelling, is generally overwhelming or merely confusing. What is noteworthy here is that not only is the disengaged patient set back, but this forebodes impending disengagement on the part of the *therapist*. Frustrated himself, he has bombarded the unresponsive recipient with too much information in a zealous move to get a response. It reveals the telltale signs of lack of attunement or, more aptly, overattunement. The compromised clinician has not only overestimated the capacity of the patient, but overextended his own interpretive prowess in an excessive, even exhibitionistic, effort to elicit a reaction. Here the endangered practitioner may be (consciously or unconsciously) sensing the recipient's remoteness—as well as his own!

> *Patient:* She did not betray me; she just got sick—it isn't her fault.

Going deeper than the patient is ready for has produced a contrary response.

> *Therapist:* Nevertheless, you may have felt deserted.

The therapist resumes his interpretive stance by challenging the patient in return and reiterating the previous point—perhaps too protective of his own position and overly reactive to the lack of synchrony with the patient.

Patient: Well, my father was there and we visited her in the hospital a lot, so I wasn't deserted.

Since the therapist's repeated insistence on his interpretation appears to generate even further resistance, he shifts his approach; to lighten the impact without retracting altogether, the therapist again reverts to a question.

Therapist: Do you think that that experience has affected your way of relating to other people in your life?
Patient: Oh, I relate to people all right.

Even this presumably less threatening interrogative form has resulted in defensive denial on the part of the patient.

Therapist: Am I pushing you too hard on this subject?

Sensing what is happening, not getting any closer to the patient's feelings, the therapist finally decides to back off. Although the patient is asked if he has been pushed too hard, perhaps it is the therapist who is being pushed too hard, into a comparable corner.

Patient: I don't mind; I know you have to do your job.

The compliant patient, devoid of authentic affect and afraid of rejection, no doubt says what he thinks will please the therapist; he is as yet unable to uncover, or reveal, how he really feels.

In order to avoid painful affect, such patients often overtly deny that they are distressed. It is a way to protect against any threatening inquiry, while in fact they are becoming more deeply disengaged. This tendency to disconnect reflects the fact that, unlike dealing with an individual's conflicts, in which ambivalent feelings and defenses can be responsive to interpretive interventions, the patient's deficits cannot be interpreted away. Preoedipal transferences do not dissolve with interpretations because they lack the libidinal energy to be discharged. Chessick (1980) has even questioned whether such self-object phenomena, which are "*not* motivated by the need to discharge instinctual tensions" (p. 208) and instead are motivated by the urge to fulfill narcissistic needs of childhood, should be considered transference in its strict sense. Nonetheless, these transference-like phenomena, if activated, only disturb the patient's tenuous sense of self.

In addition to the difficulties of treatment that accrue from the inherent nature of the detached and deprived patient are those that, ironically, are a function of the very stance of the clinician in attempting to reach and relate to those with dyadic deficits—the pivotal role of the *empathic* therapist. Thus the therapy itself can unsuspectingly suffer the iatrogenic effects of erroneous empathy. Although empathy eventually represents a mutual sharing of another's experience, part of the process of being empathic inevitably entails the *projection* of one's mental state onto another person or object; therefore, there is always the possibility that "what seems like the therapist's receipt of another's mental experience is really the therapist's transmission of his own" (Havens 1986, p. 185). Indeed, this negative side of the therapist's empathic efforts to emotionally engage the dyadic deficit patient may lead to the blurring of intersubjective boundaries as a form of overattunement. As the following example suggests, extreme empathy may lead to the therapist's special susceptibility to countertransference when working with dyadic deficit patients.[2]

---

2. An unresolved controversy persists over the participant versus observer role of the empathic therapist, that is, the extent to which he or she should (or should not) subjectively share the emotional experience of the patient. Starcevic and Piontek (1997) present three theoretical positions with regard to "the relationship between *understanding* the patient's feelings and *feeling* the way the patient feels" (p. 9, italics mine). Truax (1967), for example, has favored the former posture (i. e., feelings may in fact interfere with the therapist's understanding), Havens (1986) is largely aligned with the latter (i.e., mutual feeling is essential for understanding the other), and Greenson (1960) has taken a middle or dual position, which recommends that the oscillating therapist "partakes of the quality and not the degree of the feelings, the kind and not the quantity" (p. 418).

The Therapist's Need to Guard against His Own Disengagement:
Counterreactive Responses of Boredom, Loneliness,
Alienation, and Aggression

On the countertransferential side of the therapeutic relationship coin is the struggling therapist who repeatedly tries to meet the unreachable patient, fill the void of the empty patient, or satisfy the insatiable patient, at a place that sometimes must seem much more than halfway. Ultimately, if their converging paths still fail to intersect, the therapist can become an increasingly lonely and resentful recipient of the patient's psychopathology. In this regard, discouraged or depleted clinicians have noted the dangers of attunement when working closely with those who remain unfulfilled despite earnest and even excessive efforts in their behalf. As a result, countertransferential responses to dyadic deficit patients can include the therapist's own reciprocal feelings of detachment, boredom, fatigue, impotence, hostility, and, eventually, dread (Connors 1997, Ivey 1996).

In short, whether wittingly or unwittingly, the therapist himself becomes the repository of the patient's inner desolation and isolation. In Steiner's (1993) words, the clinician is the one who "has to carry the despair associated with the failure to make contact" (p. 95). Such prospects can give rise to the major countertransferential danger to the clinician: the risk of becoming totally detached from an already fragile bond, disconnected not only from the patient but from self. In his discussion of therapists' efforts to make contact with these insecure and emotionally incapacitated individuals, Havens (1986) has paradoxically referred to the "contagion of every affect" (p. 17), including affectlessness! In the latter instance, the therapist himself often feels empty or drifting away, as if a spell has been cast upon him by the nonrelating patient.

However, the greatest therapeutic problem ultimately becomes the clinician's unconscious confirmation of the patient's already entrenched sense of isolation and enduring belief of not being capable of or, worse, worthy of a relationship. This countertransferential propensity can be the product of defensive interactional symmetry, by which mutual behaviors or feelings between therapist and patient become obstacles to further treatment because they feed the weaknesses and special vulnerabilities of both parties (Ivey 1996). By compounding the already existing psychopathology, it thus constitutes a form of double jeopardy in the psychotherapy of the dyadic deficit patient. As one therapist empathically recognized, "the sense of abuse, inferiority, anxiety, invisibility, discon-nectedness, and despair that [the patient] invoked in me was what *he* had lived with most of *his* life" (p. 365, italics mine).

There is also the countertransferential concern that the therapist makes matters worse by reinforcing the very aloof and unfeeling type of relatedness that he is attempting to address. In fact, above and beyond the patient's resistance to forming a relationship and the disconcerting lack of discernible progress, an often profound problem for the thera-pist is to have to tolerate and overcome the patient's most potent per-sonal threat to treatment—denial of the therapist's existence. Commonly, after gentle and not so gentle strategies have missed their mark, such obliteration by another gradually causes the clinician to psychologically remove himself from the psychotherapy situation. This may start insidi-ously, with increasing lack of interest (i. e, not carefully listening, de-liberately focusing on outside matters, daydreaming, becoming drowsy). However, these seemingly self-protective devices may backfire insofar as they themselves exacerbate the therapist's increased sense of aliena-tion and abandonment.

With the gradual escalation of such feelings of fatigue and tedium, the frustrated therapist may also start to lose self-confidence. Despite rational understanding of this difficult patient, the insecure clinician will not only wonder about his own ineffectiveness with this particular in-dividual, but even seriously question his professional value in general. At the latter point, any creative attempts to revitalize the therapeutic connection may not be able to alter the steady dullness of the sessions, as the therapist himself likewise experiences a sense of emotional emp-tiness that may have benignly begun as boredom. (One telltale sign is of time passing so slowly that the tired therapist, having started the ses-sion at 6:00 pm, surprisingly finds that by 6:03 pm he has already looked at the clock twice.) Indeed, several therapists who reported clinical ex-periences with nonrelating patients have observed their own need for sleep as initially inexplicable countertransference reactions (Ehrenberg 1992, Ivey 1996, Twomey 1994).

Thereafter, efforts to energize oneself and recoup the situation by light bantering or humor can also fall flat, because the dyadic deficit patient will not easily resonate with such light-hearted remarks after being rebuffed. As the estranged therapist tries to counter these devastating feelings, neither his casual banter nor playful wit can salvage the situation.What begins as a cover for hostile teasing and covert reprisal loses its protective shield and can become a prelude to more serious sadistic and/or masochistic machinations.

The following is what transpired with an intellectualizing, obsessively defended dyadic deficit patient, who had no conception of what effect his long-winded, repetitive monologues were having on others:

> *Patient:* The intricacy of relationships in social intercourse is of rather remote interest to me. I understand sex better, though its importance is somewhat exaggerated. But it is more productive and obviously reproductive . . . this is not misogyny, mind you . . . as I have often been accused of by women. I am a man; if I were a woman, whether I would have felt the same way about the man, I don't know. Anyway, I think this has nothing to do with sex assignment; especially I am not even sure whether I am really a man or a woman, if there is such a thing. I do have difficulty, though, in living with women. To my taste they are too noisy, too emotional, too self-preoccupied with their looks and clothes, are unpredictable and disorderly. And let's not talk about their periods and PMS. But obviously I need them, though temporarily. I yearn for women when I am deprived long enough. So how does one reconcile these highly conflictual feelings? How does one carry on simply? Good lord! I was going to say, what's a man to do, but that has nothing to do with my being a man or a woman, I mean masculine or feminine—there must be a better way of saying, "What's a man to do?"
>
> *Therapist:* What's a *gender* to do!

Here the therapist directly answers the patient's desperate question with glib wit, while failing to empathically share the quandary with him.

Although playfulness can sometimes be utilized successfully when other approaches have been ineffective (Ehrenberg 1992), here it functions more as comic relief for the therapist and as a tease or putdown of the deficient patient. Bored and fatigued by the patient's ruminations, the exasperation expressed is really the therapist's alone.

At times like this, such a strained barb can easily fall flat. Usually, the greater the frustration, the more unsuitable the use of wit or other forms of verbal play. These strenuous efforts often occur for the purpose of forcing oneself to engage with—in spite of—the patient. Such veiled aggressivity in the guise of humor may temporarily assuage the therapist, but will invariably surface inappropriately each time he or she is again faced with a similar scenario. The bottom line is that the therapist has lost, at least temporarily, the capacity to be truly attuned to the patient. More specifically, the therapist's response here can be likened not only to that of the unempathic parent, but take on the qualities of the child. As Baker and Baker (1987) have described it:

> Children may seek interaction with an exhausted parent who is simply too tired to respond. They will sometimes be rebuffed by the reality of the parent's fatigue. Should these inevitable "failures" in parental self-object responses become overwhelming, the child may try to compensate for a lack by trying to be perfect, cute, bright, or wonderful. This attempt to "fix" the insult reflects the child's perception that something is wrong with him or her . . . [this] effort to be perfect [is referred to] as the "grandiose, exhibitionistic self." In other words . . . humans are so constituted that they preserve a piece of the old grandiose delusion. . . . [p. 3]

By being obliged to stay with this patient under such circumstances, here it is the therapist who struggles to preserve the grandiose delusion, as the sense of his own loneliness and the discomfort of their disconnectedness escalate. As time goes on, even the experienced clinician will begin to anticipate the therapy hours with dread. After successive sessions with this type of patient, the therapist may find himself jotting down a few discouraged lines of progress notes, such as "another tooth-pulling session," or, in expectation of premature termination, "patient certainly not suitable for psychotherapy." These revealing clinical comments may defensively disparage the dyadic deficit patient, while attempting to absolve oneself from blame. But they presage worse sessions to come.

As the foregoing excerpts exemplify, empathy encompasses an intricate and subtle phenomenon that cannot be forced or falsely imposed. Nor is it a wise presumption to expect empathic expressiveness to be a perfect panacea for the patient—or therapist. On a more optimistic note, Stern (1985) has concluded that "non-attunement" (p. 207), which refers to the unshareability of subjective experience between mother and infant, is probably limited to cases of severe psychosis. On the other hand, "selective attunement is one of the most potent ways that a parent can shape the development of a child's subjective and interpersonal life" (p. 207). It has communicative power to create and change the intrapsychic experiences of the child. Similarly, the clinician can survive this potentially devastating downward spiral course, by being able to anticipate, and avoid, the pressing problem of reciprocal disengagement—at the same time, continually trying to overcome the dyadic deficit patient's fateful flaw, the incapacity for attachment.

CREATING AND SECURING THE CAPACITY FOR ATTACHMENT: THE THERAPIST AS MATERNAL SELF-OBJECT

In light of the deficiencies of the dyadic deficit patient, it becomes the psychotherapist's crucial charge to symbolically embody, as well as realistically supply, a contemporary substitution for the early faulty or absent caretaking figure—the *maternal self-object*. The basic premise here is that such patients cannot function independently until they have had within their experience the benefit of a relationship with an idealized longed-for figure, an extension of self, who could validate their identity and worth. In psychotherapy it pertains to supplying the self-object, as well as utilizing the reiteration and reconstruction of parental failures of the past in order to understand the patient's disappointments.

Kohut (1971, 1977) has placed the patient's childhood relationship to the self-object at the core of both psychopathology and treatment, noting the fundamental need for self-object experiences to help the person regulate self-esteem and feel complete. He delineated their three major functions (which later take the form of three types of self-object transferences in psychotherapy) that serve the express purpose of meeting early basic requirements: *mirroring* (need to be recognized and affirmed); *idealizing* (need to experience oneself as part of an admired other); and *merger* (need for fusion or total oneness). Subsequently, other self-object experiences also have been recognized as necessary to maintain a balanced self: *alter-ego* (need to experience an essential alikeness or twinship); *adversarial* (need for a benignly opposing other who nonetheless supports the self); *efficacy* (need to have an initiating role in the responsiveness of others); and *vitalizing* (need for affective attunement by another who can access the inner state of the self and its fluctuations) (Settlage 1994). Emphasis is on the internalization of these missing maternal functions in the figure of the therapist; they include the earliest structures that must be repaired or replaced.

Of special significance is that object needs have been deliberately distinguished from self-object needs. In the former, the other person serves as an autonomous object that is distinctly separate from the self; in the latter, the two are not yet separable. Moreover, objects and self-objects are said to differ insofar as objects are valued for who they are, whereas self-objects are valued for the internal functions they provide and the basic needs they fulfill. As Baker and Baker (1987) have noted, what is crucial here is that "the self-object needs [sic] being met is more important than the person who meets it" (p. 2).

Since the self-object experience requires a special environment or ambience, Wolf (1994) refers to it as an "ambient process" in psychotherapy (p. 92). It is indicated for those patients (i. e., with dyadic deficits) who must have new self-object experiences in order to nourish arrested and atrophied aspects of their impaired self. It interfaces with the importance of empathy insofar as the therapist should be especially sensitive to the perceived inner state of the patient as a shared experience and respond accordingly. This provides the recipient with a caring, substitute maternal self-object who was not available in childhood. It serves to strengthen the self by consolidating the bond between patient and therapist, in order for the former to feel—perhaps for the first time—recognized, valued, and understood.

Especially when starting psychotherapy with the dyadic deficit patient, the therapist's techniques may need to be the antithesis of those frequently used with more intact patients (see Chapter 7). The therapist must empathize and affirm before he can (if ever) frustrate, confront, or otherwise risk regression. He has to provide these deficient patients with the very experience they lack and what they most long for: "the right degree of connectedness" (Cooper and Maxwell 1995, p. 125).

Being a patient with dyadic deficits inevitably entails a search, both outside of treatment and within, to find the significant figure who was either missing or very remiss in meeting early needs. Often the child has not only been traumatized, but also bears the maternal brunt. This means that the developmental tables may even be turned, in which the child becomes the receiving container of the mother's anxiety or depression, rather than the reverse. Under either circumstance, the major thrust of intervention refers to the therapist's supplying and substituting for the patient's deficient psychic structure as the patient reiterates within treatment the unresolved yearnings, expressed in a variety of primitive, primordial transferences (Kohut 1977). As the dyadic deficit patient reexperiences the insufficient ingredients of the early primary attachment, the therapist has to carefully place himself where the patient is. It is a strategic way of gently and gradually finding out how much contact and affect the patient is able to handle.

For these purposes, the therapist's clinical stance is as a nurturant, accepting, and empathic person—a maternal self-object who recreates the infantile milieu that serves the patient's unfulfilled desires for idealization, mirroring, and merger. As such, the therapist offers both approval and confirmation of the self to replace and replenish these deficits, while the patient longs for, but may painfully avoid or excessively seek, such recognition, admiration, and affirmation within the therapeutic situation.

Given the replication of this early infant environment, especially in light of tremendous pressures on the clinician that may match the infant's ungratified desires, the therapist should be reminded that the mother too was often exceedingly taxed and exhausted by unrelenting infantile demands. However, once the patient is at least in part connected to the being who gives, the therapist—unlike the mother—is advised against giving real provisions to the dyadic deficit patient in terms of money, food, or answering excessive requests. Providing a maternal self-object is not to be misconstrued as directly gratifying or actively soothing the patient, except for trying to *understand* the patient verbally and nonverbally and conveying that understanding back to him or her. Rather, he offers what Sechehaye (1951) has referred to as "symbolic realization," in that "it is not the apples themselves which count but the fact that it is the mother or her substitute who furnishes them" (p. 140). Wolf (1994) also points out a simultaneous distortion, that the patient may misperceive such understanding as love, but that, he feels, can eventually be interpreted (p. 92) (see the Empathic Interpretation: Understanding the Disappointed Self, p. 95). Moreover, Stern (1985) warns that extrapolation from early childhood experiences to the treatment situation is less than perfect. He notes that the phenomena of attunement between mother and infant and empathy between therapist and patient "are operating at different levels of complexity, in different realms, and for ultimately different purposes" (p. 220).

Being a "real" maternal self-object does not mean smooth sailing, any more than being a fantasied transference figure removes the therapist from the deleterious effects of resistance. It is particularly problematic because the therapist professionally puts himself in the place of the primitive self-object and (wittingly or unwittingly) allows archaic transferential events to transpire. Even if the psychotherapy is proceeding relatively smoothly, there are invariably regressions, disruptions, and impasses that turn the temporarily positive atmosphere into a negative one. As the need for a primary self-object means an incessant search and undoubted disappointment, the early fusion–separation scenario repeatedly presents itself in treatment, which in turn entails the continual "making and breaking"(Cooper and Maxwell 1995) of the therapeutic connection. The therapeutic trajectory for the dyadic deficit patient is thus a developmentally expected pattern, albeit an uneven course.

Wolf (1994) refers to this everchanging state during treatment as a "disruption–restoration process," whose seesawing effects absorb much of the therapist's time and energy. When the therapeutic relationship is in jeopardy, their mutual bond is likely to deteriorate either into a premature termination or an interminable stalemate. Such disruptions are bound to occur each time the fragile patient senses some nuance of the therapist's verbal or nonverbal behavior as not being attuned or attentive. It can happen at any vulnerable moment when the dyadic deficit patient feels misunderstood and has lost contact, or is unable to renew contact, with the clinician.

On the patient's part, he may perceive (rightly or wrongly) that the therapist does not truly care and appears more concerned with himself than with the patient's problems. It is believed that these overwhelming affective responses resonate with and are developmentally reminiscent of analogous affective reactions during infancy and childhood, in which the child's self-esteem was diminished or destroyed—not mirrored or validated—in interaction with primary figures. The psychotherapy experience thus becomes a repeat performance of earlier maternal failures, replete with the inconsistency or absence of love, lack of security, sense of powerlessness, and eventually loss of self—what Kohut (1977) refers to as "disintegration anxiety." The repercussions of such devastating episodes include an oversensitivity to the transience of connection and the resurgence throughout therapy of old feelings of helplessness, dependency, detachment, and fragmentation. In order to counteract these early feelings of disconnection or desertion, the therapist as maternal selfobject need not only be empathic. He or she must also be an available, consistent, and steady presence, in short, a "good-enough" mother who provides a holding function as well as offering object constancy.

Offering Object Constancy: Exquisite Attention to Reliability and Dependability

Winnicott (1958) is credited with having concretized basic guidelines for the clinician to establish an ambience for the patient in psychotherapy that would be reminiscent of the earliest facilitating experience of the mother–infant dyad; he called it "good-enough holding." It has implications for all dyadic patients, both with dyadic deficits and dyadic conflicts (see also Chapter 5). Through his introduction of the concept of such a *holding environment*, Winnicott referred to all of the nurturing aspects of the child's milieu, including actual physical holding as well as the mother's constant concern and preoccupation with the infant. A comparable term, the *holding-soothing introject*, reflects the complex endopsychic structure that underlies the growing child's object constancy and promotes a feeling of being soothingly held; such holding-soothing introjects thereby re-create positive experiences with nurturant care-takers (good objects). Thus the concept combines two types of related-ness to the mother that coexist in early infancy: the relationship to the mother as a holding environment (i. e., Winnicott's environmental mother), and the relationship to the mother as an object (i. e., Winnicott's object mother). It is believed that the former aspect of relatedness sig-nificantly surpasses the latter in importance and impact until object constancy develops (at approximately 1½ years old). The latter comes later, when the infant's object relations and ego organization are suffi-ciently developed; it refers both to the ability to perceive objects as hav-ing an existence of their own, and also to summon the memory of the mother as a comforting, tension-easing other.

The point has been made that holding is a dyadic function insofar as it is essentially a *maternal* provision that organizes a facilitative envi-ronment that the dependent infant needs, as this function becomes a major ingredient of the good-enough mother. Through it the infant ex-periences an omnipotence that is regarded as an ordinary but essential feature of a healthy child's development. It provides sufficient security so that eventually the infant is able to tolerate the inevitable failures of empathy that can have consequences in withdrawal (in the dyadic defi-cit patient) or result in rage and terror when the holding is lost (see also the dyadic conflict patient). The holding environment prepares the in-fant for these later phases with the disjunctive and unempathic experi-ences they inevitably entail. Together, the good-enough mother is thus a collective designation used to denote a mother who meets symbiotic needs by offering a holding environment that provides an optimal amount of comfort and constancy for the infant who is wholly depen-dent on her.

As implied above, the dyadic deficit patient's pressing need for attachment has several salient aspects. Many theorists have focused on the developmental desire for connection to the primary object as a matter of physical closeness, not solely for need gratification. Bowlby's

(1969) earliest work on attachment and loss, for example, revealed that the *proximity* of the maternal figure often took precedence over feeding. The continuity of the mother's presence, along with the contact and warmth she provided, preempted the satisfaction of oral needs per se.

In a more extreme position, Kernberg (1982) recently has made the particular point that very disturbed patients do not necessarily require only a warm therapist who can be internalized as a compensation for poor infant–mother interaction (indeed empathy per se can be countertherapeutic). The key factor, rather, is that the internalization of a benign dyadic interaction requires something more than, or other than, a supportive and empathic environment; it requires *constancy* of the mother. Cooper and Maxwell (1995) have recently emphasized that the establishment of a complete sense of connectedness is equivalent to having both a good internal object as well as a stable external reference point. The latter, as an environmental anchor, can be represented by the regularity and stability of psychotherapy; this assures the patient qua child of the ongoing presence of the therapist qua mother.

From the very beginning of treatment, the clinician must recognize the special power of the fusion–separation phenomenon to evoke primitive transferences and defenses as well as intense affect (however repressed). Therefore the therapist is obliged to pay special attention to the attachment needs of the dyadic deficit patient, which starts with the establishment of, and consistent adherence to, the procedures of treatment. In this regard, the clinician himself carefully complies as fully as possible with the explicit and implicit "rules" of their alliance and notices all nuances regarding the therapeutic contract they have formed— the structured and articulated basis of their bond. Any prospective departure from the set course requires deliberate explanation to the patient; such a deviation should be presented with as much advance notice as is feasible in order to be amply addressed and assimilated. Last-minute announcements can be especially perilous.

Of course, some dyadic deficit patients may look utterly uninterested and even express indifference, if not irritation, at the clinician's concerns over these procedural matters (i. e., the patient's cancellations as well as the therapist's change of schedule). In fact, these patients may be severely affected by any attachment-related alteration, thus in a state of highly defensive denial. Therefore a reasonable explanation for *any* absence or change of schedule is essential, as is the therapist's concerted phone call to the patient to express concern at the latter's failure to appear. However, the patient's need for such explanations should not be emphasized or interpreted, but just delivered. (Drawing any excessive attention to such need would only lower the patient's self-esteem and also would be denied.)

In the following instance, the therapist had previously informed the patient of an impending absence, but felt that as the date was coming closer, the subject of his leavetaking needed to be raised again, both to prepare the patient for their imminent separation as well as to reassure him of its temporary nature.

> *Therapist:* Two weeks from today, Monday the 12th, there will not be a session—I'll be out of town.

As the first order of business, the therapist makes a clear and concrete announcement to the patient.

> *Patient:* [looking unfazed, but sounding faintly irritated] You told me last week.
> *Therapist:* Am I being redundant?

The therapist must tune in to negative messages; the milder the negative vibrations, the finer the tuning. The therapist could preferably have said "irritated" because relating directly to affect can often resonate more than cognitive comments.

> *Patient:* Well, you told me, in fact a month ago, that you'll be away that Monday. . . . I mean, it's nice that you're so considerate. But, on the other hand, I began to think about that particular Monday all the time . . . and then I thought, well, you'll only be away for one session.
> *Therapist:* Only one session—so why does it matter?

The therapist tries to capture the patient's concern, as with Havens'
(1986) imitative empathic restatements of internal questions that reflect
what is on the other's mind.

> *Patient:* Well, the more you keep informing me about this same
> forthcoming Monday, the more it's becoming an issue in my
> head. I can't believe that I'm bothering to think about it. Then
> I said to myself, "What is this? Am I getting to be, you know
> ... needy; ah umm, I mean, dependent on you?" No, not ex-
> actly—it's something else. Not a familiar feeling, if you know
> what I mean . . . a kind of relationship? I don't even know what
> that means; I never had it, I think. So how do I know that I'm
> getting something when I don't know what it is? Maybe it's all
> a figment of my imagination. It's funny, though, even though
> I don't know what it is, I kind of want it. Yet I'm also afraid of
> having it.
>
> *Therapist:* It's not clear what our relation is, so is it worth having?
> You begin to want it, but then there are other feelings that come
> back, like being afraid that what if afterwards I don't come
> through?

In response to several relationship issues that the patient raises, the
therapist also casts a wide net—perhaps too wide. As much as possible,
there should only be one message at a time. Like the patient's final comment, however, the therapist's question also addresses the fear aspect
and thus ends on a threatening note.

> *Patient:* Yeah! Now that you put it this way, I definitely don't want
> it. I've got my peaceful life. This all seems to be over my head.
> [silence of 30 seconds]
>
> *Therapist:* Too overwhelming, so it's not worth it.
>
> *Patient:* Intriguing though; I sort of want it in spite of all that. . . .
> But your being away for one session isn't like you're not com-
> ing back. . . . [*silence*] You know, every time I come here, I
> wonder whether you'll be here or not. Even though you're here
> for me, it just doesn't go away . . . that sensation. . . . So the

Monday you'll not be here, it isn't that you aren't returning? I mean, I know that.

Therapist: Yes, you know that. Let me affirm it to you anyway— I'll be here for the next Thursday session.

The therapist explicitly confirms the next appointment and, in spite of the patient's denial, protestation, or expressed ambivalence (i. e., deficit-based need versus fear of attachment), reasserts his predictable, stable, and reliable presence.

By doing so, the clinician specifically reassures the patient of their unbroken therapeutic bond. It constitutes a concrete way to lessen the threat of abandonment that is always lurking in the background. At the same time, the therapist is reaffirming his future availability. This reassurance may also include the offer of special arrangements, such as post-facto contact by phone, or an additional appointment, until the patient is better able to handle even a short separation without undue distress.

Co-authorship of the Therapeutic Discourse: Formation of a "Narrative Alliance"

Since the dyadic deficit patient cannot comfortably carry on a dialogue in the therapeutic context or tell a story without active assistance (i. e., spontaneously speak about incidents in his or her life), the therapist in effect joins the patient with a dually constructed discourse—a *narrative alliance*—to which both parties mutually contribute. In contrast to a developmentally more advanced patient, with whom the therapist attends the patient's communication without concerted collaborative input, with the dyadic deficit patient the therapist is a more reciprocal and realistically present therapeutic partner in the continued construction of the narration.

More specifically, insofar as all communication is geared toward establishing and reestablishing the patient's cohesive attachment to the therapist, psychotherapy with dyadic deficit patients requires active engagement—or rather, co-engagement—with the patient. This means that the concerns of the patient are projected onto a screen, so to speak, in front of both patient and therapist who metaphorically sit side by side to watch the object on the screen and to talk about it. They engage not only in a narrative but an extratransferential discourse, whereby the focus of life events revealed in the session is purposely *not* on the fantasied or projected relationship between the patient and therapist, but on external events and consensual reality.

As applications of this type of intervention, the concepts of "restorying" or "reframing" a narrative in psychotherapy are consistent with a problem-solving orientation towards reorganizing one's experience. In this regard, White and Epston (1990) have found that as problems came to dominate many of their patients' lives, the stories they told the therapist about themselves became problem-saturated to an extent that worked against solutions; in the case of the dyadic deficit patient, the denial of problems has a comparable consequence. Therefore, concretizing conversations or narrations is designed to help the patient to refocus and to articulate particular issues as identifiable problem areas. This in turn facilitates patient access to material that is inaccessible in its current form, and thereby encourages him or her to marshal internal resources that would otherwise be unavailable. In effect, the clinician must work from the outside to the inside of the patient (and from the outside to the inside of the therapeutic situation). In this way, the clinician aids patients to refocus, to rethink and retell their personal tales.

Reframing and restorying are two different techniques that exemplify the use of a narrative alliance. Reframing has its origins in the work of Bateson (1972) and Goffman (1974), who used the term *frame* to delineate the narrow range of meaning that can surround a current situation or problem, like a picture frame, which places boundaries around circumscribed visual contents. Extended to the psychotherapy situation, however, the frame is formed around messages and their particular meanings. Reframing is thus applied to the significance of the immediate interactional context or environment for the patient. Whereas reframing refers to the immediate or current situation, restorying is generally broader and can cover past, present, and even future events.

In particular, Sperling and Lyons (1994) have emphasized that psychotherapy organized around an attachment-representational stance vigilantly attends to the patient's report of current and past attachment experiences, and it is the therapist's reciprocal task to attempt to discern emergent patterns and the ways in which these patterns are used by the patient, both to give discrete meaning to current events and in anticipation of future events. In other words, the overall goal is the "creation and reworking of a shared 'story' for further examination" (p. 34).

Emphasis on the shared story also assures that a healthy balance is maintained between the inner world of the patient and the world of reality. In strenuous efforts to enter the patient's universe, often the former is overemphasized at the exclusion or expense of the latter. For example, the empathic therapist is usually advised to expressly clarify or interpret the patient's experiences and feelings solely from the patient's subjective frame of reference, the rationale being that the dyadic deficit patient needs to find, and to remain in touch with, the validity of his or her own subjective reality. However, this should not necessarily preclude giving credence to how the patient is perceived by others, including the therapist, as part of the external (i. e., transobjective) world. It is perhaps equally essential that all patients, irrespective of the severity of psychopathology (or even because of it), can and should be exposed to alternative perspectives—once rapport has been established and the patient feels understood by the therapist. As Josephs (1994) has put it,

> To interpret consistently from the patient's point of view as though that was all that was of importance . . . could be construed by the patient as a collusive avoidance and denial of the [therapist's] subjectivity for fear of an annihilatory encounter with the [latter's] personal perspective. [p. 48]

In transobjective statements, clarifications, or interpretations, the clinician not only empathically sanctions the feeling state or emotional affect of the patient, but conveys it as a common or collective experience. This offers more than mere clinician confirmation; it extends the shared story to one of consensual validation with external reality. The patient's sense of self is thus secured beyond the treatment situation per se. It is also a way for the dyadic deficit patient to begin to establish better connections to the outside environment as an extension of—and alternative to—the therapist alone as empathic self-object.

In this regard, the narrative alliance can also be used to restore the relationship when disruptions occur. Although it is generally assumed that a professional person is rationally able to be alert to, and defend against, undesired regression of the therapeutic process, it does occur. As the prior examples suggest, being more confrontative, or coming closer than the patient can tolerate at that particular moment, will invariably evoke tacit challenge or overt denial, due to the nonmutuality of the respective experiences of patient and therapist. For the therapist, in turn, it can also mark the beginning of a deteriorating course. Unfortunately, this transpires when the clinician has been himself unable to recognize, and step back from, the wall that has been unexpectedly erected by the compromised patient. This can be compounded by the faulty self-experience of the therapist, who may begin to have comparable feelings of disconnection.

Wolf (1994) has maintained that restoration can occur, however, through an acknowledgment by the therapist of the part that he or she may have played in eliciting the affects that contributed to the disruption. At best this prompts a collaborative inquiry by both parties into each member's part in the impasse. In this regard, the therapist does not force engagement techniques, rather attempts to lay out issues for their joint examination—the resurrection of a narrative alliance.

In the following vignette, the patient has begun to talk about her symptoms and feelings, but needs the cognitive collaboration of the therapist in better understanding them, here, the extent to which they are externally or internally induced.

> *Patient:* This is the third time in the last five years that I got so severely depressed. Each time there is some reason for it, something really bad that's happened in my life, but the question is how much that is justifiable or explainable by those reasons; or, as the other doctor said, I have this illness that will come and go regardless. Of course, both ways they are illnesses, but a little different. I can't put it into words exactly, you know, different kinds of disease. Like one would have a cold and

anyone can catch it, whereas the other could be another ill-ness that not everyone would have.

Therapist: Like an allergy?

The therapist joins the patient to discuss the immediate narration, the issue of the patient's illness. The therapist's engagement with the patient takes the form of focusing on the content of the discourse (i. e., the nature and reasons for the depressive illness). As a joint venture, the clincian borrows the same texture of language and attempts to elaborate upon the patient's metaphors.

Patient: Yeah, they have the same symptoms, in fact. You know, like a running nose, scratchy throat, sneezing, headache. It would be hard to tell which is which.

Therapist: And they have entirely different implications.

The therapist sets the stage to identify the patient's predicament.

Patient: Well, yeah! First you treat them differently, I presume. Secondly, I forgot . . . I was going to say something. Secondly . . . you were saying something before.

Therapist: Their different implications?

The therapist does not leave the patient struggling with confusion, or explore or interpret the "unheard" material or possible blocking, and definitely avoids a "you heard me" attitude. The therapist helps to move the narration with the dyadic deficit patient and co-authors the narration.

Patient: Yes, they're different. If you have a cold, it will eventually go away, but if you have an allergy you are stuck with it all your life. Even though you can get the best help, you still have it; it'll come back in the spring again.

Therapist: So, if your depression is like an allergy, you're stuck with it! How discouraging!

The therapist does not focus on the transferential material, whether the patient is getting the "best help." The dyadic deficit patient does not have such a concern and would feel misunderstood, at best, by this type of interpretation or, because he is oversensitive to even minor slights, would feel accused of being ungrateful. Rather, the therapist feels for the patient and expresses it, giving a name to the corresponding feeling. This is comparable to Havens (1986) linguistic type of "simple empathic" response, noted earlier.

> *Patient:* Very! I watched my father go up and down all his life; it wasn't fun for him and for the rest of us. He was in and out of the hospital, going from one doctor to another.

The patient, in response to being synchronized with by the therapist, confirms and elaborates on the content.

> *Therapist:* And you are concerned that you'll be like him, in and out of hospitals, going from one doctor to another?
> *Patient:* It has already occurred, you know. I went through a hell of an ordeal. I almost lost everything I had. My wife left; I almost got fired.

With the therapist's active assistance in the formation of a narrative alliance, the patient has become freer to reveal his past attachment-related experiences, feelings, and disappointments while currently consolidating their own bond. This allows the clinician to again create and facilitate the original transference in order to then use it to strengthen the fragile self through mutual exploration and understanding. Both the narrative alliance and the transferential bond can work together to achieve a balance between cognition and emotion as well as between mature mutuality and primitive merger. Moreover, whereas the narrative alliance facilitates the shared story and mutual interpersonal tie, the actual words by the therapist may also serve to metaphorically seal, or loosen, their therapeutic attachment, as follows.

Consolidation of Connection through "Illusion of Fusion":
Use of Undifferentiating Language and Content

An unconscious longing for merger is always present (Cooper and Maxwell 1995, Walant 1995). In dyadic deficit patients in particular, merger and detachment occur in their most extreme forms as opposite sides of the same coin. Mollon (1993) described the basic dilemma as follows:

> if the child remains predominantly in the dyadic . . . position with mother, then his or her boundaries and sense of self are unclear. The child is uncertain about his or her origins and place in the scheme of things, not knowing who he or she is and where he or she comes from. Not having fully separated from mother, a crucial fear will be the loss of differentiation of the self, the fusion of the intrapsychic representations of self and other. . . . A claustro-agoraphobic dilemma seems a highly likely consequence, an oscillation between the twin dangers of fusion . . . and isolation. [p. 111]

Walant (1995), for example, has referred to the indissoluble bond of attachment as a "oneness/separateness paradox" that involves merging, surrendering, and uniting while simultaneously separating and individuating. Since merger, as a natural need of all human beings, is both excessively sought and tenaciously fought against in dyadic deficit patients, the primitive ambivalence regarding attachment must be faced in treatment, as both reality and, at times, a fantasy of fusion. This transpires within the context of an intense transference that repeatedly revives the archaic objects of earliest childhood, insofar as the dyadic deficit patient always longs for the original merged state with mother.

To some extent this sense of connectedness would naturally be encouraged when the therapist is empathically tuned into the patient. In addition, the therapist may have to introduce the seeds of self-object merger not only via empathy, but also by *undifferentiating language* and *content synchronicity*, which can connote an illusion of fusion. Thus as an accompaniment to bonding based on affective empathy, the therapist can utilize certain cognitive techniques (e. g., linguistic tools) to induce an illusory semblance of union. For example, such phrases as "*You* want this from *me*" or "*You* are behaving this way to *me*" emphasize the differentiation of patient and therapist, and are naturally distancing. At least at the beginning, however, this type of patient needs to relate as if he is an extension of the clinician. Thus the therapist linguistically uses such plural terms as "we" and "let's," to provide a cognitive form of fusion.

> *Patient:* I'm a little confused whether I should do something else. I can't seem to move; I feel paralyzed. It's so hard to make decisions. I've been truly floundering.
> *Therapist:* Well, let's look at the alternatives.

The therapist extends his own ego functional forces onto the patient, while joining him linguistically as well: "Let's."

> *Patient:* Okay, I can take this salesman's job; the hours are convenient, certainly, but it doesn't pay enough. The other job in the insurance company has good health coverage. I wrote down pros and cons on separate pages, gave them weight, as you suggested; both come to the same ratio. In each you gain something, lose something else.
> *Therapist:* No perfect solution?

The therapist completes the patient's thoughts, which expresses content synchronicity, in Havens' (1986) terms, saying out loud what the patient is thinking, the simplest expression of imitative empathy.

> *Patient:* No, none. Am I looking for a perfect solution? Am I being unreasonable in what I want? Do I really have good judgment about all this? I have no idea. What do you think?
> *Therapist:* We haven't identified yet the focus on satisfactory and unsatisfactory aspects of your present job, before we can compare it with other options.

Instead of accepting the patient's passive role of receiving advice, the therapist requests (using the word "we" again) that the patient join him in the therapeutic task.

Patient: You know, objectively speaking, my job is as good as the other two. It's just working with Danny that makes me want to look around.

Therapist: Then, instead of rating the pros and cons of the job alternatives, maybe we should look carefully at your relationship with Danny.

Working together, the therapist invites the patient to redefine the task.

Patient: He's just relentless; he makes me feel incompetent. . . .

While the content of the session is refocused, the therapist joins the patient's narration, without interrupting the discourse with transferential questions (e. g., "I wonder whether you feel that way, here, with me also.") The therapist makes use of the patient's statement, being especially careful so as not to make him feel incompetent in their joint venture. Since the patient appears to be in the throes of an idealizing transference, the therapist wishes to utilize the positive feelings but without further increasing the gap between them. If the therapist makes the patient feel diminished, no interpretation would change that.

Therapist: [The therapist shakes his head and utters empathic sounds rather than words as primarily nonverbal expression of empathy.]

Patient: I feel so little with him, completely useless, worthless.

Therapist: How awful! [Again, a simple empathic exclamation]

Patient: Yeah, it really is . . . the same feelings I had. . . .

In response to the therapist's empathic mirroring of the patient's feelings, the patient confirms, at least tentatively, the consolidation of their connection. In sharp contrast to the patient's work relationship with a colleague who makes him feel useless, worhless, and small, the therapist has thus offered some semblance of start toward a new sense of self.

Affective and Cognitive Inoculations:
Incremental Engagement and Understanding

The therapist needs to precisely titrate interventions with dyadic deficit patients, with careful dosage of clarifications and gentle interpretations. The major interrelated reasons for this are twofold: first, the patient's psychopathology precludes the ability to look inward in order to explain his or her deficiencies or to tolerate the pain that psychotherapy entails, and second, the purpose of such exploration necessarily is different from that of healthier patients, for whom insight is the goal. Rather, "the main point of interpretations . . . is to show the patient that he has made contact with us and been understood" (Cooper and Maxwell 1995, p. 121).

This technically means continual verbal and nonverbal adjustments and readjustments that the therapist must make in order to establish an affective baseline level that can be tolerated by the patient. Havens (1986) compares it to the act of hunting, whereby "the hunter must make sufficient noise to flush the quarry, but not so much that he frightens it into paralysis or fresh concealment" (p. 49). In the earlier case of the protesting patient, the therapist had not been successful in treading this fine line. Nonetheless, in this painstaking process of accessing the emotional life of the dyadic deficit patient through different types of verbal exchange, feeling can gradually be uncovered and expressed (albeit at times retracted and closed off anew).

As a rule, direct, forceful, or too active interpersonal engagement techniques will intimidate and confuse the patient. Rather, small "time-released" inoculations are necessary. The patient's engagement with the therapist is slow in coming and will best occur indirectly through discussion of subjects that are relatively nonthreatening and by working in effect from the outside to the inside of the patient. The therapist, while remaining accepting, nurturant, receptive, and tolerant, must search and find subject matter of interest to the patient (if he or she cannot easily do so) but which is not so problematic or emotionally loaded as to produce major resistance. This may also mean maintaining discussions not of the patient per se, but of other persons and experiences in the patient's life as the sole focus of, or route to, more self-related topics. In addition, the therapist actively avoids translating these narrations as transferential phenomena reflecting the therapist–patient relationship.

> *Patient:* I sit at my desk all day long, nothing really to do; the telephone doesn't ring; it seems like I'm cast aside. People are friendly, mind you, when I run into them, but if I don't get out of the office, or for that matter, if I don't go to work at all, it seems like no one will notice.

The patient's wondering whether the therapist notices him will *not* be the focus of the session.

> *Therapist:* Or care!

The therapist completes the missing affective element to the patient's narration.

> *Patient:* I wonder why they don't fire me. I used to have an administrative role on the unit. I still have the title, funny enough, but they just hired this fellow as manager and he basically usurps my full role. No one was telling me what was going on.

The patient apparently dismisses the therapist's search for affect and returns to his cognitive narration.

> *Therapist:* And you couldn't ask.

The therapist thus also changes the therapeutic tactic from the affective to the cognitive domain, since the patient does not appear to be ready. Instead he is preparing for the patient's self-confrontation by reframing the topic of concern, that is, the therapist goes from an *other*-oriented inquiry (i. e., the issue of blaming others) to a *self*-oriented inquiry (i. e., the patient's difficulty in being assertive). Similarly, the therapist who is unable to confront or interpret the patient's deficits themselves, may be able to explore its consequences (i. e., the inevitable disappointment).

> *Patient:* I was hoping that this was temporary and things would fall into place. Now I am, for all practical purposes, removed from the operation. I'll sit here and get paid, but then I begin to feel useless.
>
> *Therapist:* Trying to cope, but not really succeeding.

The therapist objectifies the patient's situation as a cognitive inoculation.

> *Patient:* Initially, I attempted to do a few things. I only got sort of polite responses. I'm not even sure what was the reason for all this! Occasionally I would come late, not that often, and also maybe I wasn't as aggressively shaping things up. But no one talked about it to me.
>
> *Therapist:* Yet somehow it was obvious!

The therapist, through transobjective clarification, presents the patient with a confirmatory comment. The phrase "it was obvious" objectifies the issue and implicitly joins therapist and patient, thereby preparing for the patient's self-confrontation. The clinician purposely does not say, "Somehow *you* know it," because such a statement is differentiating, separating patient and therapist, which would be too threatening and anxiety provoking.

> *Patient:* Yeah, you know, younger people are coming up; they're very aggressive go-getters; it really isn't my personality. And maybe I'm in the wrong business. So when they hired this young manager I more or less gave up my role.
>
> *Therapist:* A welcomed opportunity?

In transobjective query here, again the therapist and patient are unified through dedifferentiation. Not saying, "*You* may have welcomed this," thus separating the two, will ease the patient for eventual self-understanding.

Patient: A little bit, sort of semi-retirement. Let him battle it out for a while, check on people, write letters of threat.

Therapist: Let the new person take over all those old disturbing tasks.

Patient: Yeah, I don't get a big kick out of scolding people, bossing them around. I always thought that there must be a better way of making a living, you know . . . a kind of quiet and gentle job, no major problems all the time.

Therapist: And you now have that—and still you're not happy with it.

The therapist addresses the patient's ambivalence—his conflict over the advantages and disadvantages of his job. Conflicts that are generated by deficits are often conscious, easily recognizable, and acceptable by the patient.

Patient: I thought that this is what I wanted, so easy, no trouble. I mean in some ways it's a perfect job. I'm the boss on paper, and so no one bothers me. Jeffrey does all the dirty work. I mean, I could sit there, read the newspaper all day, chat on the phone with my wife. Actually, I bought a portable TV, which I'll bring in and have a good time—and get paid!

Therapist: Nevertheless, something is bothersome, depressing.

Patient: I wonder why! When I tell this to my neighbor, he says he wishes he had a job like that. He works in the post office.

Therapist: Feeling useless isn't a good feeling?

Again, gradually accessing affect, the therapist provides a cognitive explanation for the patient's emotional discomfort.

Patient: No, but I never realized it before. I mean, I never knew that I was useful, or if I was, I didn't give much importance to it. I did my job; that was it. I never paid attention to whether I was important or not. I never thought this way, kind of examining myself, my attitude, my thoughts. My wife does that all the

time. So strange, so uncomfortable—I want to stop that. I can't
believe that I'm indulging in this kind of stuff; this is just a
self-indulgence.

Therapist: Or just a good, solid facing your problems squarely!

The therapist provides an alternative view for the patient, in order
to encourage healthier defenses.

Patient: So maybe it's not such an indulgence, not so bad thinking
about all this stuff. Yet I think I should stop it and sometimes
I can't stop it. I'm sitting in front of my desk, just thinking about
this stuff. Lately, it's taking all my awake time; it's like a little
fire started and is slowly taking over the whole house.

The interpretive process thus takes on a "psychoeducational"quality
(Sperling and Lyons 1994). This is comparable to what is utilized in other
approaches, especially brief dynamic and cognitive therapies, as the
therapist presents interpretations in a recursive manner that allows the
patient to nondefensively share and increasingly integrate his or her
experiences. The eventual therapeutic goal, as with other interpretations
(see also the Empathic Interpretation, p. 95) is the understanding of the
disappointed self as well as a modification of internal representations.
This in turn affects the processing of current interpersonal behaviors
and feelings and modifies the perception of future experiences of self
and others. Ultimately, it is expected that this less threatening, nontransferential, didactic approach will make available to the patient a wider
and deeper range of affective relationships.

The dyadic deficit patient, after a successive series of cognitive and
affective inoculations, is daring to get closer to real feelings—the "fire"
that was ignited by the therapist has started but still smolders within.
Although a part of the patient is afraid of the spreading fire (which can
still get out of control), another part also sees it as a "little fire" and recognizes that its effects on the house that is beginning to burn are gradual.
With the assistance of the therapist as "fireman," the emerging emotions
have become less dangerous than initially feared. Perhaps the house—and

the patient—will survive. The patient's feelings have surely been singed by the blaze, but he or she is ultimately unharmed.

THE EMPATHIC INTERPRETATION: UNDERSTANDING THE DISAPPOINTED SELF

The ultimate instrument of psychotherapy—interpretation—must be subject to major modification because of the inherent developmental differences between dyadic and triadic patients. In his work on the fragile self, Mollon (1993) has compared dyadic to triadic development, explaining "the impossibility of self-knowledge in the dyadic position" (p. 112). As he theorized it, "It may be that, in the dyadic position, it is fundamentally impossible to know the self, precisely because there is no third dimension to provide a perspective. Thus Narcissus remained entrapped by the mirror of the pool, unable to separate from his own image and unable to recognize himself" (p. 112).

By contrast is Abelin's (1975) examination of the rapprochement subphase of development as a critical stage of separation-individuation, from which the role of the father and a model of early triangulation are derived. This arrival at the triadic phase has direct bearing not only for the origins of core gender identity, but on the ability to self-observe (see also Chapter 7).

More specifically, Abelin (1980) suggests that the child's entry into the phase of oedipal rivalry may be critical in order for him or her to be able to discover aspects of the self, such as one's own libidinal desires. He postulates that this occurs when the young child is able to observe the intimacy between his parents and to recognize in the father someone who is similar to himself by desiring the mother. The implication here is that without having developmentally achieved this triadic position, the child does not have the capacity to know himself; moreover, failing this, the child who has not gone beyond the dyadic position into the oedipal phase will become the patient who is unable to know the answer to the question, "Who am I?" or even the more archaic, "Am I"? (Karasu 1992).

Since self-knowledge is exceedingly difficult, if not impossible, in dyadic deficit patients who do not feel they have—or deserve to have—an independent and worthy self, the major interpretive modus operandi must be altered to accommodate their traumas, deficiencies, and profound disappointments. Thus the classic psychodynamic technique of offering an objective, so-called "neutral" interpretation of transference within a framework of frustration, if not regression, is not viable with dyadic deficit patients. This is because this type of patient needs a therapist who is not deliberately dispassionate or distant, as well as because the therapist's transferential comments, which heighten awareness of the oversensitive issue of the therapist–patient relationship and its vulnerabilities, would be so threatening as to emotionally remove the patient further from an already fragile tie. What this situation requires is a modification of the traditional transferential interpretation. Such an interpretive intervention is neither strictly neutral nor transferential; indeed, both the therapist's stance and the content of the interpretation are changed.

The pivotal intervention for the dyadic deficit patient is the empathic interpretation. In contrast to classic interpretation, which is primarily based upon the clinician's "objective" observations in offering meaning to explain events in the patient's life, an empathic interpretation is "felt" by the therapist, not just understood. It is emotionally experienced as it is presented, inducing insight in the patient through empathic sharing and acceptance, including the safety to look at oneself and the validity the therapist provides through mirroring. Empathy allows relative certainty of the acceptance of interpretation, even with difficult patients, insofar as it creates a special affective atmosphere for receptivity. Empathy is also regarded as a support, in order to allow the patient to tolerate the truth of interpretation. With dyadic deficit patients especially, the interpretive or clarifying comment per se takes a back seat to empathic resonance, as the latter becomes not just a necessary context, but the very message itself. This type of interpretation takes the form of an induction of self-exploration that, first and foremost, serves to preserve their reciprocal bond. It is a form of interpretation that carries with it, in Bleuler's (1930) early term, "affective rapport" (p. 438).

In short, the maternal self-object, as both an object and ambience, is a necessary precursor to providing a tangible intervention to the dyadic deficit patient, the empathic interpretation. Thus empathy as a general phenomenon becomes not only a way of listening to the patient and offering oneself as a self-object, it more specifically forms the affective essence of this type of interpretive intervention.

Nonetheless, in helping the dyadic deficit patient to better understand himself (i. e., who he is, as well as what his disappointments have been), the therapist must not be sidetracked by the excessive emotional needs of the patient. Although a pivotal purpose of psychotherapy with such patients is to offer the therapist as a soothing and mirroring protective figure (i. e., maternal self-object), this should neither preempt nor mask the larger psychotherapeutic issue—that the individual's need for this secure and empathic environment is really a requisite for a further aspiration—to achieve change. "Change needs exploration as well as attachment" (West and Keller 1994, p. 322). These authors have pointed out that rapport on its own, as an end in itself, runs the particular risk of leading to either an enmeshed dependency on the therapist, or the reverse, a withdrawal or escape from attachment to the therapist. The use of the clinician as an auxiliary ego or self-object at best creates a "background of safety" (Sandler 1960) or a "secure base" (Bowlby 1988), which works as a foundation. However, this crucial role of the therapist in the current situation has another agenda: for the patient to begin to unearth the profound disappointments of his or her prior attachment experiences.

This creates a sense of security with the therapist as a protective figure, which in turn facilitates the patient's capacity to tolerate and endure uncovering past and present pain that would otherwise remain repressed. Moreover, because such confrontation of one's deficits is extremely difficult to bear and these patients are particularly unable to withstand the anxiety and other disturbing feelings that are evoked, this type of exploration has to be done through a collaborative and empathic process. In this way, the "dangerous edge of insight" (Appelbaum 1976), the anxiety produced not by the symptom but by the insight itself—not merely the content of the interpretation—is affectively as well as cognitively shared between therapist and patient.

The clinician has to deal not only with the interpretation but with its aftermath.

The relationship between the therapeutic bond and the empathic interpretation also has implications for the entire therapeutic process as well as the content of interpretations. Kohut (1977), for example, refers to the ongoing course of psychotherapy and its interventions as the unfolding of the patient's disappointment. For Kavaler-Adler (1993), it also has a special function, the sharing of grief. Thus the empathic interpretation serves two interrelated purposes: to mutually experience the emotional pain of loss, and to both cognitively and affectively understand the source of deep disappointment. Some of its special themes for the dyadic deficit patient, which follow, include the fear of—and deserving of—abandonment, flight from facing the deficiency, and feelings of inadequacy both with regard to relating to others and in the expression of emotions.

Fear of—and Deserving of—Abandonment

In discerning what does or does not get interpreted, a crucial consideration involves the dual nature of the practitioner's role as a potentially reparative versus regressive attachment figure. An important dilemma inevitably ensues, which is implicit in the dyadic deficit patient's relationship—whether the therapist's primary role becomes that of maternal caregiver who offers protection and mirroring experiences that were absent or deficient in the patient's childhood, or that of the therapist as inducer of unresolved regressive yearnings that prompt a primitive transference to be played out. The concern is that one or another side will be overlooked at the expense of the total treatment. Rather, both aspects need to be adequately attended to, with each side as part of two polar elements of an "inner attachment drama" (p. 323), as West and Keller (1994) portray it.

> Within this internal drama, we can recognize the concurrence of two aspects of a conflictual situation—desire and fear. The desire component, as mentioned above, is essentially a longing for meaningful relatedness. The fear component of the drama arises when expres-

sion of the attachment desire is suffused with anxiety about the individual's own vulnerability and anxiety about the other person's responsiveness. Our therapeutic approach to this desire–fear attachment drama is to separate the desire from the fear, leaving the desire component as an uninterpreted background against which the fear component may be examined as figure. [p. 323]

Here, especially disruptive to the process of attachment is any interpretation of the patient's dependency wishes on the therapist *before* that attachment is firmly established. The patient needs to be benignly dependent (at least temporarily) on the clinician. However, if the patient is showing some signs of being disturbed by his developing dependency (e. g., cancellations, frequent rejection of the therapist's statements), the therapist must actively interpret the patient's fears of abandonment as well as its secret companion, the feeling that the patient *deserves* the abandonment.

> *Patient:* I was anxious on the way here; it's the first time I felt that way since I've been coming here. I was trying to figure out why, but I couldn't.
> *Therapist:* Would it be related to our previous session?
> *Patient:* Maybe. When I was talking about my son's going to college, for a minute I felt like crying, but no tears came out.

Although he may be inwardly moved to tears, the patient usually is unable to affectively express the grief that lies buried below the surface. In this regard, Kavaler-Adler (1993) refers to the "fear of crying" in patients who are constantly warding off a dread of engulfment in their own unbearable pain. Here

> inchoate tears from decades of suppressed pain seem to pose an unconscious threat. There is a profound fear of opening the floodgates. This seems like opening a Pandora's box of engulfing pain, in which one's own inner demons must be encountered. . . . One can fear drowning in tears that echo a loss of an object of fantasy merger. These tears also express a terror of engulfment in the very merger wished for. [p. 25]

Therapist: What stopped them?

Patient: I'm not sure. I'm not sure whether I know how to cry. I don't remember having cried in my adult years. In sad movies and so forth, when people cry I'm always puzzled by that. There, nothing stops their tears. Yet I just don't have them, period. But here, I thought they were about to come; then something abruptly stopped them.

Therapist: Maybe my being here?

The patient's reluctance to come to the session and the emotional experience of the previous session are sufficient to search out whether the patient is becoming troubled with his relationship with the therapist.

Patient: Maybe. On the other hand, I think in my focusing on my son's departure, you were instrumental in getting me to that crying point. So it's hard to understand—as if I were to do something wrong. I got scared, opening up.

Therapist: Opening up?

Patient: Yeah. I mean if I cried here, what would happen? You may console me in some way. And why is it so bad that I may want to be consoled or cared for? But I feel that it's so tenuous, and if I wanted it and you didn't console me, then what? But I know you would, not hug me maybe, but you'll say something consoling. I know that.

Therapist: Maybe the tenuousness is related not to whether I'll say something consoling to you now, but whether I'll always be there to console you.

Here the therapist, by interpreting the patient's fear of crying within the therapy situation, also addresses the larger issue of the dread of abandonment and the anticipatory mourning process that the patient is going through. It should be pointed out that the therapist emphasizes the fear of abandonment, not the fear of (or desire for) closeness.

Patient: Yeah, what if you'll go somewhere else?

Therapist: Like your son going to college!

The therapist connects the patient's concerns within the trans-ferential context to similar concerns, that is, the reactivation of the recent fear, outside of treatment. Such deintensification of transference by a centrifugal (i. e., outward moving) interpretation is useful here (although it would be a mistake with triadic deficit patients; see Chapter 6).

> *Patient:* I don't know how you could not, with all my problems . . .
> I mean, you may get ill yourself or move away.
> *Therapist:* Or not want to help?

The therapist focuses on the patient's sense of not being entitled to the therapist's remaining with him, of his deserving of abandonment by both son and therapist.

> *Patient:* Yeah, I can't expect that kind of commitment. Why should
> you . . . why should anyone . . . ah, you . . . why should you
> waste your time? [hesitant, voice a little cracked] You know,
> for a second, I again got that same feeling, as if I were going to
> cry, a little choked sensation in my throat also this time. It was
> surprising to me; then out of nowhere came the idea that in
> two weeks you'll be away, missing three sessions. . . . Do you
> think there's a connection?

It is important to keep in mind that any disruption of the thera-peutic relationship is inevitably linked to a lowering of self-esteem. This means that the devastating sense of disintegration and inadequacy has befallen the patient; more urgent, in such a disrupted state, the patient feels that he *deserves* the therapist's abandonment of him. In the above interchange, the therapist has intervened by companioning the patient's repressed feelings and fears of loss while helping to verbally express them. Such intrapsychic dialogue serves both to help alleviate and modify the fear of perpetual crying, by processing grief affects into conceptu-ally understandable expressions of guilt and object loss. In this regard, Kavaler-Adler (1993) concludes that "Interpersonal contact is necessary to transform the perpetual crying . . . of pathological mourning into a productive mode of developmental mourning in which the sharing of grief is allowed" (p. 25). It is the therapist's empathic sharing of the dyadic deficit patient's profound sense of loss, as well as the increased capacity to cry—in the context of nonabandonment—that ultimately reassures the patient and assuages his or her fears. In this way, the dyadic deficit patient's need to erect a wall against contact, even when crying, can be gradually diminished. As the therapeutic process progresses, such dyadic deficit patients can begin to recognize not only that they will not be abandoned by the therapist qua mother, but that they do not *deserve* to be.

Flight from Facing the Deficiency—The Inability to Connect

After the initial testing of the therapist's reliability and dependability, and with the decline of fear of abandonment, the patient may begin to talk *to* the therapist. As the latter's empathy and attempts to induce a fusion succeed, the patient begins to feel some attachment. Yet no matter how rudimentary this bond may be, it also leads to the dyadic deficit patient's wanting to distance himself from the therapist. Morgan (1995) refers to such a patient's predilection toward "destroying the knowledge of the need for love" (p. 137). As a result, the patient's silences will grow longer and he will seem to run out of material. Such a patient may even express the uselessness of treatment and want to terminate it, while still yearning to be dependent.

Patient: [silence of 1.5 minutes]
Therapist: So quiet.

The therapist does not permit long silences with dyadic deficit patients.

Patient: Nothing to report; nothing has happened since we last met.

If the patient reports that nothing is happening out there, something important might be happening right here.

Therapist: Some thoughts you might be having right now?
Patient: No, not really.

No exhortation by the therapist will bring more information from the patient. Despite the clinician's temptation to make special efforts to get a greater response, the therapist gently continues to remain affectively present and empathically tuned in.

Therapist: Wondering why you should be here?

The patient's long silences and/or statements that he has nothing to talk about are mini-absences, but they become compounded and cumulative, progressively moving toward major absences. Therefore the therapist gradually facilitates discussion of the need, the wish, the impulse to run away, because the dyadic deficit patient will not initiate the topic of attachment, and one day will just disappear.

> *Patient:* That, yes, it seems we've reached the level that there's nothing more to discuss.
> *Therapist:* The level?
> *Patient:* Well . . . the level of things to discuss, you know what I mean, the level. We can talk about my problems up to some point, then there's nothing; that's the extent of it.
> *Therapist:* The extent of it? Is that the extent of closeness that you're comfortable with?

The therapist actively introduces the likely reason for the patient's reluctance.

> *Patient:* Do you think it's the discomfort of closeness, or have I just run out of things to talk about?
> *Therapist:* Have you run out of things *to think*?

The therapist does not directly answer the patient's question. Instead he uses it to bring the patient closer to answering the question himself, drawing his own conclusion. The therapist capitalizes on the ever-present content of the internal dialogue of the human mind.

> *Patient:* You mean, all by myself? Oh no, I almost wish I had. You mean to say I should talk about things that I *think*?
> *Therapist:* [waiting without speaking, while the patient is pondering his own question]

When the patient is working, the therapist just listens.

> *Patient:* Ha, ha, well, you asked for it. I was thinking right now that this is the time to find a new therapist.
> *Therapist:* Where you'll have things to talk about below that level.

The therapist uses the formulation of the deficiency—rather than the conflict regarding intimacy—as the reason for the patient's need for flight.

> *Patient:* Yeah, that level. . . . I guess I can just go so far. I mean . . . I remember in dating girls I would go up to a certain point and then drop them. It wasn't related to sex at all, because I did that with the boys, too. I would feel like they were getting too close. I would stop all the connection in such a way that they wouldn't even know what hit them. Some of them did pursue me to find out what they did wrong. Of course, there was nothing I could tell and they did nothing wrong, so I wouldn't even respond to their questions. They never suspected that I had a problem, because when the relationship first begins, I'm okay; it's just when it gets to that level . . . what did we say? Yeah . . . then I freeze, or just cut out and then look for another relationship and bring that relationship up to that point again and move on to the next one. . . .
> *Therapist:* So when it's too close for comfort, then you have to get a new girl, get a new therapist.
> *Patient:* This isn't like the abandonment stuff that we talked about. I have that, but less. It's more like . . . I don't know how to

express it; it's like I'm this nothing person. You see, abandonment, I know what it is, I'm not even that scared of it anymore. I know the bottom line. I don't know what the next step is, I mean, what to expect. What is closeness, whatever it is? . . . Last night I was going through some old albums; in one picture we're standing. I must have been 2 or 3 years old. . . . I had this angelic smile on my face for some reason, looking at my mother whose back was half turned toward me. . . . [eyes welling] Oh . . . she was turning away, not really there for me. I must have done something I thought would please her, that angelic look I had, but it didn't matter to her, the picture brought it all back.

Having allowed the patient to bring up the subject of flight reveals that the floodgates are now open. Hereafter, with the assist of the therapist, the patient can begin to control them himself. Ultimately, if the dyadic deficit patient can face the need for flight, he may not have to flee.

Feeling of Inadequacy in Relating

The therapist's quiet and unintrusive presence promotes a safe interpersonal space—not too close and not too distant—wherein the patient can allow himself to develop a benign dependency on, and an attachment to, another. It constitutes both the ambience and the object for a more mature therapeutic relationship. Although the patient behaves as if he expects very little, if anything, from the therapist, he has invested a great deal by just showing up; in fact, the patient soon considers the clinician as the closest relation he has ever had. However, since this is usually accompanied by an idealizing transference that reactivates previously unsuccessful overendowment of parents in childhood, such transferential affect must be allowed, at least temporarily, to unfold in the therapy.

Patient: [tentatively expressing concern for the therapist after an unexpected absence] Are you feeling better?

When positive feelings are revealed through such a question, they are not interpreted as in the traditional psychodynamic approach (because leaving the question unanswered and interpreting the concern would bring the session to a halt). Rather, the therapist responds to the question with a direct answer, a form of affirmation as well as symbolic gratification.

> *Therapist:* Yes, thanks.
>
> *Patient:* When you canceled the appointments three times, I knew you were sick. Today, I expected a cancellation, that you'd phone me up to one hour before the session time. When I came here and saw your office light, I knew that you were back. This time I wasn't worried whether you'd be back or not, that kind of thing, but wondered whether I should worry about you; I mean, what's appropriate? Can I bring some chicken soup, or send you a get-well card, or come to visit? I wasn't sure whether you were in the hospital or home. Just did not know what to do!
>
> *Therapist:* So hard!

The therapist empathizes with the patient's difficulties in dealing with his emotions and the appropriate associated behavior.

> *Patient:* Yes, but then I thought, it was maybe all selfish. Then it was easy. I wasn't really worried about you. I was concerned about you because I need you; you've been my doctor for all this time. But then . . . it wasn't exactly just my needs; you know I'm sort of tongue-tied about this . . . telling you that, yes, I was concerned about your health, but I also wondered how come I was concerned about your health, I mean, besides my problems.
>
> *Therapist:* That you might care about me!

This constitutes a co-narration of the patient's self-explanation; it is not an interpretation.

Patient: [smiles] I wasn't going to go that far; I was just concerned for the moment. Why do I have such a hard time? . . . So inarticulate. I get this complaint from Lillian, and in fact from everyone, that I don't express my emotions. I do, but rarely; then I go back to my closet, the emotionally safe closet. Occasionally I venture out. The other day, Lillian put her arms around me and said, "I love you." So I replied, "I love you too." I think I meant it. Then I quickly changed the subject and asked, "All right, what are we having for dinner?"

Therapist: Scary!

The patient runs away from the therapist and the therapist tolerantly becomes empathic: two steps forward, one backward (or at best sideward) with dyadic deficit patients.

Patient: I was scared, even before her hugging me. You see, in the closet I'm always scared; and when I leave the closet temporarily to come out emotionally, it isn't that I get more scared, I just don't know what to do, how to carry on. What do you do after you've said, "I love you?" Do you understand what I mean? These are little emotional tests that I'm subjecting myself to. But these tests are not clear. It seems, in fact, that I'm the one who is setting up my own tests and then trying to pass them. Afterward, I wonder whether or not I've passed the test.

Therapist: All these self-imposed exams with vague criteria, so how do you find out what your grade is?

Patient: I have no way of knowing. So I run back to my closet.

Therapist: Where you know all the rules.

Patient: Like second nature . . . emotionally invisible.

Therapist: And you became too visible once you felt you might care about me?

This provides an empathic induction of the patient's self-exploration.

Patient: Because caring about you is a little disorienting. You see, I grew up in an emotionless house. I don't ever remember my

> mother initiating a touch; I have difficulty in remembering any memories of physical contact with her. I must have had, or some loving, caring feelings, but it's as if she never existed. I remember my clinging to her legs even as old as 5 or 6 years; she used to push me away, saying that I was too old for that. It wasn't a sexual thing; I just wanted to touch her, to sense her warmth, even if it was just a physical warmth.

When the patient begins to express idealized feelings toward the therapist, simultaneously the unfulfilled need and sense of inadequacy in relating may get sharply exposed. It is a necessary step, however, towards self-exploration of profound feelings, which have persisted since childhood, of impoverishment and failure to relate to mother.

Feeling of Inadequacy in Expressing Emotions

While past and present perceptions, cognitions, actualities, and meanings of events, fears of abandonment, and inadequacy feelings in relating are discussed, the therapist attempts to make linkages between them repetitively, and at times even to a seemingly excessive degree, without expecting the patient's full collaboration or emotional resonance with the material. But, as in the old saying, "Even if the message is not received, that does not mean that it is not worth sending." Once the patient begins to experience some emotions and feels safe enough to own them and express them, it creates quite a bit of conflict and confusion both outside of treatment and somewhat chaotic sessions in treatment. Any attempt at interpretation of the patient's sense of inadequacy in feeling, even well into the treatment process, requires considerable security in the relationship with the therapist.

> *Patient:* It isn't that I fear intimacy, I just don't know what it is! So when she complains that I'm holding back, I don't know what she's talking about. Am I really holding back? If so, what is it? I'm not conscious at all of holding back. I try, but it seems something is missing; always, she ends up being unhappy.

Therapist: And you end up . . . ?

Patient: I end up feeling inadequate with her. As I've said many times, obviously I lack something. And I don't even know what it is, never mind remedying it. She's really something. She says, "Now, right this moment, how do you feel?" Of course, if I have any feelings at that moment, they all evaporate by her zeroing in on me. Then I feel, if anything, like trying to get away from her, to be all by myself.

Therapist: Are there such moments here, too?

Defensive battles are best fought in the transferential field, but only after some attachment between patient and therapist is secured.

Patient: No. At the beginning a little bit; I felt inadequate here too. I think she does expect something that I may not be able to deliver. But you don't do that. She keeps after me, as if I'm doing something on purpose, depriving her. Then I feel like I'm no good, just no good, period.

Therapist: Oh . . . how awful!

This simple empathic statement serves as a short emotional utterance by which the other's feeling is acknowledged and shared; it adds emphasis by being exclamatory. By such pointed means of affective expression, such as strong tone of voice, the therapist encapsulates the difficulty that the patient must be experiencing in tolerating the events described. Havens (1986) suggests that these exclamations or "accented adjectives" answer the need for an emotional reorientation in order to stay with the narrative. It pulls the speaker back from what has been recounted, pausing so that both parties can absorb the experience. Havens also alerts the clinician to the observation that, if used deliberately (or too often), such interventions can be unctuous or patronizing. Rather, they need to be spontaneous moments of shared pain in order to empathically express emotional attentiveness and attunement.

Patient: I don't understand why she just doesn't leave me. You know, if I'm that bad, why hang around? I may be better off without her. She wants to get very close to me, she says. I'm there as much as I can be. What is this intimacy business anyway? I'm trying to keep my head above water. There's no point in making yourself so needy to someone else.

Therapist: You're worried that your feelings will make you dependent on her?

Patient: I don't know what I feel! I feel like I'm not normal. I don't feel the way others do, talking about feelings. It's kind of empty. Maybe that is all I am, no feelings; I don't know. But I know one thing, though—one should always be independent, never making another person indispensable.

Therapist: That's the reason why you wouldn't agree to an extra session?

Patient: Maybe. Because here too, I can't make you indispensable. . . . I come here just to have enough connection.

Therapist: Or you come here just to have enough *dis*connection.

Patient: Hmmm! . . . You know, it was more painful to have my parents back, even though I had such craving and yearning to see my mother, than when they were away. I used to get adjusted to her absence. I don't react to her comings and goings anymore, I think. She was just maintaining enough separation from me to perpetuate my pain. My aunt says she should never have had children.

By sharing the patient's pain translated through multiple empathic interpretations of his or her sense of inadequacy in expressing emotions, fear as well as deserving of abandonment, and the flight from facing the inability to connect, the dyadic deficit patient can eventually recapture and transcend the grief of the lost, deficient, or disappointed self.

THE EMPATHIC INTERPRETATION: USE OF PRIMARY AND SECONDARY GAINS OF DEFICITS

The deficits of the patient may be used by him or her for a variety of primary and/or secondary gains, and both of these types must be interpreted by the therapist. The clinician does not confront the deficiencies per se, but the ways in which the dyadic deficit patient uses them to protect the fragile self (i. e., for primary gains) as well as for other gratification that is not integral to the illness per se (i. e., secondary gains). In the same way that the conflicted patient often gets extra benefits from the perpetuation of his or her neurotic symptoms, such as the added advantages of special attention, being nurtured, or not having to meet the everyday demands of reality, so the dyadic deficit patient may sustain his deficiencies for reasons that are elaborations of, but not necessarily inherent to, the deficit itself.

Some major uses of the patient's deficits for primary gains, which are usually unconscious, include: satisfaction of dependency yearnings as he or she continues to maintain maternal merger; remaining helpless as a way of avoiding painful affects, that is, as an antianxiety or antidepressive device; or, of most compelling paradox, sustaining *insecurity* as a secure base in order to remain intact, an extreme measure to fend off the even greater threat of total disintegration of the self. The functions of secondary gains, which can be preconscious and therefore more accessible to both patient and therapist, may be related to the compensatory glorification of one's pathology, partly to maintain a privileged position of victim, and partly to assuage the fear of moving on in spite of one's presumed handicap. Whether a particular deficit-related behavior can be used for primary and/or secondary gains may be a matter of degree for any given patient, which in turn reflects his or her particular psychopathology. For example, the perpetuation of the person's symptoms as a litany against parental figures may have a secondary-gain function in the dyadic deficit patient (whose hostility is not a necessary mainstay of illness), but have a primary-gain function in the dyadic conflict patient (who may need to express or act out unresolved aggression against others).

Another distinction is that the dyadic deficit patient's need for loving and caring accompanied by low self-esteem and self-worth do not represent conflicts, but deficits. Thus these needs will not go away with interpretation (see Making Contact with a Nonrelating Patient, p. 53). In fact, offering interpretations tends to add insult to the already existing injury. Instead, the therapist has to set the stage for the patient to receive these supplies initially from the therapist himself, later from others, and hopefully and eventually from within. The latter experience of self-supplying psychological strengths from within, even when it does occur, is always a relative phenomenon and may never come to fruition in some patients.

On the other hand, the patient's use of deficits for secondary gain, that is, using his deficits in the same way that the neurotic patient uses his symptoms, will help to undermine their entrenchment. Thus the therapist can interpret the patient's *use* of deficiencies—as a way of securing supplies both in the therapeutic relationship outside, both in the present and in the past—but, again, he is not to confront the deficiencies themselves. This approach applies even when the patient seems eager to make his or her deficiencies the focus of the sessions and is willing to indulge in them—as if the deficits themselves are some sort of conflicts.

In this regard, Russell (1993) has noted some patients' confusion between unrealistic wishes (that underlie their unconscious conflicts) and real needs (that are a function of environmental deficits). It is believed that having suffered repeated trauma and empathic failure can easily interfere with the ability to know the difference. They are so needy that they cannot distinguish between excessive desires and realistic expectations of need gratification from others. In fact, such attempts of dyadic deficit patients to present deficits and losses as conflicts not only reflect their own confusion between the two, but has several wish-fulfilling, secondary-gain advantages, as noted above. At bottom, however, all of these gain-related behaviors can be expressions of the underlying wish to be compensated for past sufferings (Connors 1997).

Maintaining Dependency: Guaranteeing Supplies and Holding onto Mother

Maintaining helpless dependency in order to gratify deep yearnings for nurture and attachment to another is the patient's way to guarantee supplies, to hold onto mother and subsequent maternal representations. This type of patient may thus perpetuate a sense of helplessness in order to secure the therapist's commitment and protection that was missing in the past. The dyadic deficit patient may even undermine himself in life in order to convince the therapist how desperately and definitely he is sick. The therapist in turn needs to interpret the patient's maintaining of sickness or helplessness as a way to hold onto the therapist, just as he once thought that was the only way to hold onto mother.[3] Such an interpretation follows below. It should also be pointed out that preparation of the patient for interpretation of secondary gains usually facilitates resonance with the therapist, which can be a precursor to interpretation of primary gains.

> *Patient:* You wouldn't believe how sick I am. Since treatment, I'm getting worse. My husband says I can't even make minor decisions; I call him many times a day just to touch base. If he's ten minutes late coming home, I get into a panic. And he keeps saying that if I don't stop this, he's going to leave me. But I can't help it. I feel so useless, so worthless. . . . Am I really that helpless, or am I exaggerating, as he says I am?
>
> *Therapist:* Do you think you're maintaining that sense of uselessness just to secure your dependency relationship with him?

With dyadic deficit patients, the direction of interpretations directly follows the narrative content (i. e., if the patient is engaged in out-of-session topics) until a transferential impasse occurs.

> *Patient:* I don't know. If so, it certainly isn't working. My husband is getting pretty disgusted . . . in fact, it would be better if I weren't so clinging to him. He's going to leave me! The funny part is that I wasn't that dependent on him before I began the treatment. You've got to help me, Doctor; I can't work . . . I'm a very sick person.

---

3. This theoretical understanding of the patient's pathology may or may not be correct. The question has frequently been asked, "Are all intelligible interpretations equal?" I believe that the interpretation that evolves consensually between therapist and patient is more equal than others. In that sense, the empathic interpretation need not be technically correct—the only condition for its "rightness" is that the patient must resonate with it.

Therapist: You think I'll stop treating you if you start working.

A centripetal (i. e., inward-directed) interpretation follows, again a shift onto the patient's narrative content focus.

Patient: Well, you might. But you see, I wouldn't blame you either. You see, people don't understand—the fact that I'm not stay-ing in bed doesn't mean that I'm okay. So people stop caring if you, you know . . . the only time I felt taken care of was as a child when I was sick. It seems like my parents only gave me something when I was sick, or accepted my weakness, my sick-ness. So I feel if I were useless, Joe wouldn't desert me, and if I tell you how badly off I am, you wouldn't terminate the treat-ment. On the other hand, if I tell you all the bad things about myself, I'm afraid they will just be confirmed. If I keep them in my mind, it's still a little safer, but by uttering how useless I am, I feel confirmed as being useless. I don't know which one is worse—to be abandoned, or to be confirmed that I'm no good.

Therapist: Between a rock and a hard place!

Patient: I think this therapy made me worse, Doctor. In the past, I wasn't even worried about people leaving me. I didn't care. Joe thinks I'm having this problem since I began treatment. I can't live like this. Not that Joe has changed; he's behaving the same way as before. Some treatment! So tell me, is this going to go away? I mean, I have become really sick.

Therapist: Just to make sure that I do maintain your dependency on me.

Patient: You keep saying that! [little laugh] I don't know what it would be like if I were not dependent or sick. What sort of relationship we would have? I have no idea. . . . I was so upset when I got better from meningitis. I knew that my mother wasn't going to remain the same; almost like I lost her twice.

Therapist: We'll have to stop.

Patient: Oh, is it time? I have 5:47 P.M.—you have 5:50 P.M.? I see that's why . . . I thought you started five minutes early.

Therapist: Let's synchronize our watches. [the therapist dials the time information number] Okay, it is now 5:52 P.M.

The therapist does not comment as to whose watch is correct. Rather, by the words,"Let's synchronize," he concretely and metaphorically attempts to join together with the patient, even at this stage of treatment.

Patient: [correcting her watch] May I ask one question, though? Do you think my not working really had something to do with my dependency?
Therapist: Well, maybe to secure the dependency! Let's talk more about this next time.

The therapist does not comment on the patient's trying to stay in the session a little longer—another sign of her insecure dependency; it is not yet time to do so.

Patient: Okay, see you then, Friday. [standing up on the way out, looking down at her wrist] Whose watch do you think needs to be fixed—mine or yours?

The above query, an "exit line" (Gabbard 1982) that was not part of the session per se, nonetheless has special significance. Like the French term, *esprit de l'escalier* (spirit of the staircase), it refers to retorts that consist of a residue of unfinished thoughts upon leavetaking. In therapy, as in theater and life itself, such departing retorts can possess the power of a final pronouncement. What the patient casually whispers, or perhaps blurts out, at those parting moments, may represent the culmination, not of what has already been revealed during the actual hour, but what the patient has been unable to say. Knowing that he or she will not immediately have to face the consequences of the last utterance, which has been presented as an ostensible afterthought, can give the patient courage to say what might not otherwise be said (even if the patient doesn't recognize its import).

In particular, Gabbard's examination of clinical exit lines indicated that they had a special role as a "defense against the feelings evoked by the experience of separation" (p. 586). Such lines can thus serve to soften the blow of abandonment, while acting as a bridge between the therapy hour and the external world of the patient. In the dyadic deficit patient's attempt here to extend their time together, the exit line phenomenon no doubt specially reflects "a fantasied continued relationship outside the session" (p. 580). Since the therapist typically does not want to prolong the session with a reply, it may provide the patient with the more specific fantasy that he or she has somehow triumphed over the set time limit. The patient's exit line has thus accomplished several functions for both patient—and therapist. The patient has fended off his hurt at being cut off too soon, simultaneously leaving a lasting impression on the therapist's thoughts. It also is grist for the clinician's mill, by placing in bold relief the patient's dependency problems and his or her defensive denial of responsibility to depart on schedule (especially if it is the patient's watch—not the therapist's—that needs to be repaired). If the latter is not the case, then it is explicitly a parting warning to the therapist, who may yet have to compensate the needy patient with more time in the future.

Maintaining "Curative" Symptoms: Using Helplessness as an Antianxiety, Antidepressant Device

One of the common gains of having deficits is to hide behind them in life, especially to avoid experiencing depression and anxiety. These symptoms serve both as secondary and primary gains of the patient. Therefore, interpretation of them requires a degree of carefulness and empathic fine-tuning that may not be necessary in dealing with simple secondary gains. For some therapists, using banter when dealing with the secondary gains of the symptoms may work, but it never works as a bridge to primary gain symptoms.

> Patient: You know, I worked so hard and for the first time in my life put together this deal. Would you believe I got the bank to give a small loan and fund these two fellows to open a laundromat? I was the go-between. To everyone's amazement, things worked out; now they're in business, and they don't even call

me. I'm the odd guy out. I spent so much time on this; I was going to talk to the guys, then wondered whether I deserved something here. You know, have I really earned it? So I said the hell with it and I just let it go.

Therapist: Nevertheless, it feels bad!

Affective attunement is utilized to set the stage for empathic interpretation.

Patient: Maybe I'm getting too old for all this. I'm an insecure person to begin with; to be involved with business encounters makes me anxious, even the social situation. Why should I push myself even to call someone for a date? You think that I should? Nine out of ten times I get rejected.

Therapist: Discouraging!

Patient: A little, but also, you know I might be harming myself— my body—by subjecting myself to all this anxiety; the stresses, you know.

Therapist: Have I been pushing you into stressful job and social encounters?

By asking the above question, the therapist turns the direction away from the outside world, as well as away from the self-imposed anxiety, towards their relationship in treatment.

Patient: Not necessarily. I mean, I also want to do all those things. But they, all these encounters, end up lowering my self-esteem even further. Maybe I'm just nothing, this little old fellow, with no special skills or specialness of any sort. What am I trying to prove—to be appreciated and loved at this age? [silence of 30 seconds] I never got that when I was a child, never felt special, so why after all these years am I working so hard—for what? I'm still this incompetent, inadequate kid.

Therapist: Is the anxiety to confront these guys so powerful that you're willing to portray yourself as incompetent and inadequate, the same kid you were so many years ago?

Interpretations must be carefully calibrated to maintain synchronicity with the patient, to be presented with concreteness and specificity.

> *Patient:* Well, I am! And I don't deserve anything. [silence of 60 seconds]
> *Therapist:* Including from me?

The patient may run away from the therapist, under the disguise of again not being good enough to deserve the therapist's attention, but in fact it is done just to get rid of anxiety associated with the implicit expectation of improvement in treatment.[4]

> *Patient:* The thought occurs to me. You know, you've been so good to me, so it's hard to say exactly how I feel. . . .
> *Therapist:* You feel you don't deserve me, so you don't want to confront me with my pushing you into this stressful world.
> *Patient:* Yeah, that also makes me anxious. You don't fully understand how anxious I am; all the time it's a miserable life. I'm anxious, I'm depressed, feeling insecure, inadequate.
> *Therapist:* You feel the worst, in order not to feel bad.

Once again the patient's *use of* his deficit is interpreted, but not the deficit itself.

> *Patient:* I feel bad enough already—why do I need more? Is there more? Incidentally, I mean how much more anxiety is there to come out? Do you think I should sit with these guys and have it out?
> *Therapist:* Do I think you deserve your share of the deal, or do I think you can tolerate the anxiety of the confrontation?

With the deficit patient, the therapist is a full participant and the co-author of interpretations.

---

4. Interpretation (rewording Noel Coward's sentiments with regard to wit) ought to be treated like caviar—never spread it about like marmalade.

Patient: Damn sure I deserve it. As far as anxiety, how bad can it get? It couldn't be worse than what you put me through here. Those sons of bitches . . . can you believe what they're putting me through?

Here the patient is beginning to realize that his excessive efforts to avoid anxiety have denied him other of life's benefits, such as his fair share of a work deal. It is a step in the direction of greater sense of self and greater tolerance of anxiety (or depression), mitigating some of the secondary gain need to maintain his prior portrayal of himself as a helpless and undeserving person.

Maintaining Cohesiveness: Sustaining Insecurity as a Secure Base to Remain Intact

The dyadic deficit patient learns how not to get attached in order to prevent potential abandonment. More damaging, however, is that this type of patient believes that he is not worthy of love. He presents himself to the therapist in a worthless light in order control the damage of not being loved, and in a helpless light in order to prevent abandonment. The patient will also undermine himself outside of treatment (i. e., school, job, social relationships), in order to test the commitment and love of the therapist. The patient is *not* motivated to achieve, to individuate, to grow and separate.

While the therapist remains a dependable and accepting figure to whom the patient can attach himself, the patient's self-defeating behavior is interpreted both in the present, to test the nature of the relations with him (i. e., minimum signs of love), and in the past, historically with the mother. The therapist also interprets the patient's nonattachment as a way to prevent well-deserved abandonment. In addition, the patient's sense of helplessness and all other secondary gains are subject to interpretation, viewed as efforts to secure connectedness with others (e. g., the therapist and the mother), as well as to contain anxiety and depression.

If all goes well so far, the patient is now prepared for the interpretation of the primary gain of maintaining the deficits—the effort of the self to remain intact or whole. Paradoxically, so entrenched are these failings that in the absence of such deficits (e. g., helplessness, low self-esteem), the patient feels as if he or she is becoming unglued, fragmented—as if it is the deficiencies themselves that are holding him together and keeping all of the pieces intact. The very sense of self of the patient is in effect defined by these deficits. Thus their absence becomes associated with the dissolution of that sense of self. In fact, this insecurity is the only *secure* base the patient ever knew! In short, a secure attachment to the therapist, and insight into the secondary gains of the deficits, are requirements before embarking on attempts to deal with the primary gains.

> *Patient:* My son called from the boarding school, saying that he was having difficulties with some kids and that the teachers didn't like him. He said to me, "Please come, Mom, I need you." I felt so good, even though it was very inconvenient. So I drove up, and by the time I got there he was already fine. I could have strangled him! Anyhow, we had lunch together; everything is okay and I came back. When I called him, he didn't have time to talk. I felt so hurt. Here I drove over 100 miles in one day. He's the only person I have some relation with, I thought. Well, I was ready to write him off; I felt he had abandoned me.
>
> *Therapist:* You want to write him off before he does it to you.
>
> *Patient:* Yeah . . . it isn't some kind of retaliation though; I just can't stand that feeling of being left behind, cast out. I feel like I'm coming apart. I know we talked a great deal in the past about my fear of abandonment by you. I think I'm okay with that here, but it's still not a substitute for real life out there. I have to establish some sense of permanency with people. I never got attached to my husband for the same reason. I feel like he could leave me at any time. Of course, he's equally afraid of getting close to people. I wish he could go and see a therapist too. So, we are some pair, but I thought that with my son things would be different. I truly feel close to him, well sort of, but now that he has begun his teenage stuff I can't stand it. It tears something inside of me. I can't explain the pain and the dread.

Did I spend all my life to avoid this pain? I feel like I'm coming apart. Do you know what I mean? It isn't just anger, or anxiety or feeling upset; it's quite different. I may just go crazy or become nothing, as if falling into a black hole, a bottomless pit, no end to it and completely empty. A nightmare of nothing there. [silence of 1 minute]

Therapist: How frightening!

Patient: You have no idea . . . I would rather go back to my old uninvolved self, gladly.

Therapist: Just not to experience that dread, the sense of coming apart?

Patient: What is it? . . . Would you believe I find solace at work, of all places, which I used to complain about. I have the old detachment at work, thank God. I don't have to roll up my sleeves and get involved. I'm afraid that if I do and make a commitment, then they may ask me to leave; then what do I do? But now, I'm just there, doing my work in an acceptable way. So if they ask me to leave it won't be a major trauma, and I won't have to have the sort of engagement I can't manage. Yet, I feel like I'm always in limbo; nothing seems definitely permanent.

Therapist: Except your sense of insecurity.

The therapist actively participates in the development of the interpretation, or even provides one if the patient struggles too much.

Patient: Yeah! . . . I guess I never felt secure with my parents. I felt deserted as long as I remember and I sort of liked that. I was completely indifferent to them too, not *playing* indifferent; I was just fine. I wasn't going to need her. But why was I so needy? My son doesn't do that to me, he never did. He's secure enough, I guess.

Therapist: Hmmm.

Patient: And there's really no reason for that. He's a typical kid. Once his needs are met, then off he goes; it isn't that he stopped loving me, or would leave me, anything like that. But I feel like I want to feel abandoned. Do you know what I mean? Isn't that queer? Even though it upsets me, depresses me, I'm going out of my way to feel deserted, while no one really is doing it. How could that be?

Therapist: It's the home-base feeling that you return to.

The therapist gives an explanatory interpretation: the patient's only security is his old, familiar feeling of being unattached, thus unabandonable.

Patient: My home-base feeling?

Therapist: Your feeling secure in that familiar sense of insecurity.

The therapist does not say, "You heard me," or remain silent, and does not inquire as to why the patient did not hear.

Patient: Yeah, I thought that's what you meant. I know that sense, and I'm comfortable with it; as bad as it is, it doesn't mean the bottom. There's something else there which seems more dreadful.

Therapist: Hoping that your son would recognize your hurt, get close to you, and remain attached.

The (uncomfortable) therapist unnecessarily shifts the focus onto how the patient is using her insecurity toward certain secondary gains.

Patient: To play such a silly game with a kid, it's really amazing; I shouldn't be subjecting him to such nonsense. He's attached fine enough; he probably can't and shouldn't do more—he can't meet all my needs.

Therapist: Especially the past unmet needs.

This represents co-authorship of content with an interpretive lead.

Patient: You mean, I want him to heal my past, too. I guess I did with you, too; almost no reassurance was sufficient. I guess in

no way can I undo the past. No point in insisting on that; the past stays there. Then will I always be dreading moving on?
Therapist: Rather than remaining solidly insecure!

The therapist recovers—always one message at a time.

Patient: It's beginning to make sense, I guess. My son? Poor kid, and others . . . poor people; they have no idea what I'm putting them through.

Here the patient has begun both to feel more secure and to better understand her insecurity. Through the empathic experiences with the therapist as a "maternal self-object" for greater security, soothing, and a sense of being understood, the patient becomes empathic. This is manifested in her expression of empathy towards her son's feelings, which she had earlier been incapable of.

WORKING THROUGH DYADIC DEFICITS: SHARING A DELAYED MOURNING PROCESS

Psychotherapy with dyadic deficit patients, which is pivoted upon attachment issues and their resolution, especially the repressed yearning for merger, inevitably means the need to mourn the missing mother. Treatment thus strives to complete a "delayed mourning process" (West and Keller 1994, p. 327). To the extent that the dyadic deficit patient is a person experientially bereft of mothering, such a bereavement process has been both unfinished and unexplored. What is required is the progressive integration of the patient's profound sense of loss into the therapeutic course as well as the eventual understanding of the deficiencies and defensive behaviors that have characteristically occurred.

Working through the dyadic deficit thereby entails enabling the patient to experience the positive feelings of closeness and merger in relation to the therapist, along with the disappointment and sorrow in old and new objects. Both of these come from affective and cognitive connecting and reframing of past and present. More specifically, such microinternalization of the therapist by the patient as an idealized maternal self-object is an ongoing, sometimes painstakingly slow process of assimilation and change. Its solidifying influence is facilitated only after the patient has first established some secure attachment to the clinician as a caregiving figure, then gradually attaining insight into the unconscious use of his or her symptoms for primary and/or secondary gains, which are derived from and integrally related to the deficits.

Induction of Transmuting Microinternalization via Continued Cognitive and Affective Vaccinations

The term *transmuting internalization* was originated by Kohut (1971) in order to distinguish it from a somewhat similar term, *identification*. In the latter, the totality of internalization of another is implied, whereas in the Kohutian concept it is a piecemeal process, as in my more diminutive revision of the word, a *micro-internalization*. This differentiation reflects Kohut's concern that if the therapist actively assumes a role of idolatry as prophet, savior, and redeemer, he thereby encourages only gross identification; this necessarily obstructs a gradual integration and transformation of the patient's own psychological structures and of the progressive building up of new ones. In transmuting internalization, however, aspects of the idealized self-object are slowly and partially internalized, then reassembled in the psyche of the patient. This means the piecemeal assimilation of an ongoing identificatory process, including recognition of realistic imperfections of the self-object, as new contributory aspects of the therapist are continually internalized and integrated into the emerging self.

    In short, the former reflects the nonspontaneous establishment of an object relationship with sweeping identification, the latter a spontaneous establishment of transferences and minute processes of internalization and reinternalization. The point is especially made that these phenomena are not mutually exclusive. Indeed, with certain patients or personality types (e. g., persons with dyadic deficits), massive and unassimilated identification processes can easily occur on two occasions:

either relatively early in the psychotherapy process, as precursors to or harbingers of small-scale, structure-building transmuting internalizations, and/or relatively late in treatment, during the beginning of the terminal stage, as the patient once again falls prey to the impending impact of recently relinquished, or only partially repudiated, primitive self-objects.

> *Patient:* When I asked how long it would take for me to be, you know, what I'm supposed to be, to find out what I want, or who I am, all that stuff, you said, "It depends." I felt very angry with your answer. I felt like you're saying, "Look, you're a loser, but I'll take care of you the rest of your life."
>
> *Therapist:* Plus not being reassured.
>
> *Patient:* I don't know whether you'll take care of me for the rest of my life. I'm not sure I want that. What I was trying to convey is that it meant that I was a useless person, a loser, that I might need you for the rest of my life. If you said, "Look, we have one month to finish the work," I would be very anxious, but the idea that I'll be in treatment for a long time is very depressing.
>
> *Therapist:* Between the choice of anxiety and depression?
>
> *Patient:* Do you think that means that I'm getting better? If so, I'll tell you it isn't such a good feeling. No, let me take that back. What I meant was, it's a feeling that is positively there, a feeling; it isn't a *bad* feeling. But the feeling itself is not all that comforting, because I'm weaker now than before. First, I didn't care whether you existed. Then there was that feeling that you'll abandon me; I was so upset, it was awful. Then I got over that. Then later, I dreaded not feeling anxious. But the feelings were not really related to you. Now, when you say that this is an open-ended process, I'm getting angry at you and depressed in our relationship. I mean, don't get me wrong, I like you and I don't mind remaining in contact with you, but what does that mean? I was supposed to take what I learned here and find people out there. Well, no such luck, at least so far. Not that I haven't tried, you know. So when you say, "Well, the treatment

is open-ended," gosh, I do get upset. What if we terminated before I find good relations out there, or get depressed thinking that I'll always need you? It's like a yo-yo—depression-anxiety. Something else . . . this yo-yo illness of mine, I mean by remaining ill is also a means of failing you. I feel guilty for being responsible for your failure . . . I mean I feel bad for you . . . I can't believe what I'm saying . . . me, gushing this sentimental stuff. . . . Speaking of sentimental stuff, I had a strange dream this morning. . . .

The very act of putting the experience into words gives form to previously unformed experience and moves the ego to a higher level of organization. This is especially true when the patient lives the emotions associated with the experience fully and undiluted in the sessions. The patient ultimately becomes both an experiencer and the observer of inner life and gains the point of view of observer. To describe one's condition in detail and in depth is an essential step towards transforming it.

Patient: I watch my son with amazement. He's so self-confident, I mean. Where did he get that from? Neither my husband nor I am that way. We, in fact, are both quite insecure people. To me it's a real wonder to watch him assert himself with me— what he wants, what he likes, what he doesn't like, calls me names. Can you believe he says I dress like a dyke? I can't even get angry because I'm so impressed and puzzled with his self-confidence. I mean, to be able to confront me like that. I could never have done even anything remotely like that to my parents. It would have never occurred to me to comment on their way of dressing. I guess I never felt that they would even pay attention to what I thought. I was to be content that they didn't mind my presence. . . .

Therapist: What a contrast! [In the past, the therapist would have made some empathic sound or statement.]

Patient: Joey knows that he's loved. There's nothing that can change that fact. So he's free and confident. I guess that's the secret. I never felt loved. I thought they just tolerated me . . . but I came to understand that the worst part of my elaboration on my family situation was *not* that they didn't love me, though that's for sure. What really came out was that I also presumed I was unlovable. I think that was the most damaging.

Therapist: An inevitable misinterpretation.

The "inevitable" aspect is an expression of sympathic understanding, while the "misinterpretation" aspect is a cognitive reframing of the situation.

Patient: Because of that, I end up relating with insecurity to everyone I meet. It's not a question of whether they'll like me, but that I'm unlikable, period. So I was only grateful if anyone threw some crumbs of love to me. But by and large I didn't expect anything, even crumbs. And whenever I wanted some love from someone, it got excruciating to see whether I'd get it.

Therapist: Even when you got it, it was never reassuring.

Patient: I just remember earlier sessions. After I stayed away for a long time—emotionally, I mean—I then began to look forward to our sessions, but, God, I was so insecure, as if the whole thing was my imagination. I kept thinking, how could I feel secure enough in a relationship, even if it is with a therapist? I felt like it was so fragile, as if it would blow away any time. That was harder than not having it at all. Now, I'm more confident at work, home too, but it all seems like it's not deeply grounded. Maybe it's like learning a second language, learned with conscious effort, hard work, rather than a naturally occurring mother's language. This new learned security, self-confidence, and entitlement are again like the learned language, not fluent. Can it be perfected, to get close to the maternal language?

Therapist: Is that . . .

Patient: [patient interrupts] This is no reference to your accent. Well, maybe it is, too. But if I could get my self-confidence as fluent as your English, I would be satisfied. What I need maybe is to throw myself into it, so that I'm immersed, a sort of Berlitz in self-confidence.

Therapist: Are you suggesting that we should meet more frequently?

Patient: I don't know. You raised this issue once before recently, but I feel that now I may be ready for it. I needed some confidence even to ready myself. It's so exciting and also again a little frightening. . . . I mean, what if we meet frequently and you find out there isn't much there to work on?

Therapist: Why not quit while you're behind?

Patient: [Laughs] Behind? Not ahead? I feel as if I've lived an "unfelt life," so much work to be done. I don't even know where to start. If you said, "Quit while you're ahead," I would have thought that you overestimated the success. Do you know what I mean . . . as if so far I haven't lived—was that what you meant?

The patient is emotionally present, talking to the therapist about himself, about the therapist, and to the therapist.

Despite the apparent progress that the patient has made, insight-seeking interventions, interpretations with full sexual and aggressive dimensions, and/or complete interpretations with genetic emphasis and transferential focus will have to wait for the patient to move up the subsequent stages of the psychological ladder. This may take a long time in some patients and may never arrive in others. In the former, the therapist patiently works and makes haste only gently; in the latter, the therapist comes to terms with the limitations of the patient—as well as his own—and remains committed in light of undue demands, disappointments, and, of particular peril with the dyadic deficit patient, impending disengagement.

The working-through process with dyadic deficit patients embodies empathic failure as a traumatic reenactment of the original pathogenic self-object experience, seen anew in light of an empathic environment to internalize a present nonpathogenic self-object. Like other transferential phenomena, it entails a reiteration of old relational patterns and experiences, with displaced distortions and/or primitive projections superimposed upon the clinician. For West and Keller (1994), the ways in which the therapist is woven into this "inner attachment drama" largely derive from the unmourned trauma of chronic failures in caregiver responsiveness, from which a spectrum of disavowed feelings, from re-pressed desire to despair, may be evoked.

However, they also believe that the dyadic deficit patient's initially persistent and eventually episodic disappointment in the therapist is not necessarily regressive. They suggest, rather, that

> When the therapist . . . does *not* act the role assigned to him or her in the person's inner attachment drama—a discontinuity of experience results. Such a refusal to be cast into playing a role in this drama can precipitate the best kind of corrective emotional experience. Over time, this experiential discontinuity favors accommodation of the therapist as a new and different coactor. . . . [p. 326]

Although the conscious and unconscious processes of comparing past to present attachment experiences inevitably arouses painful feel-ings about what one hasn't had, of wasted and missed opportunities, this comparison also sets in motion a mourning process in which the pa-tient can grieve, and eventually overcome, these otherwise irrevocable losses. Indeed, it is the *discrepancy*, that is, the therapist's relating in a totally different way from the early maternal figure, which serves as both reminder of the past and promise for the future.

Similarly, Wolf (1994) has suggested that amid the therapeutic course of disruption and restoration, the self state inevitably starts with regression or disorganization of various aspects of the self structure that are consistent with the archaic experiences of early childhood. However, as the psychotherapy proceeds, a more cohesive configuration can begin to be created that is in harmony with the current relationship with the clinician. Thus the disruptions and disappointments gradually dimin-ish and are transformed. They are hopefully replaced by the restoration of an empathic ambience of increased connection and validation that undoes and transcends the past. The patient's self-esteem is eventually enhanced in tandem with the strengthening of the self, which is in contrast to the archaic experience with the self-objects of childhood. Whereas interpersonal interactions between mother and child had for-merly left the patient feeling inadequate and despairing, this deficient scenario is gradually reversed in the therapeutic situation, and the dyadic deficit patient may eventually gain a new and stronger sense of self.

Pine (1990) has also incorporated the dyadic deficit patient's developmental history of empathic failure into the developmental course of the working-though process. He refers to those patients who respond with a profound sense of having been failed to what in others would be experienced as relatively minor "misses" of where they were emotionally. He portrays this particular experience as a very powerful one—a deep sense of wound, of psychological abandonment or callousness—that takes considerable time and sensitive interaction to heal. In this regard he concludes that

> The work toward healing is itself . . . a central part of the [therapeutic] work. That is, it does not simply heal a breach that then enables "the work" to go on, but is itself the form in which the tendency to *experience oneself as having been failed* gets worked on and ultimately worked through and understood. [p. 126]

It has been observed that those very patients whose development has been seriously arrested at a level that failed to meet their early needs for mirroring and validation of self often show dramatic results in psychotherapy (Goldberg 1973); this has been attributed to their finding a therapist who understands them (without excessive sympathy or indulgence) and who offers them the special opportunity for passage through a past developmental phase, from which they can then move beyond it (Basch 1980). Kohut (1971) earlier suggested that as a result of the working-through process

> Ultimately the patient, paralleling the gradual achievement of an internal relinquishment of the (narcissistically cathected) [therapist], may discover with calm but deep and genuine pleasure that he has acquired solid nuclei of autonomous function and initiative in his everyday life and in the mode of his perception and understanding. . . . [p. 167]

In short, for the patient such a process "becomes an experience of being understood, an experience of efficacy in having an influence on the [therapist], and, finally, an experience of being vitalized by the affective attunement with the [therapist]" (Wolf 1994, p. 95). Similarly, in describing the therapeutic effects of the good maternal self-object milieu for the infant and its implications for the working-through process, Basch's (1994) conclusion for the child aptly applies also to the patient, for it is he or she who is eventually able to incorporate the sense of a new cohesive self as separate from others. If and when this is accomplished, the dyadic deficit patient will be able to

> accept without a sense of permanent loss that fact that his selfobjects are selves in their own right and have needs that at any given time may disregard or even be in opposition to his own. . . . He may come to recognize and understand that the selfobject needs of others are as significant and as worthy of respect as are his own. [p. 27]

5

The Dyadic Conflict Patient and the Projective Container

PSYCHOTHERAPY SCENARIO

Treatment of *dyadic conflict* patients entails working with unstable individuals who show marked inconsistencies, rather than across-the-board deficiencies, in their ego development and object relationship to the therapist. They may have sufficiently intact reality testing and relatively established interpersonal relations to give the deceptive appearance of adequate functioning, or even success, in certain arenas of their life. However, they are especially vulnerable to regression—and aggression—under stressful or conflictual circumstances. Basic developmental problems reflect their faulty object constancy, thus inability to integrate positive and negative introjects or affects of love and hate and, as added insult to that injury, the inadequacy of soothing and holding introjects to keep hostile impulses at bay. Particular weaknesses of ego and object relations are expressed in their major maturational difficulties with regard to adaptation and self-protection (i. e., primitive defense mechanisms, such as splitting and projective identification), identity formation (i. e., diffusion of boundaries between self and others), frustration tolerance (i. e., excessive need for gratification), and impulse control (i. e., emotional volatility, especially rage reactions).

This means that as psychotherapy reiterates early traumas, which are in turn recapitulated in the patient's turbulent relationships of adulthood, core conflicts around aggressivity continue to occupy a pivotal position. Moreover, as the dyadic conflict patient's unmet wishes for intimacy remain riddled by fears of engulfment from an intrusive and rejecting maternal figure, an unrelenting hostile–dependent transference can claim the clinician's full time and attention.

In accordance with this, the therapist's expressed empathy as a therapeutic tool is received differently from that of the dyadic deficit patient. Because it is so easily subject to distortion, it may be too enticing (leading to excessive gratification and idealization of the therapist) or too threatening (leading to a heightened sense of intrusion and paranoic misperception as pity). As an agent of change or cure, it should only be offered judiciously; in particular, it is not appropriate as a unilateral antidote to assuage the dyadic conflict patient's signature affect of anger. Rather, the containing function by the therapist of the patient's malevolent impulses becomes paramount, as the clinician not only assiduously structures the therapeutic situation, but also absorbs, organizes, and transforms through cognitive translation (i. e., explanation, clarification, interpretation) all negativity. The clinician even encourages aggressive expression *within* treatment, without retaliation.

Such arduous requirements of the therapist can also have undesirable repercussions. They may be accompanied, at least initially, by unrealistic rescue fantasies, which are invariably doomed to fail; thus both practitioner and patient end up separately suffering their respective disappointments. In addition, caught in a vicious cycle of projection and introjection, acting out still remains a major temptation and impending danger by either party. Here the formation (and role reversal) of a "victim-aggressor" dyad easily emerges as the predominant transference/ countertransference configuration. In fact, the perpetually persecuted therapist, feeling berated and betrayed, may not only begin to believe the patient's—and his own—projected badness, but behave in hostile or punitive ways that foster this self-fulfilling (and object-fulfilling) prophecy. At the same time, the compromised clinician's counteraggression, as well as boundary transgressions under duress (i. e., pressured to meet excessive or intrusive demands), can reflect reciprocal problems to those of the patient. Ultimately, both must survive this disruptive, and sometimes mutually destructive, therapeutic course.

OUTLINE OF INTERVENTIONS
FOR DYADIC CONFLICT PATIENTS

CASE EXCERPTS WITH THERAPIST COMMENTARY

Somewhere between the poles of irrepressible desire for mother and morbid fear of closeness to her or engulfment by her resides not only the dyadic deficit patient, but the dyadic conflict patient. While both may yearn for a sense of symbiotic bliss with the maternal figure and suffer profound disappointment at her absence, in the former it most often takes the form of detachment and withdrawal to fend off deeper depression, catastrophic loss of self-esteem, and "disintegration anxiety" (Kohut 1977), whereas in the latter, conflictual hostile and destructive impulses can come closer to the surface and be externalized. Thus, dyadic conflict patients may be more prone to sudden, uncontrolled outbursts of enraged aggressivity and acting out against self and others (Kernberg 1992).

There is a decided difference between anger and rage. Whereas some degree of anger and aggression is considered normal and even healthy, the intensified form of rage is regarded as pathological, a malignant product of self-object failure (Kohut 1984) or frustration during the oral period (Kernberg 1992). In addition, nonpathological aggression directed against objects, which seeks to remove the obstruction to gratification, should subside when the need is met. But archaic aggression in the destructive form of primitive rage, which has earlier origins, does not necessarily stop when the self-object is reestablished. Rather, "rage seeks revenge" (Baker and Baker 1987, p. 6). What distinguishes dyadic conflict patients is that they want to get back at the frustrating figure. So long as the conflictual feelings remain unresolved, these individuals are unforgiving, and try to destroy the source of frustration even after insufficient supplies have been replenished or presumed misdeeds have been rectified.

For dyadic conflict patients, therapy can thereby become a way of life that is vengeful instead of reparative. To them, it is not necessarily for *validation,* but for *vindication.* Unlike the dyadic deficit patient, for whom psychotherapy may be an insatiable source of self-confirmation, for the dyadic conflict patient it provides a more aggressive purpose: the retaliative pursuit of destruction. They use the therapist not solely to satisfy their positive dependency needs for support and sustenance, but for negative reasons of assault and reprisal. Such patients may go into treatment in large part expressly because they need to have "a libidinal object to attack" (Rosenfeld 1987, p. 22). These patients "are consumed with an intense, often unconscious hostility against the primary object, as a consequence of which they are driven into a chronic conflictual pattern," in Cooper and Maxwell's (1995) words, "a repeated cycle of destruction and search" (p. 119). In psychotherapy, this destructiveness can manifest as sudden, blatant breaches of the therapeutic relationship and disruptions through regressive outbursts or flagrant violations of rules. In addition, a chronic companion to destruction is distortion, which may more insidiously manifest as persistent paranoid misperceptions. These can take the form of "therapeutic misalliances" (Langs 1975, Meissner 1993), in which the maintenance of trust is perpetually undermined by primitive projections and defensive distortions.

In light of the above, the dyadic conflict patient characteristically conveys an unaccepting and unyielding attitude, with an overall demeanor of negativity, aggressivity, and undue demand. This invariably occurs regardless of—and even because of—the therapist's natural attempts to be reasonable and accommodating, at least initially, in order to set the receptive stage for treatment. Despite concerted clinical activity to be positively engaged by generating some semblance of acceptance, succor, and/or support in their interactions, the patient's hostility and unresolved rage towards both self and others appears to be fused with an incessant need to overtly or covertly counter the clinician's capacity to care. As Kernberg (1975) has put it, "In very simple terms, the experience of giving something good and receiving something bad in return, and the impossibility of correcting such experience through the usual means of dealing with reality, is a dramatic part of the [therapist's] work" (p. 61). The pivotal therapeutic question thus becomes: How does one deal with the dyadic conflict patient's tenacious attempts to thwart treatment and to test the therapist's mettle at every turn?

REMAINING ENGAGED WITH THE NEGATIVELY
ENGAGING PATIENT: CREATING A SAFE
AND RESILIENT CONTAINER

A primary pathogenic influence in the early childhood of the dyadic conflict patient has been portrayed as the "parental difficulty in assuaging and regulating the child's angry feelings and reestablishing a viable developmental relationship" (Settlage 1994, p. 30). Four pathological consequences of such repressed anger have been proposed: fear of the powerful combination of repressed rage and omnipotence fantasies; fear of loss of control over repressed, angry, and rageful aggression; omnipresence and readily triggered emotional volatility that interferes with structural integration; and injury to the self that manifests as feeling bad and unworthy of love, with one's needs felt to be unacceptable. As these primitive hostile impulses, accompanied by persecutory and feelings and fantasies, pervade the clinical picture, the major thrust of intervention is invariably the need to deal with aggression, whether covert or overt. This means having a handle on the patient's aggressivity, as well as on the therapist's own.

Insofar as the affective ambience can be unexpectedly (or expectedly) pervaded by the patient's hostility and hatred, the therapist has to be perpetually prepared to be the therapeutic target of unresolved rage. Cooper and Maxwell (1995) have aptly suggested that a major function for the clinician, as both real and symbolic object, is thus to provide "an unbreakable container" (p. 118), strong enough to survive repeated attacks on it. Such a figure has to be able to withstand the dyadic conflict patient's rageful reactions, along with the inevitable distortions and projections that are colored by unresolved and seemingly unmitigated contempt. What is equally essential is that at the same time, the patient needs to begin to experience the (maligned) therapist's nonmalevolent survival as a precursor to his own. If the clinician succumbs to, or reciprocates the patient's object hate, then the patient certainly cannot be expected to control or overcome it.

As with dyadic deficit patients, Winnicott's (1958) work is also applicable here. In particular, he has theorized that when the infant must face frustration and resultant aggression, the good-enough mother offers support within a setting of basic empathy and holding. Those attributes enable her to meet the infant's omnipotent needs without having to challenge them overtly, so that the young child has a gratifying human context for a subjective sense of self. Thereafter, it is her failures that gradually show the growing child that he or she is likewise not omnipotent. Similarly, psychotherapy can become a holding environment by providing protection for the patient (against his own as well as others' aggression), along with freedom to cognitively examine his or her internal self and to shift back and forth between fantasy and reality.

As a more specialized concept, Bion (1962, 1967) elaborated upon the calm receptiveness or "reverie" needed by the mother in order to contain the infant's feelings. Such receptivity was capable of translating confused and projected sensory data into meaning; this in turn permitted the infant itself to begin to establish the capacity for reflection and ego functioning. Alternatively, if the mother was unavailable to provide this calming function, she would be inadequate as a containing external object, and the infant's early envy and hatred of the good object would cause it to attack the very object upon which it desperately depended.

While this container concept is similar to Winnicott's (1958) holding environment and Kohut's (1977) self-object experiences, it is more focused in its overall role. Thus the containing function is Bion's conceptualization of the maternal figure being used expressly for tension regulation. Within the context of the calm receptiveness provided by the therapeutic setting, the therapist is similarly seen not as a real object, but as a container, into which all the anxieties and other unwanted feelings on the part of the patient are absorbed. (When these affects are not merely held at bay, but transferred or transformed, the concept is also similar to Kohut's [1971] transmuting internalization.)

In more recent views, Winnicott's theory of the container function can be construed as "a designation for the basis of any relationship between two or more people, whether infant and mother, man and woman, or individual and society" (Moore and Fine 1990, p. 32), and in Campbell's (1996) definition refers to "all those elements (in mother, analyst, etc.) that help the infant or analysand hold parts of the self intact and separate from the object" (p. 15). Comparably, the therapeutic situation can become the contained calm world or object wherein the patient is able to deposit or hold his or her anxiety, anger, and other feelings, so that they not be acted out. Failing this, however, like the infant vis-à-vis the mother, the therapist too may become subject to aggressive attack.

In its broadened form, according to Lewin and Schulz (1992), by such holding (or containing) is meant not only an environment or ambience but

> an action, literal or symbolic, that has the effect of supplementing the existing psychic infrastructure so as to render what may be an overwhelming situation less overwhelming, thus providing the patient a degree of increased security that allows for continued developmental effort and experimenting with new ways of experiencing. [pp. 116–117]

They also recognize the complexity of the concept by their observation that every holding action is simultaneously to some extent concrete and literal and to some extent abstract and symbolic. In the case of the dyadic conflict patient, the holding/containing function is literal to the extent that the therapist is the direct recipient of, and resilient receptacle for, the patient's strong and suddenly shifting emotions. It is he or she who must therapeutically hold the reins. This complex function is also symbolic in that it embodies more than the actual therapist per se, but becomes the unconscious representation and primary motive force of treatment—the abstract signifier of the early idealized, but more often malevolent, maternal introject. It is this figure as a current object upon whom the patient's unresolved rage can be transferentially expressed and redirected, without retaliatory risk. The therapeutic bottom line is that, since dyadic conflict patients are themselves unable to accomplish certain ego functions such as impulse control, some other person—to wit, the therapist—needs to be able to perform those very functions that they would never be able to accomplish on their own (Zetzel 1971).

The point also must be made regarding these patients, that the holding or containing environment does not have the primary or sole goal to provide a corrective emotional experience that is significantly different from childhood experiences, although it may wittingly or unwittingly do so. Rather, it is utilized here for a preparatory purpose, to provide the foundation for subsequent essential exploratory, confrontative, and interpretative work. Indeed holding, soothing, or containing do not suffice. In this regard, Adler (1993) warns that "Therapists who believe that their caring and love for their patient is the major factor for therapeutic change to occur are vulnerable to countertransference feelings involving their [own] grandiosity and omnipotence" (p. 203) (see also Management of the Patient's Chronic Hostility, Rejection, and Demanding Dependency, p. 166).

In the final analysis, a critical therapeutic distinction must be made: while holding is primarily an affective concept, containing is essentially a cognitive one. Therefore holding is more closely associated with the fundamental need of dyadic deficit patients, containing with that of dyadic conflict patients. In the latter model, if the infant has projected part of his or her psyche, especially uncontrolled affect, onto the mothering figure, it must be contained by her in order for healthy development to occur. This means that she not only absorbs the emotions, but "translates" them into specific meanings and reflectively acts upon them. This significant transaction results in a transformation on the part of the infant—from primitive projective identifications to meaningful thought. Indeed, this same transformatory process becomes the basic goal and course of the therapist's interventions with the dyadic conflict patient.

Establishing Stability, while Allowing the Patient's General Attitude of Reluctance and Negativity to Surface

From the very beginning, the therapist should establish clear guidelines that set limits as the acceptable "rules" of treatment. As a basic tenet, those practicing psychotherapy with hostile, aggressive, self-destructive, or acting-out patients (Chessick 1977, Kernberg 1975, Masterson 1976, Waldinger 1987) have emphasized the need for supportive continuity and stability of the requirements of psychotherapy. It includes the importance—at the very onset—of keeping regular appointment times as well as starting and ending sessions promptly. It also means making structural expectations circumscribed and consistent. As Moore and Fine (1990) have noted "The regularity of visits, rituals of coming and going . . . and very continuity of the objects, spaces and textures . . . all contribute to a metaphorical holding that can help contain the disruptions that occur during meaningful treatment" (p. 206). At the same time, the therapist's own responsibility in posing limits and abiding by them both provides a model and sets the stage for clarification of the patient's reciprocal responsibilities in meeting therapeutic requirements.

This is also a tangible way of placing "assignment of responsibility for the preservation of treatment to the patient" (Sledge and Tasman 1993, p. 143). It is an intervention that imparts power to the patient through direct recognition of the part he or she plays in behaviors during the treatment process. Although adherence to these procedural matters may seem minor, they can become an internalized foundation for other socially accepted and expected nonaggressive acts.

In negotiating such a therapeutic contract with the dyadic conflict patient who struggles with destructive impulses, the therapist must be firm, but without being so strict or inflexible as to be himself harsh, hostile, or punitive. As Plakun (1993) has advised, formation of the contract should always be a mutual, collaborative effort, not imposed by the therapist, so that the terms of the agreement "do not scare off the patient through their potential to be perceived as rejecting" (p. 139). In fact, early in the therapeutic endeavor, it is the making of these very necessary basic contractual arrangements, such as negotiations for the fee and even the hour of the sessions, that can become an arena for the dyadic conflict patient to demonstrate the nature and degree of reluctance and resistance. Whereas these procedural events themselves have limit-setting as well as containing functions, the negotiations to arrive at them are an opportunity for allowing emotional responses, especially aggressive affect, to surface. These preliminary arrangements serve as an initial indicator of—as well as opportunity for—the expression of fundamental feelings, often suppressed resentment, of the patient toward psychotherapy. Perhaps as important, they can also act as a prelude to more pervasive negativity, anger, and aggression yet to come.

Therapist: How about Thursday at 5:00 P.M.?
Patient: No, I can't make it at that time.

When the patient gives no excuse for rejection of the therapist's offer, the therapist has to register, but not confront it—at least not yet. The preliminary purpose here is to secure the affective frame of treatment by allowing the negative responses to occur and, at the same time, to assess to what extent such an initial response does or does not reflect a real negative disposition, which has yet to be confirmed by its repetitive and seemingly intractable nature.

Therapist: 6:00 P.M.?
Patient: No, Thursdays are no good for me.

The therapist again does not confront the negativity, but patiently accepts it by offering the patient yet another option.

Therapist: Ok, let's see. I have next week, Monday, 6:00 P.M. is available.
Patient: Monday evenings I go to gym.

At this third refusal, the therapist moves on to another level of accommodation, by shifting to the patient's calendar instead of his own. At the same time, his own resentment is beginning to rise.

> *Therapist:* Let me hear your calendar. Which days and which times are better for you?
> *Patient:* Well, Mondays and Thursdays are definitely inconvenient.
> *Therapist:* [with quiet control] And the other inconvenient days are Tuesday, Wednesday, Friday, Saturday, and Sunday?

As the therapist is unsuccessful in repeated attempts to accommodate this patient, he may naturally be increasingly frustrated, or even start to feel personally rejected, by the latter's apparent need to keep presenting new obstacles. However, the therapist must also recognize that the dyadic conflict patient may in fact be expressing this repeated reluctance *because of* the former's continued accommodating attitude.

Offering alternatives may appear to be a perfectly reasonable response on the part of a helpful and accepting therapist, but is flawed from a therapeutic point of view. Such an approach can covertly encourage suppressed anger to escalate by not permitting, or at best postponing, the direct expression of negativity by the dyadic conflict patient. With these demanding and emotionally unstable individuals, such a stance is technically inadvisable on two counts: (1) it can lead to the patient's heightened fear—or possible acting out—of impulses as they reach uncontrollable proportions; and (2) it can increase the patient's distortion of reality, and of the therapist's idealized role, by meeting excessive requests instead of having these patients more realistically face their disappointments or confront their suppressed feelings of frustration and anger. Masterson (1983) portrays such common clinical responses of gratification of the patient's wishes, by succumbing to unreasonable requests or demands, as a form of unconscious collusion. Under these circumstances the therapist is resonating with part of the patient, the "rewarding split-object-relations unit," which may manifest as attempting to rescue or trying to provide these patients with a better childhood experience than the primary parent did. Such motives of the conscientious and often overly taxed therapist—to save or to at least satisfy the dyadic conflict patient—however honorable and without awareness, are ill-fated.

> *Patient:* [irritated at the therapist's remark] No . . . no . . . [looking at his calendar] I am so goddamn busy. It's very difficult to carve out any convenient time. Coming up here and then going back, you know, it takes a good two hours of the day!

Like the dyadic deficit patient, this patient is obviously not humored by the therapist's retort. This is typical of dyadic conflict patients, who do not usually appreciate offhand remarks, nor do they easily engage in light banter, especially in the early stages of the therapeutic relationship. These patients are especially sensitive to the thinly veiled hostility associated with such comments, and thus have little tolerance for the potential put-down that may reside behind a presumably humorous or witty response.

> *Therapist:* Do you also wonder whether it would be worth it for you to make such reallocation of your time to see *me*?

Under the circumstances, the therapist seizes the opportunity to forge ahead with a clarifying query. When the therapist does offer a clarification, confrontation, or interpretation of the patient's resistance, such a comment or question has to be crisp, unambiguous, and highly personal (e. g., the therapist refers to "me" instead of using a more general reference to the therapy).

> *Patient:* [sarcastically mimicking the therapist] I don't *wonder* whether it would be worth it; I know that the chances are you won't be able to help me.

In this instance, the patient has fended off the therapist's sarcasm, not by denial or withdrawal (as with the dyadic deficit patient), but by retaliation expressed by his own resentment. The patient barely begins to interact with the therapist when he immediately reverts to a resistant response, although at this point in the therapy it is not blatantly aggressive. Nonetheless he cannot get past a defensive wall of relatively mild sarcasm and negativity (nor can the therapist, for that matter). As Stone (1993) has pointed out, an important function of the therapist is as an "early-warning device" (p. 265), the capacity to be "like earthquake sensors designed to detect weak tremors that might be harbingers of much worse tremors to come shortly" (p. 266).

Tolerance for—and Survival of—a Therapeutic "No-Win" Scenario: Absorbing Indirect and Direct Negative Affect

The pivotal therapeutic stance of absorption of the patient's negative affect refers to the nonretaliatory role of the therapist of tolerance of an incessant "no-win" scenario, as well as unscathed survival in the face of severe and seemingly intractable aggressivity. This absorbing of indirect and direct negative affect invariably includes the dyadic conflict patient's adverse reactions to the therapist's empathy, negative criticism of content explorations, argumentativeness at interpretations, and, of special significance, resorting to the definitive defensive maneuver of the dyadic conflict patient: *projective identification.**

Derived from object relations theory, *projective identification* refers to a situation in which one individual projects subjectively insupportable or undesirable elements of his own self onto another, thus liberating himself of them. The concept of projective identification was first described by Klein (1946/1952); other later work has elaborated not only on the patient's part in this defensive process, but on its interpersonal aspects and countertransferential significance (Ogden 1979). As Adler (1993) explained, "The patient, using projective identification, wants

---

*The meaning of this concept is not always consistent. Some theorists use the terms *projection* and *projective identification* virtually interchangeably, believing that there can be no projection without a recipient (container) with whom the projected part is to be identified. Others suggest that there is an implied distinction between the two: *projection* designates only a defense mechanism, whereas *projective identification* involves a fantasied object relationship (Moore and Fine 1990). This author takes the latter position, also differentiating them developmentally: projection is considered to be relatively advanced, whereas projective identification is more primitive.

to get rid of an unwanted aspect of himself or herself, or an aspect to be protected" (p. 198). The latter may consist of an affect or self or object representation, whereby the projected part is "placed into" the recipient of the projection, who in turn can either "contain it" (Bion 1967) or also attempt to get rid of it (in which case it gets reinternalized by the projector). According to Moore and Fine (1990), in projective identification "parts of the self and internal objects are split off and projected onto an external object, which then becomes identified with the split-off part as well as possessed and controlled by it" (p. 109). Its defensive functions include: fusion with the external object in order to avoid separation (especially when used by a dyadic deficit patient); or (more often in dyadic conflict patients) to take control of the destructive, so-called bad object, which is a persecutory threat to the individual; and to preserve good aspects of the self by splitting them off and projectively identifying them in the therapist for safekeeping.

The containment capacity of the recipient is partially determined by the nature of the projection (i. e., its intensity and primitive quality), and in part by the nature of the recipient's own ego capacities (i. e., the extent to which the projectee has repressed or split off unresolved aspects that resemble what has been projected). As both an intrapsychic and interpersonal phenomenon, both aspects are relevant in determining the final fate of the projective identification experience. Most significant is the fact that the projector (here, the patient) unconsciously behaves in such a way as to provoke the recipient (here, the therapist) to act toward him- or herself in a manner consistent with the projection.

More generally, these patients will relentlessly complain about the treatment no matter how badly they are in need of it, and directly or indirectly reject whatever the therapist offers while desperately dependent upon him or her. Full-blown offenses about anything and everything may come out of nowhere, puzzling the unsuspecting therapist. Unfortunately, it is naive to believe that giving accepting attention to the content of the patient's material will undo the repellent litany—it won't. In fact, expressions of empathy may simply generate anger because the patient experiences it as too intrusive, an early reminder of mother. Similarly, the therapist's interpretations of content material and of transference are invariably rebuffed.

Nonetheless, there is "a method to this madness" of absorbing the patient's repeated negative assaults. While the dyadic conflict patient may begin with seemingly trite complaints about objects or impersonal events, which are only remotely related to the real source of his or her rage, these eventually will lead to more personal and interpersonal discharges of affect. Such unauspicious or insidious responses thereby serve as a precursor to revealing profound malevolent feelings and a start in recognizing their real targets, which in turn can be redirected *toward the therapist* for further expression and exploration. Ultimately, concerted containing of the patient's hostility discharged toward the therapist can be understood as part of a more general pattern of relating to important others (Waldinger 1987).

Patient: Oh, it's freezing here! Is the air conditioning on?

Every negative statement that the patient makes, no matter what the subject but especially about content that is related to the therapist (i. e., the clinician's office, neighborhood, furniture) is brought into the treatment as a reflection of the patient's relationship with the therapist. However, the therapist waits until a negative pattern can be identified; a single comment by the patient is not sufficient.

Therapist: No, it is not on.

Here the therapist simply addresses the patient's question by answering it, without commenting upon it.

Patient: Well, maybe I'm getting a summer cold or something. Anyway, when we met for the first time the other day, you said we need to meet at least a few times before you can answer my questions. I don't know whether I have the time for that; I mean you already know my history—you should be able to tell me how to get rid of my headache.
Therapist: You are already disappointed by the pace of my work!

The therapist does not say "our" work. This is in sharp contrast with what the therapist says to dyadic deficit patients in order to establish or secure their bond. When the dyadic conflict patient is negatively engaged, however, saying "our" or "us" will be perceived as appeasing (if not intruding) rather than alliance building. This is especially true when the therapist is the one meant for the patient's aggression. Thus the therapist uses "I" or "me" as a form of lightning rod, to draw the undiluted negativity and anger upon himself.

> *Patient:* I don't know what your work means! I can't just keep coming here to talk, while you're trying to figure out what makes me tick. It's only making me sicker. I'm here suffering, can't you understand? I don't think you do. How would you like to have a pain in your head all the time and not be able to sleep? You wouldn't be sitting there cozily, asking all kinds of far-out questions about my sexual life, my drinking habits, my relationship with other people. Besides, I've got to solve the problem with my wife fast. I've got to make fast decisions. I mean, where are you coming from!
>
> *Therapist:* You also feel that I'm slowing you down!

Here the patient has not only split good from bad in his primitive distortion of the therapist's purposes, but has begun to blur the boundaries between them. Through role reversal, the patient has in effect taken the therapist's place and is telling *him* what to do.

> *Patient:* Well, try not to. Here I've got Helen, this crazy woman, to tackle; if I take her to court, everyone is going to suffer, including the kids. If I don't, she'll keep pushing me around, get me upset, disturb my relationship with my sons, which isn't in such great shape to begin with. You know, it would have been so easy to deal with a normal woman. The kids will be with her one weekend and with me another. What's the big deal? It's just common sense. Maybe that's why I have these awful headaches. [bangs his fist on the side table]
>
> *Therapist:* Exasperated!

The therapist attempts to express affective attunement with what the patient must be feeling at this moment, by making a "simple empathic" sound (Havens 1986). Although it was a spontaneous effort on the therapist's part to share the patient's frustrating experience, it was received through the same unreceptive filter as all of his other responses.

In this instance, the patient was particularly provoked by a simple empathic expression. The painfulness of, and resistance to, attunement is not entirely unexpected and has been observed by other clinicians (Seinfeld 1991, Walant 1995). Seinfeld (1991) has in fact suggested that for those patients with faulty object relations who are easily engulfed, "empathy can be as ensnaring . . . as any other intervention, even more so because, like pure honey, it tempts the patient into its sticky, thick warmth" (p. 38). In addition, therapeutically empathy has been deliberately differentiated from sympathy (i. e., the former literally a form of "feeling into" another, the latter "feeling with" another), but to the dyadic conflict patient they may seem the same. Sympathy can be closer to pity or feeling sorry for another, often an outsider's anguished and even maudlin response to those perceived as less fortunate. As Moore and Fine (1990) have pointed out, empathy is "relatively neutral and nonjudgmental, unlike the related phenomena of pity and *sympathy,* from which it should be rigorously distinguished. Pity and sympathy lack objectivity [and] encourage overidentification . . ." (p. 67).

Both may be wasted emotions, erroneously regarded as excessively or insincerely sentimental, when expressed to a dyadic conflict patient with primitive aggression. For such patients, who can neither truly self-soothe or be soothed, either can be rejected from their interpersonal filter. Taken further, Chessick (1993) has expressed the view that when such patients react with angry disruption or suicidal or other acting-out behavior in the face of paternalistic counseling or "feeling" approaches, their response may neither be a manifestation of psychopathology nor of transference. Rather, it may represent their intuitive (and realistic) recognition that what they are receiving is inappropriate to their intense personal suffering, thus another desperate and disappointed instance of nonempathic encounter.

Patient: You must be kidding! I really don't need sympathy! I need some real help for these headaches.

Therapist: You made some connections between your headaches and your conflict with Helen. Tell me a little bit more about that.

The therapist reverts to a less affective approach in order to counteract the prior outburst, without changing the subject.

Patient: Tell me a little more! What more is there to say? She really is driving me crazy. I can't believe that I was married to this woman for 10 years. What kind of a person am I that I even stay in this marriage? I know all that. So what? You've got to help, can't you understand?

As the above excerpt reveals, the "good" therapist, who is empathic, understanding, helpful, engaging, insightful, and available to accept angry feelings and therefore earnestly attempts to interpret the barrage of negative transference, will still get nowhere with the dyadic conflict patient unless he is also prepared to accept the fact that this type of getting nowhere—a therapeutic "no-win" scenario—is part of the therapeutic process. Under such circumstances, it has been recommended that the therapist not bend over backwards in working towards renewed rapport or strenuously trying to get the patient to like, admire, and appreciate him.

Rather, the "best antidote" (Basch 1980, p. 75) (and possibly easier approach) when working with negative patients is for the clinician to focus on himself—to try to like oneself better while working with an unlikable patient. Therefore, the therapist's survival of this stage (only temporarily so intense, but always present in diluted fashion) depends on anticipating it and monitoring the dyadic deficit patient's—and his own—reactions of hurt and rage. It is especially essential that the therapist find ways to avoid or control the countertransferential temptation, especially the projectively identified tendency, toward retaliation or self-destruction (see Reactive Fine-tuning: The Need for Vigilance over Subtle Retaliation, p. 157).

*Allowing Microexternalization: First, Facilitating the
Expression of Anger and Rage; Then, Turning Aggression
Away by Redirecting It Toward the Therapist*

Not only does the therapist need to detect and anticipate small and large affective quakes in order to appropriately absorb the full extent of the patient's aggression, but he should *encourage* the expression of emotion within treatment. It has been suggested that affects, such as eroticism, can serve a binding function by providing structure to assuage the ego's internal chaos (Giovacchini 1990); similarly, anger may act as an organizer of the dyadic conflict patient's disorganized state, phenomenologically portrayed as a "pacifier"(Giovacchini 1993, p. 241). Moreover, attacking another may be less devastating to the psychological structure than being attacked (Chessick 1993). To create a safe environment for the patient to express strong emotions such as murderous rage and hatred, the therapist needs to allow the patient to air all complaints, while simultaneously taming his own desires to defend himself, even in view of fully justifiable situations. This means that the therapist makes no attempt to soothe the patient when the patient is angry. In fact, he or she seeks its full discharge.

As Plakun (1993) has pointed out, however, the need for direct expression of feelings should not be misconstrued as implying that therapist and patient should continually engage with a lot of affect, in angry or tearful confrontations. "Affect must be engaged in a way that generates more light than heat" (p. 142). For this very purpose, the therapist generates an atmosphere of protection—not simply a safe haven (as with the dyadic deficit patient), but a veritable fortress if need be—wherein the patient may openly vent all of his resentment and anger, without any risk of reprisal. The creation of such an environment includes the crucial requirement that the clinician *not* lose control of his own impulses in counterreaction to the uncontrolled patient.

Maintaining the position of safe container of the patient's aggression is not easy, as the therapeutic relationship remains a continual testing ground, and often battleground, for the patient's rage—as well as the therapist's resilience against it. For example, the patient may pick up any subject and confront the therapist just to make him feel wrong, incompetent, unhelpful, or the like. There is no point arguing with the patient as to who is right or who is wrong. This only perpetuates an "aggressor–victim" or "superior–inferior" therapist–patient configuration (Meissner 1993) that is the hallmark of unsuccessful interaction with the dyadic conflict patient.

The only thing ostensibly accomplished by pointing out the patient's "one-down" position is for the therapist to assuage his own injured feelings by "proving" to the patient that he is really good or competent. But such feelings are very fleeting. At best, the patient has only given in on one specific point, his negativity temporarily suspended only to emerge again in connection with another issue. Moreover, if the patient caves in and submits to the therapist for a period of time, it will be at the expense of treatment insofar as the patient's need to see the therapist as "wrong"or "bad" will go underground, his negative feelings will be suppressed—if indeed the patient doesn't drop out of the process altogether.

The focus of the sessions, rather, should not be that of requesting or soliciting the patient's compliance, nor should it consist of the therapist defending himself against the patient's attacks, or of getting involved in a "who is right and who is wrong" debate (that very argument would put the therapist in the wrong). First and foremost, the therapist must not interfere with the patient's needs to be negativistic. It should be emphasized that such negativity by the patient represents a form of interpersonal relating; like Fairbairn's (1954) libido aggression, it is not discharge seeking, but object seeking. Therefore, at least initially this negative interaction, which is a form of microexternalization, should be left alone.

It is only *after* the patient expresses his anger, frustration, and rage at the therapist and feels secure that he will not be rejected or retaliated against (and also recognizes that the therapist will not otherwise disengage) that the patient can begin to accept the therapist—and his or her own disappointment. The patient must evolve from his suppressed murderous rage and intolerable disappointment with holding introjects to more ambivalent feelings that incorporate both positive and negative affect, along with more realistic and tolerable disappointment.

> *Patient:* [looking directly at the therapist's eyes] What do you think? Should I marry her? She's the best sexual partner I ever had; I

> love her smell, her looks. She's the quintessential flirt, always
> in a good mood, chatty, worry free, light, a perfect antidote
> for my heaviness; she says I think too much, that I'm too seri-
> ous. But she's also so frivolous; she never reads newspapers or
> listens to the news, has no interest in the real world. She sort
> of lives in her little castle of fantasies, going to parties, shop-
> ping, constantly expecting gifts from me; you know what I
> mean? What do you think? Do you think I should marry her?
> *Therapist:* Obviously, this is not an easy decision. On the one hand,
> she's a perfect sexual partner, a playful friend; on the other,
> she lacks certain serious commitments that are important to
> you.

Instead of giving a direct answer, the therapist rearticulates the two
sides of the conflict. This is a deliberate interventive approach; the therapist is not just hedging.

Even though the patient may have attained some measure of maturation and degree of independence from the therapist, endowing him as
an expert, seeking answers from an exalted figure who will make deci-
sions for him and take adult responsibility out of his hands, is usually
regressive. Like a child, it demands that the therapist omnipotently fore-
tell his future and provide unrealistic security in an unpredictable world.
Of course, taking charge and offering "answers" to the patient can be
temporarily reassuring. The therapeutic relationship may survive on this
basis, but it cannot thrive. Sooner or later, the patient will become disappointed with the answer, or escalate his expectations with the next
desired decision. Since these patients tend to split good from bad, the
clinician easily becomes a depriving bad object.

Lidz and Lidz (1982), for example, refer to the importance of avoiding an omniscient role when treating seriously disturbed patients. They
suggest that although some patients may initially fare well with therapists who presume to know and tell the answers, it plays into a pathological belief that someone else will magically lead the way. Ultimately,
however, the patient's unceasing frustration turns the benevolent therapist into a malevolent figure, for the omnipotent person fails to provide
the desired protection. They conclude that

the therapist must try from the very start to avoid being considered omnipotent, on the one hand, and being like the parents in needing the patient, on the other. Overprotecting, or giving the impression of intuitively or magically understanding the patient, fosters one need, while masochistically accepting the patient's unbridled demands or condemnations fosters the other. [p. 306]

Nonetheless, when the therapist is asked to give advice, there is a temptation to comply. Although gratifying the dyadic conflict patient by answering a question or granting a request is not advisable under most circumstances, the worst problem with giving advice in psychotherapy, however, is that the patient may take it. The dyadic conflict patient is a special case; he asks advice—so that he can reject it.

> *Patient:* So what? That's what I said; all you did was repeat what I just said.

The negatively engaging patient does not appreciate the therapist's trying to focus on his ambivalence. He is just interested in setting a stage for attack.

> *Therapist:* You're disappointed that I couldn't come out with a "yes" or "no" answer to your question, whether you should marry her.

Dyadic conflict patients have little tolerance for carefully composed, amply articulated, soft-centered messages; they want direct answers.

> *Patient:* Well, I'm angry. Here I spent my time and money and I'm still where I was a few weeks ago. This psychotherapy thing is not helping me.
> *Therapist:* You're angry at *me* for not being helpful to you!

Here the therapist offers a "nonpunitive interpretation of the patient's aggression," one of the proposed basic principles for working with self-destructive patients (Sledge and Tasman 1993, p. 142). It is deliberately presented to the patient in both a nonaccusatory and a non-guilt-inducing manner. It hopefully identifies the precipitant of the anger, first as a way of understanding, and second as a way of helping the patient to target and control the direction of affective discharge.

The therapist may be tempted to go along with the patient's desire to make the subject less personal (i.e., "You must feel that the *psychotherapy* is not useful") and to dodge the personal attack. However such a tactic, at best, may delay the personal attack and, at worst, refuels the anger further.

> *Patient:* Yeah, that's what I just said. I get even angrier when you repeat what I'm saying, sounding as if you're saying something new or useful.
>
> *Therapist:* Hardly an effective technique of a competent therapist.

The therapist must focus on the patient's negative feelings towards him by narrowing the topic even more, in order to get all the anger, resentment and frustration out.

> [long silence]

In the ongoing interaction, the therapist keeps a watchful eye on any perceived empathic failures that he has presumably perpetrated on the patient. Although it has been suggested that the clinician retrospectively search for such failures at times when the patient has shown some self-destructive behavior that may have been precipitated in treatment, it is also ideally useful as a *preventive* intervention—to hopefully avoid the patient's acting out, a kind of insurance for the future.

> *Patient:* Well, you said it; I don't know how competent you are, but somehow I feel a little better than when I came here, though it doesn't last.

The therapist's nonretaliative attitude, while encouraging the dyadic conflict patient to express his anger and frustrations, has paid off for the time being. Nonetheless, the therapist needs to remind himself that this is only temporary; there is no guarantee that the patient is going to be in a relatively accepting mode in the next session. In fact, the odds are that he will again be angry, provocative, and rejecting, and that the clinician in turn will need to deal with his own susceptibility to feelings of retaliative aggression or rejection.

For example, it is not unusual for the patient to arrive late with a barrage of rage at others who presumably contributed to the lateness, or to directly blame the therapist. Similarly, there is the demanding hostile-dependent patient who continues to make untenable requests such as wanting extra time, phone sessions, or the like as compensation for the presumed misdeeds of others. This scenario will be repeated for many sessions until relative confidence emanates from the therapist in the ability to sustain a nonretaliatory stance. As the clinician becomes more secure in this stance—not simply as a therapeutic technique, but as a response that comes comfortably from the self vis-à-vis the patient, the patient too will begin to develop a comparable security in his relationship with the therapist.

Reactive Fine-tuning: The Need for Vigilance over Subtle Retaliation

The expression of counterreactions and countertransference by the therapist is a crucial issue with all patients, but unforgivably so with dyadic conflict patients. This is because they are said to evoke (or provoke) hate and malevolence of an equally "global countertransference" (Kernberg 1975) that parallels their own ubiquitous rage. More specifically, the pitfalls of the patient's transference rage can include the therapist's countertransferential panic and impatience (Chessick 1993).

The therapist's response to the often unrelenting aggression may have various forms and guises, the most difficult being the rejection of the patient in return. The subtler the therapist's retaliations, the more insidious and silently corrosive they may be. These can become subliminally damaging to the patient, but let the therapist off more easily. Therefore, the therapist should make every effort to avoid masking angry feelings by trying to superimpose a light mood. The patient usually does not appreciate the therapist's light humor, bantering, or even self-mockery; he may easily get offended and feel put down. Commonly, however, the patient himself may use such levities to attack the therapist.

> *Patient:* You better do or think of something to help to change my
> mood. This is no good. This depression is not as bad as it used
> to be, but is still there. I've been feeling this same way now for
> a few weeks; you haven't done anything about it.
>
> *Therapist:* Did I get you even more depressed?

Again, the therapist's somewhat defensive query isn't regarded as at all funny.

> *Patient:* [the patient's exasperation escalates] Look! I'm very goal
> oriented. If people in my shop can't identify what they can do
> and get things done [makes a cutting gesture with his arm],
> they are chopped off, gone, fired!
>
> *Therapist:* I guess I'm almost at that point of being fired.

The therapist partially recovers but still senses his own injured feelings at the patient's escalating assault.

> *Patient:* I don't know whether it's you or me; I'm not sure who to
> blame.

The patient, perhaps somewhat guiltily, half forgives the therapist, at least as a very temporary measure.

> *Therapist:* Well, I'm not about to fire you!

The therapist succumbs again to the patient's hostility and retorts once more with veiled guilt-inducing aggression. He has countertransferentially fallen into the "victim" position, with the patient as aggressor. Obviously his own negative countertransference hasn't been sufficiently worked through, and this time it pops up as a reaction formation of reassurance coated with light humor.

Patient: [snickers] Why should you? I heard that psychiatrists are ambivalence chasers! And furthermore. . . .

Once again, the patient sees only the therapist as the wrongdoer; he neither can perceive nor admit to his own failings in this situation. What's more, he has to retaliate at any hint of hostility, with the response invariably out of proportion to the realistic size of the perceived attack.

Under such circumstances the clinician has to be especially alert in assessing, and avoiding, his or her own countertransferential reactions. They can include reciprocal rage and the temptation for retaliatory retreat (i. e., to deprive the hostile patient of needed treatment). Alternatively, he may also inappropriately respond with countertransferential guilt (i. e., blaming oneself for the patient's accusations and failure to improve), and even become oversolicitous, bending over backwards to please the displeased patient. Yet another dangerous response is to self-protectively change one's theoretical stance, to view the patient's behaviors as having intersubjective meaning within the therapeutic dyad, *until* acting out occurs; thereafter there is a defensive shift to a narrower view of destructive behavior as a product of psychopathology, thus moving the onus of responsibility and blame away from oneself and back onto the patient. Ultimately, however, the therapist's—and the patient's—very survival depends on his *not* being drawn into an aggressive scenario with the patient. As Winnicott (1965) has pointed out, a crucial aspect of mother is that she repeatedly survives the infant's destructiveness; what the infant learns from this is that his or her destructiveness will not destroy the other and therefore that it can be safely felt.

"Technical" Empathy as a Major but Circumscribed Instrument

Apart from its contrast to sympathy, therapists since Kohut (1971, 1977) have explored the nuances of the notion of empathy as both a tool of observation as well as a healing agent, as its application with different patient populations has been extended. Kernberg (1984), for example, has made a distinction between *neutral empathy* (characteristic of Freud) and *maternal empathy* (characteristic of Kohut). (In the following chapter on the triadic deficit patient, I extend the latter to *paternal empathy*.) Beyond this, I use the term *technical empathy* to reflect to the special constraints on its use in the psychotherapy of dyadic conflict patients. Since dyadic conflict patients misperceive or misuse empathy, it must be titrated and used in a circumscribed way. When expressed, it must be directly targeted, as well as carefully modulated, towards the patient's pain, but not toward the aggression that is expressed or acted out as a consequence of that pain.

The therapist who does express empathy as a major modus operandi in dealing with this type of patient still has to be cautious not to reinforce the patient's anger. In the latter situation, such use of empathy can beget a chronic course of complaint and bitterness. In particular, when the patient's anger is fueled by the therapist's empathy and turned against the past, it tends to intensify quickly and suddenly spread, to contaminate current relationships. Once this process has progressed, the therapist will have a hard time containing the patient's rage—if not being engulfed in it himself.

Patients naturally do not productively regress in the height of anger and rage. Never mind having induced the anger, just allowing the regressive outburst to occur while the patient is experiencing real negative feelings and/or negative transference is extremely countertherapeutic, if not downright dangerous. However, when the release of anger, rage, and frustration makes room for the patient to experience underlying painful feelings such as sadness or loneliness, the therapist can attempt in earnest to empathize. Like the microinternalizations by the dyadic deficit patient, it sets the stage for microprojective internalizations by the dyadic conflict patient. It also serves to link the aggressive affect with its target, for further exploration.

In this regard, Kernberg (1992) has referred to the cognitive aspects of affects, which reflect their investment of self and object representations in both the ego and superego. He suggested that when a sexual or aggressive impulse or other drive derivative is examined in the clinical situation, the patient is invariably experiencing at that time an image or representation of the self relating to an image or representation of another person (object) under the impact of the respective affect. And alternatively whenever a patient's affect state is explored, a cognitive aspect is also found. Thus the patient's anger against his parents and past relationships therapeutically warrants the therapist's acknowledgment, because it can comprise a necessary cognitive connection to the affect.

Otherwise, to sustain the focus on an emotional expression for too long, or, even worse, to empathize with the patient's position through mutual anger, may become a form of countertherapeutic collusion. In addition, if the therapist is continually deflecting the anger away from himself, for conscious or unconscious reasons, this will only compound the rage and result in manifold expressions of it on later occasions. There is yet another significant scenario with regard to the expression of empathy. Even when these patients do come around and begin to be receptive to the therapist's empathic stance, it is the *therapist* who may have difficulty in genuinely empathizing with them. In fact, frequently the clinician may find himself empathizing not with the dyadic conflict patients themselves, but with their victims!

> *Patient:* After I lost my job, I was in a terrible spot. I had no money, no prospect for a new job. Then I asked Jane whether she would let me borrow the money that she's been saving to start a partnership in a small business. She refused to do it. To be married to someone for ten years and get rejected like that, it was goddamn incredible. How did she save the money to begin with? I mean, what's the message? I'm furious!
>
> *Therapist:* I see!

Recognition of what the patient is saying here is not empathy. The therapist acknowledges and confirms what is being told to him, but avoids being overly reactive or so sympathetic as to co-conspire with the patient against the presented outside target, hereby fueling the patient's anger toward his wife.

> *Patient:* Damn it! I will never forget that as long as I live. Now that I'm back on my feet and she wants this or that, she's very nice and loving. Screw that! I don't believe it for a moment. . . . Then, at times I do. When she's needy and dependent, she's

like a child, a helpless being. At those times I feel like cuddling her, protecting her. She's like an angel. Then out of the blue comes that "school principal" look, which I hate. All I want is to run away. I mean, how could it be that she's so nice one moment, and so horrible the next? It's like Dr. Jekyll and Mr. Hyde.

Therapist: Hmmm.

The therapist remains contemplative, purposely not siding with the patient in his anger at his wife.

Patient: She says to me, "You're crazy, what did I do, what did I say that makes you so furious? You're like your mother; the whole family is crazy." She starts crying; that angelic face returns, then I feel bad that I've been hurting her.

Therapist: How confusing for you—first feeling angry because she hurt you, then feeling guilty that you've hurt her!

Here the therapist empathizes not with the outer-directed affect of anger, but with the patient's self-directed affect of guilt, his feeling bad for hurting another.

Patient: When I married her, everyone said, "She's like your mother." That isn't really true. My mother was not caring. [silent] Well, at least I think so. You know, while I was saying that my mother was not a caring person, I felt absolutely nothing, like the words were coming out of my mouth without meaning anything. I know there were no beatings or abuses, so what could be so terrible? She provided everything I needed; I lacked nothing. But I don't remember ever snuggling with her, you know, the way that my kids do to my wife. I remember this image: one day I walked into my room, I must have been 8 or 9. My mother was reading my diary. I got frightened, I'm not sure why, rather than getting angry. What on earth could an 8-year-old be writing that would be of interest to her? I don't think she apologized. Instead she said something like, "How come you don't write that you love your mommy?" I felt like killing myself; I feel horrible now, just thinking about it. God, was she an intrusive woman! I remember, even at a younger age, 5 or 4 or something . . .

Therapist: Feeling horrible just thinking about it—frightened then and feeling bad enough to consider suicide, but angry now.

Patient: And I still can't figure out whether she is a good person or bad, you know. . . .

Since dyadic conflict patients are especially invested in remaining unaware and unresponsible for their destructive nature of their anger, this also serves to point out how ungratifying self-destructive behaviors can be—a first step toward bringing such ideas to consciousness. Also, once the patient begins to see the affective connections between his rage and his sadness, the therapist can also begin to examine another basic split that has just been broached, the as-yet-irreconcilable separation of bad and good in others—and self (see also Working Through Dyadic Conflicts Via Projective Microinternalization, p. 186).

Recovery from Misdirected Empathy

The importance of the therapist acknowledging his own failures is particularly pertinent with dyadic conflict patients. The clinician must take responsibility for disruptions of the dyadic relationship that have been caused by technical errors on his or her part (Settlage 1994). Here, for example, misdirected empathy requires quick recovery in order to prevent the patient's rage from escalating and disrupting the still precarious relationship between patient and therapist. One of the major concerns is that if the therapist empathically joins the patient in his or her defensive anger, the patient's anger worsens, partly for being misunderstood by the therapist. The patient may also sense the therapist's avoidance of the deeper pain of the patient and resent the therapist for that. The therapist must recover from the consequences of misdirected empathy—by allowing himself fully to be the target of aggression. Nonetheless, as Plakun (1993) has warned, the therapist "must also be wary of his or her own potential affective withdrawal from the patient in the aftermath of [self-destructive or aggressive] behavior" (p. 142). Such retreat from meaningful affective connection can also manifest with a re-verse response—becoming overly identified with or excessively empathic to the patient. Both sides of this spectrum are problematic.

> *Patient:* My mother used to open my mail, read it, and then reseal the envelope, and listen to my telephone conversations. I had no privacy; I mean, she did not respect my privacy. I felt com-pletely invaded.
> *Therapist:* How terrible!

Such empathy by the therapist can be dangerous—it may fuel the patient's rage against his mother.

> *Patient:* I would confront her with that, and she would deny it. She'd say, "Who? I opened your letter? You're crazy, why would I do that? Who cares about your letter?" Then I wondered whether I was imagining it; maybe I *was* crazy. I would lock myself in my room, curl up in my bed to regain my senses. I'd pull my hair, dig my nails into my arm, just to experience pain so that I'd feel something real, like I existed or something. . . . Then I'd feel like I need her; I hated that, that I needed her. I felt like I was getting unglued.
> *Therapist:* How frightening!

Empathizing with the patient's self-directed feelings is a produc-tive use of empathy.

> *Patient:* I was frightened, but frightened for no obvious reason. From all outside appearances, my family looked stable; we were not homeless. I didn't worry about food or clothes, or toys, things like that, and my parents were well-meaning people.
> *Therapist:* They meant well, but you were still frightened. So there was some limitation.

Patient: Some limitation? Some limitation! A child who has no food or toys would be better off than one who . . . you know. People who don't care shouldn't have children; intrusive people shouldn't be allowed to raise kids. Can you imagine a little kid trying to assert himself as a human being, constantly made unimportant, unwanted on the one hand, not being let go on the other? People who have this kind of limitation should not have children; it's no excuse that they're entitled to have some limitation. What about me? Does anyone care? I hate them, I really hate them; I mean, I can kill when I think about it. Limitation, my ass!

Therapist: Was I giving them an excuse for their behavior by naming it a "limitation"?

The intensity of the patient's emotion in the narration of content is usually transferentially loaded. Therefore the therapist, at the first opportunity, will try to bring the subject back to their relationship.

Patient: You have no idea what they've done to me; you have no idea, you didn't grow up in that household.

Therapist: I will not suggest that as an excuse for my limitation.

The therapist is struggling.

Patient: You better not. It's bad enough that you don't understand what I had been through and what I'm going through. Your limitation is that you always look at things from every person's point of view, sort of a nonjudgmental judge.

Therapist: It's the kind of limitation a therapist shouldn't have.

The therapist is unsuccessfully attempting to diffuse the anger by generalizing.

Patient: Not if he's going to help the patient.

Therapist: I shouldn't be a therapist to you, given my limitation?

The therapist finally recovers and makes himself the proper target.

Patient: [laughs] At least you're asking that question. My mother
never wondered whether she was right or not. As far as she
was concerned, she was a perfect mother and I was the sick
one, or demanding one, and maybe I was. Or was I? I really
don't know, I can't figure that out.

Therapist: Confusing, not knowing who was who.

Forgiven, the therapist goes back to an empathically explorative
mode.

Patient: Even now, it is. Imagine how it was for a little child. I remember one day I was at the front door . . . amazing, I never
thought about this incident before; just incredible—where was
this memory hiding? Wow! I was standing in front of our main
door. . . .

It is only after the patient's anger has subsided that he is able to
come up with an early memory. In the heat of hate and rage, all he can
do is to protect his pain or otherwise fend off further exploration by
dissociation or denial.

MANAGEMENT OF THE PATIENT'S CHRONIC HOSTILITY, REJECTION, AND DEMANDING DEPENDENCY

Walking the Tightrope of Narcissistic Alliance/Paranoid Collusion

If the therapist survives the initial rejection and angry stages of treatment—allowing the patient to express negative feelings at the therapist
without retaliative rejection, as well as taming his own narcissistic injury
in view of the patient's explicit devaluation—he may eventually arrive
at a relatively stable, trusting, but not necessarily an easier state of relating to the patient. In the incessant search for the primary object in
psychotherapy, Cooper and Maxwell (1995) refer to the "constant need

to reenact the scenario of merging and breaking" (p. 121). Like the dyadic deficit patient, there is always a continual process of severing, then transitory reestablishment of object relations with the therapist, of "losing and fusing" (Lewin and Schulz 1992), disruption and connection.

At the junctures of this "dissolution–restoration cycle" (Wolf 1994) of the therapeutic process, always on the verge of severed ties, the patient will bring in a barrage of material to the session for discussion (mostly about negative relations with others), yet always expect the therapist to side with himself independent of the merit of the situation. Here the patient is recruiting the therapist, for purposes of collusion, to engage in a primitive narcissistic/paranoid alliance. At the same time, a subtle and chronic hostility remains just below the surface, waiting to emerge at any opportunity. This is especially the case when the therapist inadvertently, or even justifiably, presents the side of the other individual for the purpose of providing an objective perspective.

> *Patient:* My boss wrote me this long memo: you haven't done this, you haven't done that, you should do this or that—I really hate his guts. I feel like telling him to go to hell, to say, "You know what you can do with that memo. You know I have no dignity left here." But I bite my tongue because I don't feel like looking for another job; it pays well.
> *Therapist:* What's the nature of those "10 commandments" of his?

The therapist is tempted to ally with the patient against outsiders (here, by exaggerating the displayed self-importance of his boss).

> *Patient:* Oh, I don't know. He wanted the evaluations to be finished last week. I was to correct some mistakes in the ads, prepare the annual report; you know, kind of bureaucratic nonsense.
> *Therapist:* Is all this bureaucratic work part of your job? Or is he just dumping on you things that someone else isn't doing?

If the therapist rewords the patient's narrative (i.e., from bureaucratic "nonsense" to bureaucratic "work"), he must be careful that it is not just a form of countertransferential disapproval. He has to be alert to any message that implies that the patient is distorting his side of the story, exaggerating his position, and therefore unjustified in his complaints.

> *Patient:* I presume he could have someone else do it, but it's my job to do all that; I just hate it. No one really cares about the substance of the matter. They're all interested in looking good on paper.
>
> *Therapist:* Does he have a choice?

The therapist explores whether the patient can put himself in others' shoes and look at himself, to have another perspective on the subject at his own peril.

> *Patient:* [irritated] It's easy for you to suggest that! You sit here; you are your own boss. People come to talk to you and pay, and off they go! What do *you* know about the institutional idiocies? Some of us, you know, don't have that luxury.
>
> *Therapist:* You wish you had a job like mine.

Whenever anger is displayed, the content that brought it about is deliberately dropped. Instead the therapist and patient relationship is focused on—here, the envy.

> *Patient:* I would like to, of course, but . . . it's your good luck, but that doesn't mean that you should be so judgmental towards others, because you don't know.
>
> *Therapist:* And you wish I had *your* job.
>
> *Patient:* [laughs] No, no, no. I wouldn't wish that even on my enemies! Do you think I would be better off . . . ?

The therapist may have to finely tune to the patient's primitive needs at the initial phase of treatment in order to keep the patient, but perpetuating this, while very tempting, is ill-advised. If the therapist joins the patient in his mistrust, suspicions, and battles against others under the guise of the therapeutic alliance, he thus creates a paranoid collusion that alienates the patient from everyone, if not endangering the two of them.

Systematic Deintensification of Negative Transference: Transference as Content

Sessions should remain relatively content-free, until the negative transference and its affect has been deintensified. For this purpose, all negative, emotionally loaded material is brought into the relationship between therapist and patient, and the therapist attempts to rechannel the patient's emotional expressions of being angry, irritated, and disappointed. The therapist deliberately makes no connections to the patient's early relationships, because doing so will dilute the transferential anger and, substitutively, may generate a litany against the patient's parents or other significant figures. If the latter is encouraged to occur, most likely negative feelings will only snowball and come back upon the therapist in an avalanche.

> *Patient:* He's the worst boss I ever worked for. He's not fair, he's not honest, he's not knowledgeable, he's not even smart.
> *Therapist:* Hmmm.
> *Patient:* This new guy he hired is six months junior to me; my boss gave him all the good accounts. And the kid doesn't know his elbow from his ass. He comes in late every morning and leaves early. I'm there all the time, working my ass off and what do I get? All these complaints and insults. I'm really mad; who the hell is he? I mean, how dare he humiliate me? I can't stand that; the man is completely insensitive. He calls me in, very friendly after what he did, gives me a big hug. "Look" he says, "we're like brothers, a great team." I almost puked; God, trying to make friends with me. He says, "Jerry, why are you so angry? Smile, we'll all have a good time." I'm not going to work for these guys, lower myself to their level; I have my dignity— no way.
> *Therapist:* Have I also been lowering your dignity here?

The therapist enters the picture from the most emotionally-loaded arena, without easing in or diluting the transferential intensity.

> *Patient:* Well, you keep saying that I should keep the job. You don't just come out and say that, but I know that's what you're thinking. When you ask, "What are the pros and cons of your leaving the job?" that's what you're saying, rather than saying that these are bad guys hurting you and I should get the hell out of that place. I'm not sure what's in your agenda. Is it to help me— or something else?
>
> *Therapist:* Something else?
>
> *Patient:* Well, you tell me; now the ball is in your court and don't play this mind-fucking game with me.
>
> *Therapist:* Am I suggesting that you stay on the job just so you can pay my fee?

The patient's direct confrontation is responded to with equal directness.

> *Patient:* I don't know, you tell me. I should slave on this horrible job so you can get paid. Don't you see that this is no good for my morale? To be subjected to their running me down just isn't good for me, period.
>
> *Therapist:* Do you *also* wonder whether I'm good for you?

The therapist says "also" because he does not want to dismiss the patient's reality (i. e., that the others are not good for him). This patient will be offended if the therapist says, "I wonder if when you talk about the job not being good for you, in fact, the only thing you are really talking about is that I am not good for you." Furthermore, in making such a shift, it is important to make the connection personal: i. e., "I am not good for you," not "*the treatment* is not good for you." The impersonal approach will not really protect the therapist's self-esteem. The patient is complaining not about the treatment, but about the therapist. Dodging will bring only more stones thrown at the therapist, or worse, no stones.

*Remaining Centripetally Focused Despite Discouragement
or Derailment by the Patient*

When the therapist brings the patient's (past or present) outer-directed anger into their relationship, the patient may insist that the therapist is wrong in his interpretations. If the resistance is intense and nonabating, the therapist may reevaluate whether the preparatory stage needs further attention, especially in the arena of trust. Otherwise, the therapist should remain centripetally interpretive despite the patient's discouragement.

> *Therapist:* You're quite upset at your boyfriend for hardly acknowl-
> edging your birthday. I wonder whether you're also angry at
> me for not having wished you a happy birthday!

Here the therapist acknowledges his own empathic failure. As Settlage (1994) has suggested, this open acknowledgment can serve to restore—or preventively avoid—another disruption in their relationship.

> *Patient:* No, you're not my family; you're not my friend. I don't
> expect that you will remember my birthday. A therapist doesn't
> have to remember his patient's birthday.
> *Therapist:* I shouldn't remember your birthday?

The therapist makes it personal, rather than interpreting the patient's defensive dilution. The latter will only make the patient argumentative—feeling criticized.

> *Patient:* I don't think so. You must have a bunch of patients; how
> can you remember everyone's birthday? This is not a social
> relationship. [looks irritated] Anyway, enough of that; I want
> to go back to the subject of my boyfriend's behavior.
> *Therapist:* Irritated by my intruding myself into this birthday issue?

The therapist uses the emotion displayed by the patient to bring her back to further discuss their relationship, in spite of the patient's intimidating attitude.

> *Patient:* I'm not sure what you're trying to do. I don't care whether you wish me a happy birthday or not; I don't even know yours. This is not a real relationship; I don't expect real things.
>
> *Therapist:* So that you don't have to express your disappointment?
>
> *Patient:* How can I expect those kinds of things? I mean, this is a professional relationship.

At this juncture, the patient's overendowment of the therapist begins to come through. But, as Kernberg (1992) has pointed out, this is the opposite side of the aggression coin, a primitive idealization of the therapist, which temporarily disguises and fends against the deeply rooted hostility. Eventually, however, the two may begin to merge into a more realistic appraisal (see Working Through Dyadic Conflicts, p. 186).

The therapist's attempt to reassure the patient that their relationship is real and caring does not work. However, the therapist must remember that this is not the critical purpose here; rather, the crucial point is to have the patient express her hurt.

> *Therapist:* It's a kind of relationship in which it's hard to express hurt and disappointment.
>
> *Patient:* I mean, what purpose would that serve? I got angry a couple of times in the past when you kept asking this kind of thing. When I didn't tell you of my anger, you kept saying, "You're afraid of your anger and mine." Maybe that was true once. Well, it no longer is. Besides, you never can truly expect, you know, to trust. . . .

Exposure and interpretation of the dyadic conflict patient's repressed aggression is a matter of timing, when the patient is ready to do so. As Settlage (1994) has suggested, often it is easier and more effective to broach the subject at a time when the patient *fails to* express appropriate anger, rather than when she is overreacting with uncontrolled rage.

> *Therapist:* You can't really expect to trust me after you express your anger and disappointment?

Patient: I really don't care.You're not my mother; I can't expect that, not that she would have remembered. I also don't need you that way; you're just my doctor. How pathetic that would be if I just wanted to be loved by you!

Therapist: Especially if it seems like it's not forthcoming!

The therapist dismisses the genetic material and pursues the transferential issue, in spite of the temptation to get off the track.

Patient: I think it's insensitive of you . . . my talking about my birthday last week, you couldn't remember; I can't believe that. You never forget to give the bills on the last session of every month. So you couldn't be so senile! When it comes to your interests, you're damn right there. . . . Okay, now you got what you've been asking for! Yes, I'm hurt and furious at the fact that you didn't remember my birthday. But why do you want to hear all this? Are you some kind of masochist?

The therapist purposely makes no connections between this material and the patient's early relationship. Such an approach may temporarily dilute the transferential anger, but in fact it will go underground and intensify. The therapist thus remains with the centripetal explorations without genetic interpretations, in spite of the patient's reluctance and active discouragement.

The expression of rage, interjected by its antithesis, an idealizing transference, can eventually become modulated and serve a therapeutic function. Buie and Adler (1982) and Kohut (1971) have emphasized this salutory side of the aggression coin. Waldinger (1987) has stated their position as follows:

> They view the analysis of negative transference as a preliminary step that clears the way for the emergence of the more fundamental idealizing self-object transference. This unrealistic positive transference is ameliorated by what Kohut termed "optimal disillusionment," a process by which patients gradually notice discrepancies between the idealizing holding introject and the actual holding qualities of the therapist. [p. 270]

These authors conclude that, to the extent that each disappointment is "optimal" and not overwhelming, it can prompt the patient to develop insight into the unrealistic aspects of his or her positive feelings for the therapist. For the dyadic conflict patient, this applies as well to pervasive *negative* feelings, as the two begin to more realistically converge in the course of treatment.

Suspension of the Centripetal Emphasis—Temporarily Only (i. e., When the Patient Is Under Severe External Stress)

As Settlage (1994) has emphasized, the therapist must recognize the power of libidinal and physical separations to evoke preoedipal transferences. Since reactions to separations, disruptions, and interruptions is such a sensitive subject, the therapist must tread especially softly at this time. When the patient happens to be involved in a critical issue in his current life, any confrontation of devaluations or other attacks on the therapist may be difficult for the patient to bear. Typically, the patient will talk about the particular concern in his life during the entire session and only at the end of the hour may remember that he has not devalued the therapist yet. Thus, as soon as the therapist announces the ending of the session, or the patient spontaneously recognizes the fact that the time is up, he will typically interrupt his narrative of current problems and launch an attack on the therapist.

The therapist would be best off simply receiving such anger at the end of the session without any concerted reactions, so as neither to delay the ending of the session nor to further provoke the patient. In the subsequent session, however, the therapist can take up the subject somewhere in the middle of the session, when an appropriate opportunity arises. If the patient is still in the midst of the current crisis, he will likely dismiss the confrontation quickly, although not necessarily in a less hostile fashion. The therapist thus makes his observation, but respects the patient's sense of priority and urgency by following the content of the patient's narration.

> *Patient:* [on the way out] I just spent 50 minutes telling you things that I already know. Okay, now you know them too, but it's

not productive at all. I know no more than I knew when I came in. You should be more active—give me some advice, something. Just telling you what horrible things happened since the last time I saw you is not good. This was a waste of time!

Therapist: That should be the topic of the next session. See you on Thursday.

The therapist registers the negative reaction of the patient, and addresses it in the next session.

Patient: I'm exhausted, goddamn! What kind of life is this? I feel totally overwhelmed. My wife and her lawyer keep bringing up all sorts of irrelevant stuff—deposition of this, deposition of that. Why do they do that? It's just wasting my time. Now I *have* to respond; why couldn't this be solved amicably?

Therapist: Last session on the way out, you mentioned that seeing me is also a waste of time.

Patient: Oh, come on. Don't be so insecure! I can't be bothered with you now. I have enough on my plate to worry about. This woman isn't just wasting my time, she's wasting me. . . .

The patient's scolding of the therapist by calling him insecure is partly accurate. (Or is this a product of projective identification?) The therapist who deals with an angry and devaluing patient usually feels somewhat insecure. Nonetheless, when the patient has a serious problem on his hands, he needs specific reality-based assistance from the therapist. Even at times the real-life problem-generated issues take precedence. They provide a center for the therapist and patient to ally (albeit temporarily), while allowing an occasional moratorium to their transferential interactions. This relatively peaceful coexistence may last as long as the life stress persists. Thus the patient's animosity and devaluation are not gone and forgotten, but simply suspended, only to be resumed after the crisis is over. It is very important nevertheless to check the transferential aspects of the patient's negativity, even in the midst of such crisis.

INTERPRETATION OF DYADIC CONFLICTS: PROJECTIVE AND OBJECT-CONSTANCY BUILDING INTERPRETATIONS

The traditional approach (i. e., the original conflict/working through model), which is based on intensified and interpreted transference regression, requires the presence of two conditions: (1) the patient must have a positive transferential disposition, and (2) the patient possesses a structural conflict. The latter implies a certain developmental phase in the maturation of the individual; the patient has already stabilized his nuclear self and has established the tripartite psychic structure (id–ego–superego), and now can take a certain distance from and look at his psyche. This *triadic conflict* is fully represented in the patient's mind and is conducive to resolution by insight.

Patients with dyadic conflicts, however, will not satisfy either of the above requirements. First, the transferential disposition of these patients is a negative one, and deliberate intensification of it will, at best, bring about a premature termination. Second, these patients have not stabilized their nuclear self. The tripartite psychic structure is not formed sufficiently to contain intrapsychic conflict as an independent mental representation, to be resolvable by insight (see also Chapter 7). These patients cannot take distance from themselves without risking fragmentation; their self is in the process of just becoming, even though deficiencies in the structuralization of the representational world may also present themselves as conflicts.

Therefore the therapist must carefully differentiate internalized triadic conflicts from failed structure-building interpersonal ones. These dyadic conflicts are actually still serving the formation of object constancy—they are not something to be interpreted away. More specifically, they are the glue that is required for internal cohesion. Thus, objective interpretations of dyadic conflicts are facilitative of this process of object constancy and psychic structure formation, in contrast to empathic interpretations (as a precursor to the induction of self exploration) wherein therapist intersubjectively fuses with the patient. Here, with the dyadic conflict patient, the therapist "projects" interpretations onto the patient, as he or she experiences them.

The interpretations of dyadic conflict are formulated in their interpersonal context (dyadic relationship between therapist and patient), rather than within an intrapsychic context. The therapist is not a neutral outsider, reflecting on the patient's internal struggle (e. g., "I wonder whether you feel guilty for the thought that . . . "), but an insider, engagingly providing one end of the dyadic pole and simultaneously interpreting the interpersonal conflict between them (e. g., "You are not sure whether you should trust me or not. . . .").

To a patient with dyadic conflict, the therapist is an individuation-phase contemporary self-object (in contrast to an attachment-phase contemporary self-object wherein the therapist provides primarily an empathic presence, as with Kohut's "deficit patients"). The therapist's role with the dyadic conflict patient is more complicated, that of a differentiating self-object, while allowing the person to securely individuate and maintain a benign attachment.

After the patient is relatively secure in the therapist's nonrejection, he will still continue his rejecting/angry attitude, and furthermore, often with greater intensity. As an early sign of attachment at this stage, the patient's fears of being eaten up or swallowed prompt strong emotions bordering on paranoia. At such times, the therapist interprets the patient's yearning for closeness while fearing engulfment, yearning for dependency while fighting for independence—but all geared toward *their* relationship. They need to be acknowledged as defensive maneuvers against receiving and giving love (Settlage 1994). These interpersonal conflicts are relatively accessible. Once some stability with the therapist is established, the patient will easily recognize such conflicts and be able to elaborate on them.

Interpretation of Rejection of Others as a Preventive Measure

When the therapist interprets the patient's angry feelings as the need to reject the therapist, it can serve as a reciprocal preventive measure—in order to contain anticipated rejection. If such insight is well received, the dyadic conflict patient may suspend anger temporarily and begin to talk about underlying self-doubt.

Patient: [10 minutes late and furious] I got stuck in traffic on the way up here. I gave myself more than a half hour; this time of the day it's always a problem. I really hate coming here at this hour.

Therapist: You were not happier with the other times I offered.

Patient: In reality, no time is good. I've got to either leave the job early or get up early.

Therapist: And for what?

Patient: Yeah! I don't think I complain just to reject you before you reject me, as you said last time. Maybe I am rejecting you, but not for the reason you say. It's because I don't think this has been helpful at all.

Therapist: And what kind of reaction are you anticipating from me?

Patient: I don't know. I'm sort of wondering why you don't say, "Okay, if I'm not useful, don't come, period!" When I came here the first time . . . [silence] . . . I thought to myself, why should this man spend his time with my silly problems? What's in it for him? Except maybe money; but you seem to be doing okay there, so what I wondered is what did you get from it.

When the patient makes himself vulnerable, any counterbalancing statements on the part of the therapist such as, "Don't you think you are being a little too hard on yourself?" or "Why?" "You deserve . . ." etc., are characteristically considered to be patronizing and unconvincing. The worst effect is that such attempts will be perceived by the patient as that of not being understood.

Therapist: My initial nonrejection was not reassuring.

Patient: No, it made it more suspect.

Therapist: So since then, you are trying your hardest to elicit "inevitable" rejection from me—so that you don't have to feel rejected!

Patient: [smiles] You think so? How sad, if it's true. [silent] . . . You know I always expect that. . . .

Interpretation of Need for Closeness while Fearing Engulfment

After the dyadic conflict patient is relatively secure in his relationship to the therapist, he will still continue his rejecting and angry attitude and, sometimes predictably enough, with greater intensity. This is a sign of the patient using rejection and anger as his way of attaining a reassuring level of engagement and separation. The patient's fears of being eaten up or swallowed by another prompts strong emotions that border on paranoia. The therapist actively interprets these rageful and rejecting responses as the patient is trying to protect his boundaries in order to prevent perhaps his or her greatest fear—engulfment by the therapist.

> *Patient:* Look, I don't need therapy, so why do I keep cancelling sessions? That's why. I don't need twice a week for sure. I mean, we did what was needed. Now I know a little bit about myself, that's enough. Now I have to get on with my life. You keep implying that the work is not finished; well tough, that's life! The problem with my girlfriend is really *her* problem. She wants to know exactly where I am, who I'm with every minute of the day. What is this? If I'm preoccupied, she needs to know what am I thinking! She's constantly asking whether I love her. I feel stifled. Then, of course, I stopped calling her; I don't answer the telephone . . .
>
> *Therapist:* [interrupts] And you cancel sessions or show up late.

This is one of the few patient indications for short latency of response time by the therapist. Opportune moments in the patient's narrative are seized if relevant to the immediacy of the patient–therapist relationship, even though it may seem interruptive to do so; in fact, in such instances it is conducive to their therapeutic engagement.

> *Patient:* You don't believe that I cancel sessions because I don't need them. I don't really feel stifled by you, except when you

go after this "why am I late" kind of stuff. Then I feel like running away.

Therapist: When I'm being excessively intrusive?

Patient: The intrusiveness that I can't stand, especially with her— I feel like I'm disappearing.

Therapist: Disappearing!

When the content is synchronous with the process of the patient-therapist relationship, the therapist joins the narration.

Patient: I can't stand that feeling. I need my distance. Of course, I want you to be concerned about my absences, but I guess at the same time I want you to let me be.

Therapist: So it isn't so much whether you need further therapy, but that you would like to monitor the degree of closeness you're able to tolerate with me.

Patient: That's a real problem for me, you know. But am I that different? Don't other people need their space as much as I do? I need my space, to be alone, unaccountable . . . the famous boundaries issue. There are various diameters of fences; those further away are not that high. The closer you get, the higher the fence has to be.

Therapist: With barbed wire.

Patient: [laughs] In fact, electrified.

Therapist: You want to be close to me and, at the same time, not to be intruded upon.

Patient: And engulfed. Marie says I'm like a porcupine. . . .

It is especially advisable that the therapist avoid reiterating the patient's worst scenarios, that the clinician not identify with these patients' negative introjects. If the practitioner allows himself to become susceptible to the patient's particular transferences, if he is unable to keep himself from treating the patient as his girlfriend does, for example, he is in clinical danger of becoming yet another "bad" engulfing figure that the patient will run away from.

INTRAPSYCHIC STRUCTURE-BUILDING INTERPRETATIONS

Projective Empathy and Projective Interpretation

The dyadic conflict patient would like to force the therapist to experience how the patient himself really feels. It is natural for the therapist to empathize with the patient's projected part-self within himself, thus projectively with the patient. Yet the patient, with his unresolved anger and his demands, is requesting unilateral empathy for his underlying feelings, his dilemma. It is a kind of shotgun empathy request imposed upon the therapist by projection of all the badness of the patient; it is also a way of diminishing the therapist in an impasse. Meanwhile, the therapist must be prepared to contain the negative affect, to receive the experience of the diminution and pain, and to ground the patient's self-empathy. The clinician of the dyadic conflict patient must also recover from the attempted diminution, to reassure the patient that his aggression can be safely owned and expressed.

> *Patient:* [long silence, staring into the distance]
>
> *Therapist:* So silent!
>
> *Patient:* Nothing much to say; nothing happened since I saw you last time. Coming here and telling you about my problems doesn't serve any purpose. You've got to help me, something, I don't know what. . . . The other doctor that you sent me to wasn't helpful either. The medications he prescribed were too expensive and useless.
>
> *Therapist:* Even my consultants are no good?
>
> *Patient:* [getting more and more negative and demanding] No, they're not, honestly. I heard that cognitive therapy is the best treatment for this kind of problem. Why don't you give me some cognitive therapy? I mean, do you do that kind of therapy?
>
> *Therapist:* And would you also like to know whether I'm any good at it?
>
> *Patient:* [grins] Well, you must be good at something.

The therapist feels the hostility.

Therapist: I'll find a cognitive therapist for you. Next time I see you, I'll make the arrangements and give you a name.

Patient: This woman at work knows a cognitive therapist; she thinks he's great; maybe I'll go to him.

Therapist: Concerned that my cognitive therapist will also be no good?

Patient: [smiles] Maybe concerned.

Therapist: Maybe convinced.

The therapist accentuates the negativity of the patient.

Patient: Well, I don't know. You sent me to two different consultants; nothing good came out of it. . . . Meanwhile, I can't make a decision as to whether I should take that job offer. What do you think? And don't ask me what I think. If you were in my place, would you take it? And don't ask me, "What are the alternatives?" and don't tell me, "It must be a difficult decision." I don't want to pin you down on this, but . . .

Therapist: No . . . you only want me to feel useless.

Projected interpretations of the patient's attempts to reduce the therapist and of his or her angry demandingness are delivered without preparing the patient for them. It is an unfreezing technique. Even though this is done after having relatively recovered from the pain and hurt by the patient, the therapist does not say either "I am hurt" (which constitutes a confessional burdening on the patient) or, worse, "You hurt me" (which constitutes blaming the victimized patient).

Patient: No, why would I do that?

Therapist: So that I could understand you better? To feel the way you always feel?

Patient: Yeah? [silent] . . . You think so? I mean . . . I never intended to make you feel useless . . . nooo . . . you mean . . . well, it's absurd for you to think that. . . .

Along with all the aggression and negativity absorbed by the therapist, it is recommended that, whenever possible, he should also provide opportunities for reparation by the patient (Sledge and Tasman 1993). Although the therapist may neither expect nor need any apologies, they should be gracefully accepted. Importantly, they may signify the patient's own empathic recognition of the real limitations of the therapist and of his or her mutual responsibility for transgressions that may have occurred.

The confrontation of initially projected interpretations may cause further contention, but it is expected that the patient will come back to the subject eventually with greater accessibility.

Projective Integration: Projection of a Bad Self to Complete the Self

The dyadic conflict patient's attribution of negative qualities onto the therapist (i. e., nontrustworthiness, manipulativeness, self-interest, sadism, lack of caring, or intrusiveness), used together with anger and rejection, serve various purposes. It is a way of relating to the therapist, engaging him and also keeping him away; it is also a way of making the therapist feel diminished, so that he can really understand what the patient is going through. These alternative purposes may represent different stages of the patient–therapist relationship. Thus different interpretations of the same behavior of the patient would require the therapist to recognize respective stages of treatment, the nature of their relationship, and the level of the patient's accessibility along the way.

One more step in the hierarchy of interpretations reflects the patient's attribution of negative qualities to the therapist for the purpose of completion, whereby such qualities are projected onto the therapist in order to maintain a sense of self, to feel whole, in particular to enhance the cohesion of the good and bad aspects of the self. In contrast to integration by introjection, wherein the patient identifies with the therapist and becomes whole by microinternalization, in projective integration it is the the projected part that serves to complete the self. It thus constitutes a form of integration that occurs not through microinternalization but through microprojection.

Patient: There is really something wrong with me. My mood changes too quickly. I was depressed all afternoon. Then I got this call from a woman who I met last month. We made a date. My mood changed immediately—like a different person. Where is my sense of self, that I could be so dependent on the outside—whether it's a woman or a business opportunity? What does that all mean? It's so disturbing.

Therapist: Hmmm.

Patient: That I'm at the mercy of other people, that I have to rely on other people to make myself feel undepressed.

Therapist: Is it just to feel undepressed?

Patient: No, there's this anxiety or agitation, as if some dreadful thing is going to happen. It looms so large over me that I can't focus on anything else. I can't read, I can't listen to music, I can't exercise, nothing.

Therapist: All consuming.

Patient: A terrible way of living. Being wanted by other people is so important; to need other people so badly.

Therapist: Hmmm!

Patient: Also, am I picking the wrong people? People are so unreliable. They don't return calls, don't answer letters. If they do, it's because they have their own agenda. Everyone is out for himself. People are selfish, only looking after their own interests. They don't give a shit about me, really.

Therapist: As one of the people out there in your life, you must wonder whether I really care about you, whether I have my own agenda.

Again, even at this stage, the therapist picks up a negative emotion-loaded topic and brings it into their relationship, just in case.

Patient: Well, we went through this so many times before. I don't know. Speaking of selfishness, you haven't changed to the evening session time. I asked you at least three times. No, I don't trust you; you're nosey and you crowd me; shall I go on some more . . . ?

Therapist: And you want to make sure that I have those terrible qualities.

Patient: It's not that in comparison I feel better; that's not it at all . . . [long silence] . . . I'm not sure whether I believe what I say about you, either. You know what I mean. Maybe I'm the one who's selfish, no good. My mother always accused me of being selfish; maybe she's right, but somehow I can't stand feeling that way. You know, there are lots of people who are selfish and so forth; they don't care; in fact, they may even get some hidden joy out of it . . . or me, if I face the fact that I may have those terrible qualities, sometimes I fear some dreadful thing will happen. Rejection? I don't think so; it's too powerful to be explained by that. So what is it?

Therapist: Something more fundamental.

Patient: Yeah, it shakes my roots. I feel like I'm disintegrating, dissolving. And when you don't quarrel when I say those bad things to you, I feel secure; isn't that bizarre? I would think that one wouldn't feel secure in being with such a bad person. I seem not to be able to just dump the bads on you and walk away happy either, though. It sounds crazy or perverse or something.

Therapist: Puzzling?

Patient: Well, what if you decided that you had enough of me? I know people usually move away from me. I went to a party on Saturday. I felt like after a few words or an interchange with people I meet, they tend to inch away from me. I wonder whether I do to them what I do to you and they can't take it; I mean, who would want that? What is really with me?

When a patient acknowledges and owns his pathology by asking, "What is wrong with me?" instead of constantly asking what is wrong with everyone else, he has moved up the developmental ladder.

Although the patient's question reflects some semblance of introspection, with the dyadic conflict patient interpretations are geared not primarily for insight-oriented change, but for object constancy, for intrapsychic structure building. The therapist remains trustworthy, nonintrusive, and noncontrolling, thus allowing benign dependency to develop without interfering with the patient's projected and distorted assertions. On the one hand, the therapist will detoxify these patients' microprojections and, on the other, will provide a corrective, contemporary, differentiating self-object relationship for microinternalizations.

WORKING THROUGH DYADIC CONFLICTS VIA PROJECTIVE MICROINTERNALIZATION

The essential change in the dyadic conflict patient occurs through microinternalization of the clinician as contemporary "container"—here via the vehicle of the therapist's microprojections. Microexternalization is a special step in the process of self-formation wherein the other (the therapist) provides part of the projected self-defining counterpart to the patient. It is only after such a containing presence that the therapist may expect any microinternalization by the patient.Ultimately, it is through this projective process that the patient will gradually develop object constancy and consolidation of the self.

More specifically, as the therapist survives the patient's microprojections and still provides an attachable as well as separable object who is not engulfing, the patient begins to feel accepted but not threatened by the therapist. He or she slowly comes to feel valued and neither diminished nor abandoned, in spite of the perceived badness. In addition, through projective interpretations, the therapist helps the patient to build an intrapsychic structure. As the patient integrates his or her own bad and good within the temporary "gluing" presence of the therapist, the patient at the same time begins to identify with the surviving therapist. Thus the dyadic conflict patient gradually may start to accept the bad and the good in others as well as the self.

Toward Accepting Bad and Good in Others

>   *Patient:* I've got to change the job, get rid of Helen, and start with
>   a clean slate.

Therapist: And get rid of the therapist!

Patient: With Helen I get no affection, no love. How long do I have to stay in this relationship with her to figure out that she can't give me what I need? It's like an obsession. I'm stuck with her. She won't leave me alone. When I try to extract real affection from her, it's like getting water out of a stone. The funny part is that she tells me, "I can't give you what you want, Fred, I just can't; you're too demanding for me, so go and find yourself a mother. You're looking for someone who would love you in spite of you. I'm not that kind of woman. Go away and find a mother!"

Therapist: A motherly mother.

Patient: Yeah, certainly not *my* mother; she means an ideal mother. Strangely enough, my mother used to say similar things, like "Don't be such a baby; stop demanding!" You know, it still hurts to remember her saying things like that. I wasn't that demanding; it was she who was demanding and intrusive. When I wanted her attention, she'd be busy with her card games, hairdos, bowling—you name it. Then she'd come home and not want me to spend time on the phone with my friends. She would even stand over me, listening to our conversations. I don't think she gave a damn about *me*, but she'd want me to cater to her. She would send me out after school to get groceries so that we'd have something to eat together, always playing up to me. But I never got what I wanted. I mean, where was she all day! I saw how controlling she was with my younger brother, so I must have been equally exploited throughout my childhood. Then she would insist that we write love poems for her. . . . If I told her all that, she would deny it.

Therapist: All your life you've been writing her love poems!

Patient: Yeah . . . what a sap. Knowing what a terrible mother she was and still believing and insisting that she was a good mother. You know, the other day when you looked like you weren't listening, I didn't think you stopped caring about me. You apologized and then I felt very good. You're also a person. You said you had a fever. Well, the other times too . . . sometimes you're off, but you know I think you're all right. . . . Like every-one else, you have your shortcomings too. I guess the same goes for my mother, too. I mean, in reality, she was neither that good nor that bad.

Therapist: Somehow you couldn't reconcile those two aspects of your mother.

Patient: You know, when for the first time I began to doubt whether she was really a good person when we were discussing her intrusiveness, I began to have these anxieties, deep, shaking me, like, I mean, do I exist? Who am I? What am I? The other day I had this awful dream. I was in a dark alley; this monster-like creature was coming at me; it was wearing a mask, but I can see from the side that it was a human.

Therapist: Hmmm.

Patient: I wonder whether that's me or my mother. I wasn't scared in the dream, for the first time. I usually have nightmares like this, wake up in a sweat; this time it was like in a circus, or a zoo; I was curious rather than frightened. . . . [silence of 60 seconds]

Therapist: Any further thoughts?

Patient: Does it mean that it's okay now? I don't know . . . I don't need to have Helen's kind of people around me; they're clearly not good for me. I don't have to search for goodness in every person. Everyone may have goods and bads, but some people have more of one than the other. I need to be with people who are by nature less demanding, less selfish. Obviously, this may reflect some problem of mine, whatever it is. Some people seem not to tolerate my needs, even though I think my demands have severely declined. But you know, other people are needy too, maybe two needy people don't make a good match. I have to stop looking to find my mother types and trying to make bet-ter people out of them.

Therapist: That's the obsession you referred to earlier?

Patient: I keep doing it again and again; I can't believe it. It's really hard in the face of evidence. I'm still trying to make an all-good mother out of bad women.

Therapist: And your own mother?

Patient: Especially my own mother, my own bad/good mother. She was most likely struggling with her own problems. I see her now, a strange woman. I don't think she knew what motherhood really was all about; she was herself quite possibly badly treated, poor soul . . . not unlike Helen. . . . With my mother I didn't have the choice, I mean I couldn't choose obviously who is going to be my mother. But Helen . . . it's something else. I'm willing to see the bad and the good in others, but I can still make choices, can't I, when it comes to spouse and friends. . . .

Therapist: And your therapist?

In working with dyadic conflict patients, the therapist never rests.

Patient: [laughs loudly] I had a dream about you the other day. . . .

Toward Integrating Good and Bad in the Self

As the therapist anchors the patient, the patient will increasingly present vulnerabilities to the therapist. This will include talk about negative qualities, undesirable traits, and his or her basic sense of badness. Gradually, however, these patients will microinternalize the therapist's projections and begin to anchor from within. They will start to accept themselves as they are, some good, some bad.

Patient: I'm really nothing, you know, if you think of it. I went through the schools, all that, but underneath, I'm a selfish person; I mean I don't have a single real friend, not a single intimate person I could call on if I really had to. What kind of person am I? I'm no longer as much an angry person, which must have been so obnoxious, don't you think? But I'm this nothing person, inflicting myself on good people.

Therapist: Good people, bad people!

Patient: Yeah! But still I feel for people who have to put up with me.

Therapist: Isn't feeling bad for people who have to put up with you a good trait?

Patient: [a little laugh] Well, you seem to find the pony in every pile of shit, but I guess that's not a bad trait either. You know, two years ago I would have never accepted that I'm no good— I just couldn't. It would never have occurred to me to be concerned about what I'm doing to other people, either. So it is progress, I guess. All these years, I wonder what I inflicted on my kids. My son hardly used to relate to me; now, we do a few things together . . . I've got a lot of undoing to do. Can I do it? Do I have in me care and love for others; am I so damaged that it will take another 35 years to undo it?

Therapist: Or maybe another two years.

The therapist refers here to the length of time the patient has been in treatment.

Patient: Yeah, maybe it won't be 35 years here. [long silence] And I even feel sorry for you. Things that I put you through; gosh, why didn't you just throw me out? What a pain I must have been all that time. You must have seen something that I didn't and figured that I'll come around. At least I honestly began to question myself rather than hurting people, even those who cared about me. I guess you too. [short silence] Can you believe that I could come to say something like this? This doesn't make me anxious at all. You know, in fact, it feels good to say things like that. The other day I said to Nancy, "You know, Nancy, you're a good wife." The words just rolled out of my mouth. I felt so good saying it. She looked at me and said, "What? Are you okay?" You know, they're all so accustomed to my being critical and irritable that they think I'm sick or something when I say something nice. In reality I'm not that bad. I mean, I don't really hate people. You know, I could be nicer; another 3 years, I presume . . . is this a hostile comment? I mean toward you. . . . I got to tell you this joke, but please no interpretation! Okay? Now, what is a psychiatrist? Well . . .

> a psychiatrist is someone you go to half crocked, and leave
> completely broke. Ha, ha, ha! . . . But now, you don't deserve
> this.

The patient has begun to accept himself as both bad and good, but instead of totally separating the two, eventually can start to integrate them into a developmentally more mature form of ambivalence (see also Chapter 7).

Even conflicts arising in the dyadic stage are a kind of deficit, yet they are essential elements (a form of cement) of the psychic structure building, not necessarily to be interpreted away or resolved but to be contained, used towards the solidification of patient's self. It has been suggested that containment has the potential to lead to structural change (Adler 1993). To the degree that the therapist can contain the patient's projections, the dyadic conflict patient has the possibility of reinternalizing these projections, now modified by the containment process. He concludes that

> Although most containment experiences are only relatively success-
> ful (i. e., how many therapists can always empathically interpret in
> the face of the patient's rage and interpersonal provocation?), there
> is an incremental experience over time in successful therapy that can
> allow the patient to reinternalize modified projections. [pp. 198–199]

Taken further, it is believed that these cognitive translations and transformations within the context of the holding environment, with the clinician as "projective container," ultimately themselves become safe, resilient and good (but not *all* good) introjects that heal the patient.

6

The Triadic Deficit Patient and the Prosocial Introject

PSYCHOTHERAPY SCENARIO

Treatment of *triadic deficit* patients entails working with paternally deprived persons, either due to actual absence or through the destructive presence of an abusive and antisocial father figure. Traumatized by or bereft of good fathering experiences, they are thus either missing a primary model or have introjected an immoral model for proper socialization and ethical values. This means that such individuals may be lacking the internal structures to either recognize or to respect right from wrong and therefore to be able to obey societal standards or honor appropriate authority; in treatment this can manifest as a disregard for the doctor's (i. e., therapist's) "rules." In addition, these patients tend to externalize their problems and to favor action over reflection; their imagination seems absent, their inner world inaccessible. In terms of amenability to psychotherapy, they are seen as sustaining a cognitive style that is the antithesis of introspection and psychological-mindedness.

For both situational and intrapsychic reasons, triadic deficit patients come to therapy reluctantly and remain in treatment unreliably; even when such patients do agree to a contractual arrangement, there are likely to be broken or compromised promises. Since triadic deficit patients have frequently formed a *false self* as a front for meeting environmental demands, they often function on a superficial or deceptive interpersonal level that conceals their real feelings. They may even have a secret world of antisocial or duplicitous behaviors (e. g., adultery, addiction, petty crime). Thus triadic deficit patients will easily disengage from relationships, or only temporarily engage by using others—including the therapist—through secretive or unscrupulous means of manipulation. Their prime purposes are characteristically those of meeting self-serving motives and expedient needs.

Just as the psychotherapist becomes a substitute maternal self-object for the dyadic deficit patient, so the clinician for the triadic deficit patient must become a paternal stand-in and moral representative; as such, he serves as both a real and a symbolic figure, a father object and a prosocial introject. In these capacities, he supplies what has been deficient—the earlier standards that were either unestablished for socialized behaviors and meeting responsibilities or, with the more developmentally deviant individual, substitutes for the defective internalization and idealization of antisocial figures.

Insofar as therapy represents a microcosm of the rule-abiding social world, limit setting here is a crucial therapeutic function, as the clinician carefully structures sessions while confronting transgressions and violations as well as their rationalizations. Moreover, comparable to the maternal empathy offered to meet affectional needs of the dyadic deficit patient, the therapist offers *paternal empathy* to meet affiliative needs of the triadic deficit patient. Like the former, it too has its therapeutic constraints, that is, it should not be utilized to express synchrony or sympathy with the patient's projected complaints against others, but must be primarily reserved for self-blame and guilt, in order to reinforce the internalized rudiments of morality.

Of special consideration are the countertransferential tendencies to overempathically embrace the triadic deficit patient by becoming not only his or her ombudsman in mediating societal matters but an accomplice against authority. Alternatively, in retaliation to threat or betrayal, there is the danger of taking punitive or vengeful measures in a vindictive wish to destroy the destructive patient. These act as ineffective and inappropriate antidotes to the special difficulties of treating persons with this particular psychopathology: they cannot serve to relieve the therapist's pressing sense of responsibility for the other's immoral behavior or allay anticipatory guilt over bad deeds that could conceivably be prevented; nor do they rectify wrongdoing through personal policing and punishment. For those vulnerable psychotherapists who are most prone to be overly moralistic or easily manipulable, such defensive behaviors are rarely successful in reducing irrational fear of contamination of the clinician's own ethical conduct. Amid these countertransferential tendencies with the triadic deficit patient, perhaps most pertinent is the need to see past the defensive subterfuge and to continually seek the human true self behind the antisocial facade.

OUTLINE OF INTERVENTIONS
FOR TRIADIC DEFICIT PATIENTS

CASE EXCERPTS WITH THERAPIST COMMENTARY

Triadic deficit patients, whose psychopathology may include various forms of antisocial or immoral acts of delinquency, substance or sexual abuse, crime and violence, as well as lesser forms of philandering, lying, cheating, and manipulating, are thought to be the "least loved" by their therapists (Strasburger 1986, p. 192). This is due to the unaccepting and often punitive feelings that they engender in their caretakers and those who treat them, which in turn tend to mirror the overriding response of the social structure and its sanctions—unconscious or conscious rejection—in particular the sentiment that their problems are those of moral degeneracy, of "sin more than sickness" (p. 192). While both patients and sinners share the same fate, in that the two categories may be subject to stigma and victimized by others, triadic deficit patients (compared with other types of psychopathology) are often considered outsiders; they are especially scorned as offenders of society rather than viewed as victims of illness, thereby unsympathetically looked upon as legitimate recipients of disapproval, blame, and retaliatory malice.

Behind this stigma unfortunately resides an overall failure, by society and therapists alike as their agents, to go beyond an automatic reaction of aversion, fear, or anger, and instead to see "sociopathy as a human process" (Vaillant 1975). The former refers to the reluctance to place on the same universal continuum "all the standard psychiatric categories, all the stuntings, cripplings, and inhibitions . . . and also the character disorders . . . the diminutions that result from drug addiction, psychopathy, authoritarianism, criminality . . ." (Maslow 1970, p. 131). More specifically, unlike other psychopathology presented here, there is a particular resistance to maintaining triadic deficit disorders within a maturational paradigm—clinically and humanely—and thus dealing with "sociopathy as developmental delay" (Kegan 1986). In the latter light, the therapist must especially bear in mind that these particular patients who present to treatment have been the recipients of a special slice of deficient maturation: the lack of, or unsuccessful passage into, the triadic relationship of childhood. This transition has profound developmental importance, both societally (Lacan 1957) and sexually (Mollon 1993) (for the latter, see also Chapter 7).

Relating to the the role of the father in particular, Lacan (1957) has suggested that the entrance into the oedipal (or triadic) position may be synonymous with passage into a symbolic mode, with the paternal figure seen as representative of the outside world, especially the law and the social order. In fact, above and beyond the Oedipus complex per se and its many manifestations in the sexual life of the individual forevermore, Lacan sees as equally universal to these drives and desires the necessity to subject those same impulses and urges to the keepers of the law, such as society, kinship, or family units.

More broadly, the structural shift from the dyadic to the triadic is considered a radical and universal transformation of the human being, in short, a significant movement "from a dual, immediate, or mirror relationship to the mediate relationship . . . of the symbolic. . . ." (Lemaire 1977, p. 78). Whereas the *imaginary* is considered a maternal function, the *symbolic* becomes a paternal function. In this way, the developmental passage into the triadic position is seen as having profound psychological consequences. It reflects not solely a more cohesive sense of identity and of self boundaries, but of the social and symbolic order. It metaphorically means knowing one's place in the larger affiliative scheme of family and society.

In looking at the psychopathological side of this transition, Mollon's (1993) examination of the fragile self expressly goes beyond dyadic deficits when he refers to a "failure to establish the triadic position: the exclusion of the paternal dimension" (p. 110). Whereas the self disturbances depicted in Chapter 4 in dyadic deficits can be understood in terms of an early relationship with the mother, Mollon's clinical observations suggest that there is an additional aspect that occurs further on in development—"the failure to progress from the dyadic relationship with the mother to the triadic or oedipal position which allows a place for the father" (p. 110).

He posits that entry into the triadic (or oedipal) position necessarily involves a radical restructuring of the self. As the relationship between the paternal and maternal figures is increasingly acknowledged, the child must to a great extent separate from the mother to accommodate the father. This important transition also allows the youngster to progressively recognize the classic consequences of the primal scene and to thereby prospectively place him- or herself in an equidistant position as the product of two parents—with whose intimacy he or she will inevitably compete. This of course concords with Freud's (1923) view that the Oedipus complex always occurs in both positive and negative forms—thus for both sexes the primary oedipal wish is to remain close to mother as well as to ward off the rival father.

More specifically, Mollon (1993) addresses the pre-triadic exclusion of the paternal figure, which he refers to as "the foreclosure of the father" (p. 113). He suggests that the father is not repressed (by which Freud [1915b] referred to the defensive denial of an *internal* perception of an instinctual need), but rather (as later depicted by Freud [1918]) reflects the dismissal of an *external* perception that is disavowed or repudiated. The attitude toward the paternal figure within the dyadic configuration can become one whereby the father is dually shut out from the mother–infant dyad. The father is not allowed his normal place in relation to the mother and in relation to the child— the authority of the father, as equal to that of the mother, is not accepted nor is the father's sexual relationship with the mother with its significance of being the origin of the child. [p. 113]

Whereas the former aspect (i. e., authority) is most pertinent to the triadic deficit patient, the latter aspect (i. e., sexuality) is more applicable to the triadic conflict patient (see also Chapter 7).

Mollon (1993) goes further to suggest that a critical factor determining the child's fate of failing to enter the triadic position may be the mother's desire to denigrate the role of the father, which in turn coincides with the child's oedipal wish. He predicts that

This malignant alliance between the mother's wish omnipotently to do without the father, and the child's oedipal desire to remain close to the mother and exclude the father, may trap the child in a developmental cul-de-sac from which it is increasingly difficult to escape. [p. 112]

The triadic deficit patient thereby suffers from a variety of developmental deficits and delays that pertain to a missing or faulty triadic relationship. Two major scenarios are implicated in triadic deficit development: the absentee father and the unprincipled or abusive father. Although some triadic deficit patients may victimize and/or abuse others in adulthood, they have themselves expressly been the victims of the physical or psychological loss of their father or, worse, an exploitative, unprincipled, and perhaps abusive paternal figure. Such a father, by not having provided an appropriate role model, has also affected the child's relations with his or her mother, insofar as this unavailable and non-self-respecting father did not respect the mother either. Thus the individual has grown up without a healthy role model for identification, for competition and mastery, or even the normal aspiration of father's love.

For the female patient, it also means an abortive process, the failure to have gone through the stages of competing with mother for the father's interest, because the mother was not loved by the father. As a result, as a young girl she has lost her respect for women at large as well as her self-respect and, further, feels undesirable to other men. For both sexes, the crucial issue thus becomes not having had an idealized male object as a role model of men, or having had an idolized *bad* paternal role model for identification.

In addition to this unsavory scenario, such children did not need to compete with their father for the mother's attention and grew up not respecting women. In the above ways, the deficit of the father signifi-cantly impacted on the mother as well, and the mother, insecure in relation with the father, may not have herself been able to provide a focus for the child's interest and challenge as a maternal object or model for affection and affirmation. The consequences are compound: while the father is not trusted or is idealized as an antihero, the mother is deval-ued (the mother's role in reciprocal devaluation has already been noted). The child either ends up suffering from these paternal losses as he yearns for the missing father, and/or identifies with the negative figure and becomes like the unprincipled paternal object in fact or fantasy. In their study of the phenomenon of deceit, Gediman and Lieberman (1996) believe that patients who frequently lie suffer from identifications with parental figures with faulty egos or superegos who have lied to them (perhaps presenting themselves as better than they really are). Their children, in turn, tend to defensively idealize the impostor parent (Gottdiener 1982). Similarly, Bollas (1989) suggests that lying can be reparative for the patient, because "lying functions as another order of self and object experience, an order that consistently helped [the patient] to recuperate from the actual absences [or failings] of the parent" (p. 179).

Whereas the patient who has had an absentee father may be treated with individual psychotherapy (albeit with great difficulties), in the case of the abusive father and the antisocial adult individual psychotherapy may only play an adjunct role. For these patients, being in a long-term, highly structured environment where acting out is strictly controlled is an absolute necessity. Individual therapy may supplement the main treat-ment of reculturation and resocialization with external controls, reedu-cation, and rehabilitation-oriented group activities.

Let's return to the first group of patients, who do not identify with or idealize a bad father figure, but primarily suffer from paternal losses nonetheless. These are deficits, not conflicts, and are not unconscious. They are not repressed on the basis of superego inhibitions; at best, they may be consciously suppressed, and the patient may be reluctant to talk about them. At worst, the patient may act out his sexual and aggressive impulses unchecked. Such patients may not believe in the authority of basic social structures (i. e., religion, marriage, friendship, law) nor follow the values that they represent. Depending on the patient's social status, he may even be involved in antisocial acts such as white- or blue-collar crimes. Short of being actively criminal or delinquent, these individuals may less blatantly lack the formation of sincere and honest goals and the development of proper ideals; in such instances, for example, they may make superficial financial gains or other mercenary interests the focus of their life, at the expense of interpersonal relationships and real care, concern, or fidelity to others.

Triadic deficits also have important implications for the formation of a false self. Winnicott (1968) has theorized that if the person's environment is either unreliable or unacceptable because it is itself unprincipled, a hidden self forms. The individual fends off this unsatisfactory scenario by devising a false self, which has a dually difficult task: the duplicitous need to hide the true self while at the same time attempting to meet the demands of the real world. When there has been a deficiency in the holding or containing aspects of infancy, the tremendous anxiety that this early experience evokes is offset by the erection of a false self, which serves to salvage the situation by saving the infant from total disintegration (as in dyadic deficit patients); in other instances (as in triadic deficit patients), the false self may mask the true self by forming a secret life. (In healthy adaptation, there can also be a false front, the less pervasive and pathological development of conforming or socially expected attitudes and behaviors.)

Stern (1985) has shed some additional light on this subject by suggesting that the earlier mother–child relationship may have already been amiss, prior to the triadic deficit. In such instances, the infant may have been the recipient of a particular type of misattunement, which not merely altered the infant's experience, but "stole" it, resulting in "emotional theft" (p. 213). Thus the intersubjective sharing of experience between the maternal figure and her child resulted not in a positive communion, or did so only temporarily. The danger here is that the mother may have attuned to the infant's state, establishing a shared experience, but then changed that experience so that it was really lost to the child; the child was, in effect, left hanging. Usually this would occur when the mother has attempted a prohibitive or preventive act, in which a moral lesson was not accomplished in a straightforward manner; instead, the mother varied her behavior midstream in a way that the child was no longer able to follow and, in so doing, she "slips inside the infant's experience by way of attunement and then steals the affective experience away from the child" (p. 214). Stern (1985) makes the intriguing point that in such examples,

> one of their main features for the infant is the danger in permitting the intersubjective sharing of experience, namely that the intersubjective sharing can result in *loss*. This is likely to be the point of origin of the long developmental line that later results in . . . *children's need for lying, secrets, and evasions, to keep their own subjective experiences intact.* [p. 214, italics mine]

In the above regard, these dyadic deficits may interface with, and even compound triadic deficits. Thus triadic deficit patients have perhaps not learned the moral lessons of either parent. In adult life, they may then behave as if they are obeying the dicta of society, but not out of guilt. They will act as if they are making friends, or as if committed to causes, because of the desirability of such traits; however, in reality they do not engage in enduring relationships, considering others in general as dispensable. Solely out of self-interest, the only relationships they may be able to maintain are strictly temporary or situational ones, dissolving quickly after some self-serving motive has been satisfied. This type of patient is interested in succeeding without any formulated goal, doing everything he or she can to accomplish this, given the limitations and circumstances. Those triadic deficit patients who have managed to sustain a good-enough dyadic relationship with their mothers may seek and get attached to one or more women (maternal persons). In such instances, like dyadic deficit patients, they characteristically establish highly dependent relationships, and are frequently disappointed; they also are likely to exploit or abuse sexual relationships and social connections.

Good (1995) has suggested that these patients frequently enter therapy conscious of their premeditated attempts to manipulate or deceive the therapist. "Basically, a part of them wants a meaningful experience, but another part, a more malignant part, does not want to enter an honest process of relating to another as this would mean a lack of control of the other" (p. 155).

Any threat to a specific relationship, business failure, or physical illness is what typically brings such patients to treatment, and all they may want under such circumstances is the re-establishment of the status quo. In answer to the question of why these reluctant and deceitful patients come to therapy, Winnicott (1965)'s response can be offered: that the false self brings the true self to therapy. The critical therapeutic question thus becomes: How can the therapist foster the authentic self throughout therapy and, for his own sake as well as the patient's, how does he deal with the discrepancy between the real individual and the duplicitous disguise (or even, how does he tell the difference)?

BEING WITH AN ANTISOCIAL PATIENT: DETERMINATION DESPITE A CONDITIONAL ENGAGEMENT OR FALSE FRONT

The fundamental issue here is how best to engage a dismissive, deceitful, and often disengaging person, and to sustain determination despite having to do therapeutic work with a patient who does not believe in treatment or the therapist and who implicitly and explicitly expresses his lack of confidence in both. On the surface, the patient shows neither fear of intimacy nor of engulfment; in short, he or she displays no dependency, thus is emotionally unengageable. In contrast to the dyadic conflict patient, who attacks and diminishes the therapist as a way of relating, however negatively, the triadic deficit patient genuinely lacks trust in the therapist and is not at all interested in forming a clinical bond by being critical. Rather, this type of patient—or at least the false self—

is invested in remaining disengaged, or at most conditionally engaged, only utilizing or "using" the therapist for a specific purpose for a limited time. However compromised a connection, it is this tentative and conditional engagement within which the clinician must work.

Extra-empathic Acceptance of Rejection of Patienthood (i. e., Without "Paternal Empathy")

Triadic deficit patients tend to attribute their troubles as originating or residing outside themselves, belonging to others and to external events that are beyond their control. Thus they invariably reject responsibility for their actions and see themselves, rather, as victims of circumstance. Though they may feel sorry for themselves and try to convince the clinician of the innocence of their acts, they nonetheless disavow the patient role. A major reason is that it can conceivably implicate them by requiring them to take a hard look at the part they really play in their own unsavory lives. Once referred (or legally required) to seek psychological help, however, these patients may overtly behave as if they respect the therapist and are accepting the entire treatment process. In this way, they superficially succumb to the therapeutic situation and to the therapist; they may do so as a deliberate way of temporarily controlling their treatment and, in particular, of defensively maintaining distance.

This patient presentation invariably reflects a deceptive form of relating, in which the person is overtly or covertly manipulating the therapist and the therapy. Such a self-sufficient stance is usually sustained in order to avoid appropriate interaction, even when the patient is in the midst of serious psychological upheaval. At the same time, the triadic deficit patient may reveal his or her real neediness in other ways. Even early in the therapy, this can occur by the patient's exceeding boundaries of the basic ground rules of treatment, for example, contacting the therapist between sessions or wanting special favors.

> *Patient:* I really appreciated your returning my call. I didn't want to bother you over the weekend, but I thought I might receive some quick advice from you. I hope I didn't disturb you that much.

> *Therapist:* No, you didn't.You can always call me, and for that it
> need not be an emergency either. But do I sense that you're
> bothered about this weekend call?

The therapist makes himself very available, at least initially, and
assures the patient by expressing that availability. At the same time, it
should be noted that while the therapist questions the patient's presumed
feelings (e. g., possible guilt), he neither interprets nor confronts the
transferential issue of the extratherapeutic request. The reason is that at
this juncture the therapist wants to encourage a benign dependent relationship with the patient, who is not at all accustomed to admitting
dependency (i. e., the "needy" role). Since such an approach has its own
potential dangers, two cautions are necessary: the therapist had better
be prepared to deliver what he promises, and he should budget for more
demanding requests in the future.

Incidentally, this is only a short phase; when the patient is in crisis—the only time he accepts the patient role (albeit relatively and
reluctantly)—it is a window of opportunity for the clinician to bond with
the patient. While promoting a benign dependency, the therapist must
also understand the triadic deficit patient's discomfort at being in the
patient role and accept that feeling without expressions of empathy. This
is because the therapist's expression of such empathy makes the triadic
deficit patient feel as if he is in a one-down position, which hurts his
self-esteem; in return, he or she is likely to become even more defensive
and reject the therapist.

> *Patient:* Well, I hate to disturb people. The weekend is your pri-
> vate time. People are entitled to their leisure time without being
> bothered by someone else's urgencies.
> *Therapist:* You especially don't like doing the bothering because you
> feel you shouldn't be needing others.

In contrast to all other patient types (i. e., dyadic deficit, dyadic
conflict, and triadic conflict), the therapist's statements here are not
personalized (e. g., the clinician refers to the patient's "needing others"
instead of "needing me"). Because the patient's reaction is not personal

to the therapist, this allows the patient to maintain a desired distance and yet feel understood.

> *Patient:* Yeah, I hate that weak role.
> *Therapist:* You don't like to be on the receiving end!
> *Patient:* I'm not accustomed to being on the receiving end. I don't want anything from anyone. And when I give, I don't get anything from anyone.
> *Therapist:* How sad.

The therapist makes a mistake by expressing this generic empathy. At the initial stages of therapy these patients will negate any feelings that would make them vulnerable. Thus any such attempt will be rebuffed; at these times these patients easily feel patronized, thereby diminished. In fact, this is the opposite side of their narcissistic neediness, which they are unable to acknowledge or accept.

> *Patient:* No, not at all. . . . I like it this way. That's the role for which I'm most qualified, if you know what I mean. I get what I want when I give. So it isn't all non-selfish. I don't feel deprived at all. You've missed the whole point.

Further interpretation of the patient's denial would only result in the deterioration of treatment.

> *Therapist:* Irritated?
> *Patient:* No! No irritation! Obviously, I couldn't make it clear to you that I don't feel in need of being given to.
> *Therapist:* Is it possible that because it's so difficult for you to be on the receiving end, you end up denying some of your legitimate needs?

The therapist continues the same line of mistake, because he can't quite believe that the patient is going to reject the offered empathy.

> *Patient:* It isn't that my needs are not met. I exist, don't I? I must be supplied something from somewhere. I don't want you to

get the idea that I feel sorry for myself, because I'm not getting things I need. I think you're confusing me with your other patients. I don't deny any of my needs. I go after them and get them . . . it just isn't me. I don't really need others' advice. I mean, I understand the whole thing; there's nothing someone else is going to add or make any difference.

Therapist: And why put yourself in such a position, while knowing fully that no one can really be of some help?

Patient: I'm just being realistic. [The patient continues to rationalize his rejection of patienthood.]

Just as the triadic deficit patient scorns societal sanctions and remains exempt from their control, so he renounces the blessings of the therapist as another form of an authority's advice. In fact, the patient does not differentiate the therapist from others, so there is no transferential exclusivity in the negation. Rather, the clinician is included in the patient's overall devaluation of others and, as part of the initial intervention, he provisionally accepts the patient's need to place him in that one-down position.

Extratransferential Interpretation of Rejection of Patienthood

The triadic deficit patient is usually ashamed and embarrassed at needing a psychotherapist, the last thing on earth he felt he would ever need. The patient considers the treatment itself a sign of weakness, a form of humiliation in which he loses faith in himself. Often he will attempt to recover from shame with the use of interpersonal shortcuts (e. g., keeping to a superficial interaction that precludes recognition of problems and feelings), all the while shortchanging himself. Moreover, the patient is equally embarrassed to tell the therapist that he is embarrassed. If left unexplored, this very reaction of not sharing with the therapist the nature of his discomfort may result in prematurely terminating treatment, which is characteristically at the brink of dissolution. Under such fragile circumstances, interpretations of content are best made without transferential references.

Patient: I feel much better since our last week's chat. Things are otherwise unchanged; nothing much is happening. They've been kind of uneventful days. [Long silence, as patient is looking outside]

Therapist: And you were wondering why you're here!

The focus of the interpretation is not on the transferential "chat," but on the immediate content.

Patient: Yeah, I think that things are more or less stable in my life. I don't want to come here just for the sake of coming. I'm not worried about money or time, but I don't see the necessity to continue, unless you think that it's absolutely needed. I don't want you to misunderstand it. I do enjoy chatting with you, but there has to be an end to it. I've been here already four weeks; it shouldn't become a habit. [silence of 30 seconds].

Therapist: Habitual patient?

Patient: I guess that these days I would grab hold of anything. You know, I never knew what nervousness was until now. When people talked about their nervousness, I just couldn't believe it. I would say to myself, "Look at this grown-up man behaving like a lost kid." These people always came to me for advice.

Therapist: And you don't like to behave like a lost kid yourself.

Patient: Oh, gosh, I hate that. I don't mind being . . . I am yet to see someone I can truly look up to; this sounds too conceited, but I really mean it.

The patient's dependency fears of, or wishes for, the therapist are not interpreted.

Patient: Well, I came here with lots of stress and, thanks to you, I feel better; there should be no reason to extend the therapy. I know I still have some problems unsolved—the issue with my son will not go away, pressure at work will not go away, but I just have to handle them myself.

Therapist: Without needing outside help.

The therapist does not interpret the transferential nature of the patient's reluctance, because the therapist is only one of the "outsiders" that the patient doesn't need.

> *Patient:* Well, you were quite helpful in identifying the stresses I was under and showing me that I didn't have to be so damn responsible for everything. I'll delegate more, that kind of stuff, but it's up to me. You can't do it for me. One has to stand on one's own feet and be firm.
>
> *Therapist:* You feel bad enough that even temporarily you couldn't stand on your own feet.

The therapist does not interpret the wish that therapist would always be there, because the interpretations of these patients need to be extratransferential.

> *Patient:* I'm accustomed to solving my own problems. I don't like going to doctors, even for physical illnesses. For a psychological one, that's even worse. I must confess that I'm ashamed of being here.
>
> *Therapist:* Ashamed of being a patient!

The therapist sharpens the content.

> *Patient:* Yes, that I should need help from anyone for my problems. I've always had to take care of myself, toughing it out, so they all see me as solid as a rock. So I'm used to not needing anyone. If they ever knew that I'm coming to see a psychiatrist, they would laugh at me. They would think I must be crazy.
>
> *Therapist:* You would rather suffer than be thought of as crazy?
>
> *Patient:* First of all, I am not crazy. I know you don't have to be Freud to recognize that. There's no redeeming aspect of being here as a patient . . . oh, okay I see the time is up.
>
> *Therapist:* Relieved the time is up, so when you leave here you're no longer a patient.

Patient: [starting to leave, and then saying with a soft voice] Do I know that person who just walked into the waiting room?

Once again, an exit line (Gabbard 1982) alerts the therapist of heightened transference–countertransference manifestations at the end of the hour. Here the expression of self-sufficiency and counterdependency during the session proper belies the concern expressed upon leaving. The parting query cautiously hints at the beginning of benign dependency, and even the emergence of increasing interest in the outer world of the clinician, as well as a new sense of possessiveness. In this instance, the departing and threatened patient takes notice, for the first time, of another of the therapist's patients.

Extra-empathic Acceptance and Extratransferential Interpretation of Disbelief in the Therapist

The triadic deficit patient will show lack of interest in focusing on the patient–therapist relationship and will react to the transferential comments on the part of the therapist as an intrusion into the task at hand. In general, exploration into the patient–therapist interaction is looked upon as interesting at best, but basically irrelevant; moreover, any insistence of the therapist to make their relationship the focus of attention will only irritate the patient, without any productive result. With this type of patient, all interactions with the therapist are carefully calibrated to maintain a certain controlled distance. Even when the patient has sufficiently connected to the therapist so that he feels threatened not by their connection but by their disconnection, he still may manipulate the situation by being excessively apologetic or overly remorseful, in order to regain the therapist's favor.

Patient: I know I'm a little late, and I'm really sorry. I couldn't get off the phone with an old friend of mine who called as I was leaving the house. Though we see each other only occasionally, I consider her my best friend; we grew up together. She kept chatting about this guy she just met. I couldn't tell her that I was late, so finally I said, "Look, let me call you this evening." So I'm sorry; I hate the waste of time. And I know this has happened too many times lately.

Therapist: Have you been having some questions about me lately?

The therapist sharpens the transferential focus here, as if he is dealing with dyadic or triadic conflict patients. However, as he soon realizes, this is a mistake.

Patient: Questions about the treatment?

By rephrasing the question, the patient gives the therapist a chance to retreat. But the therapist fails to do so.

Therapist: No, about *me.*

Patient: I don't know why you keep asking whether this or that of my feelings about people out there has something to do with you. Honestly, I don't understand that. I read that in the magazine and in the books; that's how it is, but I really neither hate you nor love you; nor am I irritated at you whatsoever! I want to go back to work on what we were discussing before . . .

Therapist: I'm overstating my importance in your preoccupations.

The therapist partially recovers. It would have been better if he had said, "the therapy's importance" rather than "*my* importance".

Patient: Well, I believe the treatment has been useful. As you know, I was rather reluctant initially. I didn't know what to expect, and I was somewhat skeptical of its value. Anything that's not very scientific, you know, could be questionable in terms of its usefulness.

Therapist: Psychiatry is not scientific and useful enough!

Here the therapist has gone back to an extratransferential emphasis by referring not to himself, but to field of psychiatry.

Patient: Yes, of course, and that can't be helped. It applies to everything—some movies are better than others; some courses are
more useful than others. . . . At times, I feel I could bring more
material for discussion. I should give some thought to it and
make a list of things I should discuss, rather than coming here
completely unprepared. It's up to me.

Therapist: [responding to the initial comment of the patient] And
some therapists may be better than others.

Patient: Of course, I've found nothing special that I can complain
about you, though, you know, given the profession itself, and
what can you do. Nothing personal, but no one ever is always
. . . completely . . . you know, everyone has their limits. It's the
same with other doctors as well, or somehow it's hard to believe
that therapists could be helpful. But you have been helpful.

Therapist: You aren't convinced, though.

Patient: You think so? . . . I don't know why I'm embarrassed to
say that, but . . . I'm not . . . I usually give credit where it
belongs . . . I guess, I don't really believe, kind of unusual. I
mean, I know you are smart, but I wonder . . .

As the therapist continues to listen to the patient's doubts, he still
attempts to remain useful, credible, and valuable to the patient, always
bearing in mind that deficits will not go away with interpretations—they
have to be supplied.

THE THERAPIST AS PATERNAL SELF-OBJECT:
SUPPLYING AND FILLING THE DEFICIT

*Structure Within the Sessions: No Tolerance for, Nor
Interpretation of Violations—Setting Limits and Providing
"Paternal Empathy" Only for Self-Blame*

The therapist tries to provide what is lacking in the patient's psychic
structure—a benign paternal presence. Just as the therapist professionally becomes a maternal presence to meet the missing affectional needs

of the dyadic deficit patient, the clinican here attempts to approximate a paternal presence to meet the unmet affiliative needs of the triadic deficit patient; at the same time, as paternal self-object, he also represents a good ego ideal. As such, the clinician creates an achievable condition for obtaining father love, becomes an object for secondary identification, and offers the introduction of a value system as well as an induction of the patient as a social or community member (e. g., religious affiliation, workplace, family or marital situation), all of which provide the context for affiliative needs.

The particular difficulties in supplying and filling the needs of the triadic deficit patient reside in the fact that the very recipient of the paternal presence is typically a person who exemplifies what Gediman and Lieberman (1996) refer to as "the many faces of deceit." This includes perpetrating an assortment of omissions, lies, and disguise in psychotherapy, which no doubt mirror comparable behaviors outside of treatment. Such patients will easily exploit others (including the therapist) without shame. At bottom, these persons are usually unable, or at best unwilling, to differentiate honesty from dishonesty.

The special danger for the therapist under such circumstances inheres in the insidious and seductive nature of deception. As the above authors have proposed

> deception manifests itself not just individually, but as a dyadic, interactive, relational process, involving not just the false communication of the receiver but also a receptive Other who responds to that communication and person. The Other's reactions—belief or disbelief—are partly induced by the deceiver and partly by the personal storehouse of unconscious identifications and fantasies that touch on particular deceptions to which he or she is vulnerable. [p. 4]

In light of this clinical picture, and perhaps despite it, the therapist has to set limits on the patient's behavior in the sessions, confront his pathology, and make explicit demands. Expressions of empathy with the patient's feelings, or interpretations of them, would only encourage the patient to persist in his or her antisocial or deceitful behaviors.

Patient: [Eyes are red, slight stammering] Everyone is entitled to private time with families. I don't know how you spend your weekends, but you deserve to be with your family and children without being on call, so to speak.

Therapist: Did you drink before you came here?

The therapist dismisses the content and directly confronts the acting-out behavior when an obvious violation of limits has occurred, here, the alcoholic patient's observed transgression (i. e., coming to the session drunk).

Patient: No, not really. . . . I believe you have children because you seemed to know a lot about kids, but I wasn't really wondering. I mean, in many ways, I don't really want to know about your personal life. My internist, Dr. Daly, who referred me to you, the other day began to say something about you, that he knew your wife. I said, "Joseph, stop, I don't want to know about his personal life." I just wanted that to remain private. So I guess even if I am a little curious about your life, in actuality I don't want to find out about it.

Therapist: What do you mean by, "No, not really?"

The therapist dismisses the transferential material and goes back to the initial issue.

Patient: I stopped by; I was a little early, had a beer, that's all. No big deal. . . . Would I lie to you?

Therapist: Yes, you would.

The clinician's immediate acknowledgment and confirmation that the patient lies concords with Gediman and Lieberman's (1996) therapeutic axiom, "lies should be dealt with as soon as they are recognized, within the limits of dosage, timing, and tact" (p. 74). The therapist makes such a statement, not as an angry confrontation, but in a straightforward, assertive, albeit unaggressive manner.

Patient: [laughs] All right, I'm sorry. It'll not happen again, but let's get back to . . .

The therapist expects that it will happen again, but must not get discouraged. This is because of the persistence of pathological lying, which serves several crucial purposes for the perpetrator. First and foremost, Gediman and Lieberman (1996) contend that

> An important aim of imposture is affirmation of the false self by a real or imagined audience that can be fooled, duped, or deceived. Such affirmation by an audience serves defensive, integrative, narcissistic, and self-cohesive functions, and gratifies the instinctual drives. [p. 91]

These authors have further proposed that lying can have yet another ulterior motive, in that "the lie exposes to the other the betrayal by the parents" (p. 73). This particular motive, which peers into and plays out the past, may unwittingly take the onus of the lie away from the patient, in hopes of substitutive sympathy.

As with dyadic conflict patients, who aggress against the therapist and others, triadic deficit patients who lie, manipulate, or act out should also be offered opportunities for reparation. As verbalized above, this may start with an apology by the patient, albeit glib or expedient, but that should not suffice. It needs to be followed up with more honest and convincing expressions and actual actions of remorse. Unless the patient is given the space and time to repair wrongdoings, such unacceptable acts are likely to be taken lightly and repeated. The therapist's role here is to assist in the articulation and internalization of responsible behaviors, and to deal with potential destructive intentions and actions by helping the patient to better manage these feelings in the future. If the patient agrees to some prospective reparative act, the therapist should reinforce its merit and allow it to come to fruition to whatever extent possible. However, he himself must not renege—nor let the patient off the hook—till the deed is done.

Structure Outside *the Sessions: No Tolerance for, Nor Interpretation of Violations—Setting Limits and Providing "Paternal Empathy" Only for Self-Blame*

Since the triadic deficit patient does not appear to have the feelings of guilt that otherwise accompany a well-developed internal superego structure, the therapist needs to externally impose his value system on the patient. He does so by explicitly confronting socially unaccept-able behaviors and verbally setting limits that would otherwise go un-checked. Under such circumstances, the therapist does not indulge in exploratory questions as to why the patient has no guilt, or needlessly encourage an endless expression of excuses and rationalizations. Nor does he express empathy for the patient's dilemma, which would be misconstrued as unconditional love and indiscriminate sanction; this would only reinforce the very actions that the therapist is trying to change, by compounding the patient's need to continue his pathology.

The therapist of the triadic deficit patient instead offers a deliber-ately restricted form of empathy, *paternal empathy*, whereby the thera-pist, as social standard bearer (and, eventually, moral introject), is acutely attuned to the person's need for structure and limit setting. Sensing that this type of patient is asking for external control becomes the basis for such a paternally empathic response. When the triadic deficit patient misbehaves and, for example, the therapist tells the alcoholic not to drink, this is not presented as one who is policing the patient. Instead the therapist intervenes in empathic recognition that the troubled per-son who arrives drunk is really requesting control from the clinician, because he or she as yet lacks internal controls.

> *Patient:* My son and I had another battle yesterday. He asked me to wake him up at 6:30 A.M. So I went to knock on his door and told him to get up. Then I came downstairs, prepared break-fast, and he was still not down, so I went up and knocked on the door again. He still did not respond. I kept knocking with no response, so I opened the door. He began to yell he is sick and will not go to school. He was all covered up; I pulled the blanket to see whether he had any fever. Well, he went crazy,

screaming at the top of his voice that he hates me. What do I do with this boy? I've had it. He's failing in school and still not doing his work. Anyway, I dragged him down, hit him a few times, on the soft places mostly. Finally he left. In the afternoon he came back, very friendly, as if nothing happened in the morning. He said, "Hello, Mom, you're my favorite, you know" and he pulled me toward him for a little dance. You would not believe that this is the same kid.

Therapist: Don't hit him!

Here the therapist dismisses the sexual overtones between mother and child for possible interpretation, and does not directly respond to or empathize with her frustration. Instead, he targets in on the loss of control and tendency to physical abuse when she gets angry.

Patient: I know I shouldn't, but he's so lazy. I feel like killing him; never mind beating him up. When I was even younger, no one woke me up. I got up myself on time, prepared my own breakfast . . .

Therapist: He is different!

The therapist doesn't pursue her past, but provides a current cognitive perspective as an alternative way of looking at the situation.

Patient: With that attitude, if he could finish high school, he'll be lucky.

Therapist: He may not finish high school. Is that really worrying you?

This is a confrontation of the patient's rationalization.

Patient: The truth? I don't give a shit, as long as I don't have to be subjected to him. I have no feelings, zero. The only thing is, I'm disgusted.

Therapist: Disgusted?

Patient: Yes, even with his playfulness, complimenting my dress, or my makeup. I thought a mother is supposed to enjoy the son's flirting. But I just want him out of my life. I wonder at times why he doesn't have any girlfriends; meanwhile, my younger son always has a couple of girls calling him, going out. My husband gets too involved, starts on him. He's worse than I am . . . My father never interfered with the family. I'm not sure whether it's good or bad. I think he didn't care. We didn't really pay much attention to him either. . . .

Therapist: Neither of you should beat Jimmy!

There is obvious transferential and genetic material here, to be dealt with eventually. It is deliberately kept on a back burner because, first and foremost, the therapist of the triadic deficit patient must set limits.

FORMATION OF A COGNITIVE ALLIANCE

Cognitive Co-Authorship of Content: Encouraging Elaboration of Subject Matter

At the cognitive level, triadic deficit patients can be most cooperative, especially when (sometimes only when) the approach of the therapist is task-oriented; however, they typically do not easily elaborate on the verbal material they present. Therefore the therapist must co-author the topic in cognitive synchrony with the patient, *without* empathic or transferential interventions (even in the presence of obvious references to the therapist). To an untrained ear, these sessions can thus sound similar to ordinary conversation in its direct question-and-answer exchange, although the particular content may be very personal.

Therapist: Let's get back to your seductive overtures to your daughter. As a father, is it at all disturbing to you?

Patient: Not really . . . well, only for the obvious reasons . . . the overreaction of the family, or her friends, making a big deal of it.

Therapist: What about some *nonobvious* reasons?

The therapist almost informally expands the field, enlarging the content arena for the patient who may not be able to elaborate on the subject by himself.

> *Patient:* I didn't mean to divide it that way, and I don't know whether there are nonobvious reasons for my not being bothered; I mean, I like to tease her and sometimes she thinks I go too far—maybe I do occasionally. I can see why you would ask the question that way, but I don't know the answer. Nonobvious ones? Hmmm! I really don't know. You're implying that those obvious ones are not sufficient. So what could that be?
>
> *Therapist:* What about her *non*attraction to you?

The therapist offers another question in counterpoint to the patient's response, further engaging the patient cognitively.

> *Patient:* Oh, that. You mean the fact that I think she's a lesbian and thus not attracted to me . . . that I'm upset that I'm deprived of father–daughter love?
>
> *Therapist:* That her heart doesn't belong to daddy!

The therapist co-authors this cognitive scenario, while superficially desexualizing the situation.

> *Patient:* Does something like that really upset people? I have to think about it; I mean, it's something for novels and movies, if it's true. But I'm willing to consider . . . it would have never occurred to me in years, something like that. I guess that's why you're a shrink, Byram, and I'm not.
>
> *Therapist:* Another story of Byram, the shrink!
>
> *Patient:* I don't know, who knows? Anyhow, it's her problem. . . . Is there any way one can make her be heterosexual? Then maybe she won't mind my being affectionate with her.

Here the therapist's attempt to temporarily desexualize the situation has failed, and the subject needs to be addressed further. The therapist has apparently opened an area that the patient is unable to explore and the latter has reacted by impatiently and somewhat angrily returning to his own agenda. The use of informal terms in referring to the therapist—"Byram" and "shrink"—are not only casual and overly familiar, but considered to be signs of derogation. As such, they are deliberately dismissed here. Rather, the clinician accepts and repeats them in a sort of good-natured way, with exclamations to highlight them. Moreover, there is no attempt at systematic exploration of the negative transference, because the disbelief and inaccessibility to deep feelings are a product of the deficit that the patient is suffering; they do not represent interpretable defenses within a resolvable conflict.

Cognitive Co-Authorship of Affect: Induction of Self-Empathy

The triadic deficit patient usually comes to therapy, willingly or unwillingly, after a specific traumatic event (e. g., divorce, loss of job, major illness, criminal arrest). During such a period, in which the patient may be relatively receptive to his or her own emotions and to therapeutic inquiry, the therapist can utilize this time as an opportunity to explore the patient's feelings and to gain some accessibility to affect. As such, the therapist actively participates in cognitively identifying the patient's emotional state, as it relates to the latter's immediate concerns. This is done in order to induce genuine self-empathy and, to whatever extent possible, to allow the patient access to his or her real feelings, to feel the way that he or she truly feels. It is at these emotionally-laden, salient moments that the clinician can best reach beneath the surface of the patient's presented problems.

> *Patient:* We've been married almost 30 years. We were always together, never separated from each other for more than a day or two, perhaps occasionally for business trips. Now she's been in the hospital for two weeks and I feel lost. It's so strange because she always accused me of not needing her, that I never expressed my feelings towards her, whether or not I really loved her. Our children also said things like that. It's true that I don't

easily get close to people. But I guess no one thought, especially me, that I would fall apart like this.

Therapist: It must have been frightening to you.

The therapist cognitively searches for affect, the primary purpose being to acknowledge, identify, and explicitly name the underlying emotion for the patient who is unable to do it by himself. Moreover, the statement made by the therapist is deliberately not one of active empathy; at most, it represents a form of "passive empathy" (Havens 1986, p. 17), which reflects a stance in the quiet sharing of otherwise unexpressed feelings.

> *Patient:* No, I really don't care about that. I just want to get my act together. I want to be able to carry on in my life, to continue my job, help her . . . not to fall apart in the middle of the battle, so to speak.
>
> *Therapist:* Disappointed in yourself?

The therapist tries again. However, unsuccessful as these attempts are, they do not generate the kind of strong negative reaction in the patient he might have to direct at active expressions of empathy, e. g., the therapist's saying, "How disappointing!", which can be misperceived as pity by the patient (Moore and Fine 1990).

> *Patient:* No, I don't indulge myself that way, with the self-pity kind of stuff. I just want to get over this depression, anxiety, whatever it is and be myself again; believe me, this is not me. We never met before this occurred, so you have no idea what I'm like.
>
> *Therapist:* Confused that you could be so different?

If the therapist doesn't succeed the third time, he is still running ahead.

> *Patient:* Not really. I'm not worried about confusion, though I guess it happens. I should just learn how to cope better in view of

her illness. It's not productive or useful to her or to me that I should fall apart, be depressed, anxious, frightened, God knows what else to follow.

Therapist: To have a nervous breakdown?

Patient: Actual nervous breakdown? Like needing to be hospitalized, I don't know.

Therapist: That must be frightening.

The therapist relentlessly keeps searching for an opening for the patient's acceptable but genuine affect with self-empathy.

Patient: What's the matter with me? At times I feel so lost . . . like a child. You know, I feel a little scared. Isn't that strange . . . me, of all people?

Cognitive Co-authorship of Transference: Induction of Interpersonal Exploration

Dealing with transferential material outside of the transferential context allows the patient to reflect. However, transferential emotions, when focused upon, will not generate productive regression. Instead, such a focus will make the patient feel reduced, thus defensive. Therefore, with triadic deficit patients the therapist makes no attempt to induce or intensify transference. Whenever transference does surface and becomes available, the therapist deals with it as if it were any ordinary content and moves away from it as necessary. The therapist deliberately does not make the transference a systematic focus of the treatment. Nonetheless, he explores transferential/interactional material in the here and now when it interferes with the development of the subject under discussion. Moreover, the therapist does not focus on the meaning of the patient's deviant or acting-out behavior as an independent topic, but only identifies its manifestations within the context of the topic discussed.

Any explanations or clarifications of the patient's feelings towards the therapist are actively introduced only when there is resistance on the part of the patient to discuss certain material. However, such an interactional (transferential) point has to be highly specific, focused, and congruent with that particular evaded material. After having presented his comments, the therapist adroitly moves away from the interactional/transferential focus to go back to the avoided content. This is in contrast to the therapist's approach to negatively (dyadic conflict) and positively engaging (triadic conflict) patients, wherein the patient–therapist relationship is a steady presence in their communication; with "conflict" patients, the therapist's focus on the transference is not interspersed as needed, but supersedes all content material.

> *Patient:* I don't know what else I should talk about. I'm having a hard time making the decision. Is it possible that I do have difficulty in separation from my wife because . . . not that I love her, but I'm just that way, just have difficulty in cutting the ties with her. Or do I want to maintain both women? Is there such a thing in psychological theory? I don't know, or do I want my cake and eat it too? I guess it depends on which school one belongs to . . . [long pause] The other psychiatrist that I consulted thought that I have separation problems.
>
> *Therapist:* [briefly taken off guard, since this is the first he's heard about "the other psychiatrist"] Whether any school has the answer to your problem!

The therapist identifies the general lack of belief and trust, rather than interpreting the patient's wondering what school the therapist belongs to.

> *Patient:* Yeah, well, there's no real science to this. You seemed to explore my relationship with my mother and my father, that somehow I need a certain triangle in my relationships. If so, I'm really in trouble. I'll be miserably repeating the same situation all through my life.
>
> *Therapist:* And you don't really believe in either theory!
>
> *Patient:* Well, yes, the separation theory is simplistic but more optimistic, less exotic. I mean, I can eventually bring myself

to it; you know what I mean. I sort of understand the problem of separation and I can tackle it, if that's what it is, but if it's what you think it is, I don't know. I mean, I can't.

Therapist: You would like a theory that you could tackle.

Again the therapist makes no transferential interpretation; instead he deals with the transferential issue as if it were another content matter.

Patient: Yes, I went to see her [the other therapist] again last week. She gave me a double session. It was very useful on the one hand; on the other, again it seemed a little too simplified. She kept urging me to take a chance and leave my wife—one comes around only once, so what's the worst thing that could happen? I felt encouraged to call my wife and tell her that it was over. But I just couldn't, as if there was something missing. Then I thought about your theory: What if I repeat the same thing with Ann, too? Then what's the point of disrupting a reasonably stable, a typical marriage? All right, there's not much excitement, you know, but we have children and friends, our property. . . .

Therapist: And you wonder whether you should use me or Dr. Benedict, and towards what end.

The therapist, who was not aware that the patient had recently gone to see his previous therapist, explores the patient's manipulative disposition toward his own treatment.

Patient: Yes, I can't make a decision. I seem to have difficulty in evaluating which result I should be aiming at, so I go back and forth in my mind.

Therapist: Or is it also possible that you established another triangle that you want to perpetuate?

The therapist interprets the noncommittal attitude and duplicitous behavior on the part of the patient. Even here, interpretations are geared to the content itself, despite what seems to be an explicitly transferential reference.

Patient: [laughs] No, I don't think so. . . . I'm just trying to figure out where I would get the right help. [silence of a few minutes] Incidentally, did I tell you that the first time I didn't get the right help? My mother took me to a psychologist. Well, I used to suck my thumb, up to age 12, maybe even later; in fact, I still do, occasionally. I'm not sure whether it's sexual, you know, oral stuff, or is it a nervous habit or just plain insecurity. I mean, what is the explanation? . . . Like I read somewhere that the blinking of eyes is related to a person not wanting to see certain things.

Therapist: Hmmm.

Patient: Come on, there must be some guidelines in reading these symptoms. Aren't there some symbols in dreams, like spiders were supposed to be mothers? You're not telling me, I know, because you said before that explanations interrupt experience. But I don't care; give me an explanation about this sucking my thumb and we'll get the experience later.

Therapist: The rule of thumb is that every generalization shortchanges the individual.

Patient: [smiles] Well, I think you could make some exceptions . . . and I wouldn't mind a little shortchanging here and there. Doc, you're taking this too seriously. . . .

A general lack of belief and trust on the part of the patient can result in the kind of duplicitous behavior that the patient has unexpectedly divulged here. In fact, it may be the tip of the iceberg of other deceptive or secret behaviors that the triadic deficit patient characteristically engages in. Good (1995), for example, has written about the "art of deception" that often accompanies a "secret world" of those patients, such as prostitutes, thieves, addicts, or adulterers, who may be involved in a spectrum of immoral, antisocial, or deviant behaviors. He observes that frequently these devious persons have managed to hide their illicit or illegal behaviors from family, friends, colleagues, and spouses for extensive periods of time. In doing so, they may have had to cheat, lie, or actively manipulate others in an attempt to keep hidden their secret lives and infidelities.

Winnicott's (1965) theory of the false self that is developed in order to deal with the demanding external world, as well as the general concept of splitting (Campbell 1996), describe ways in which the primitive self defensively organizes experience in order to separate good, acceptable, or safe from bad, unacceptable, or dangerous elements. It suggests that either conscious, or more often unconscious, processes are involved in the secrecy and deception. More specifically, a proposed difference has been discerned, in that "deception is often conscious, but the need for the 'secret world' is unconscious" (Good 1995, p. 156).

Such deception may well be extended to the treatment situation, as a defensive maneuver in order to avoid being related to, or found out, within the therapeutic experience. It is presumed that even if the patients present as functioning adequately in certain arenas of their lives, their psychopathology gets compartmentalized in a way that indulges, supports, protects, or contains their secret world; in fact, this also occurs in relation to the therapist, from whom their secrets may be especially guarded.

Fairbairn (1952) early shed some light on the phenomenon of the need for secrets when he highlighted a narcissistic inflation of the ego that arose out of secret possession of, and identification with, internalized libidinal objects. He pinpointed the inner necessity for secrecy as being "partly determined by guilt over the possession of internalised objects which are in a sense 'stolen'" (p. 22). Good (1995) has more recently theorized that the secret world can be viewed as a libidinal attempt to restore the lost unity of the self and represents a pervasive need to maintain control over internal objects.

> The deceptive secret world . . . is . . . compulsively entered into as a means of control over internal objects at times of heightened psychological crisis associated with the experience of loss, deprivation or frustration. As far as their real needs have not been acknowledged, but have been replaced by excitement, the destructive part of the personality has seized control and the narcissistic organisation has resurfaced. [p. 156]

Here the patient's having another therapist and managing not to mention it reflected a form of infidelity. Once such a secret is divulged and the patient's duplicity has been inadvertently revealed, however, this inevitably becomes a time at which the therapist of the triadic deficit patient may himself be most susceptible to countertransference reactions. This is both because of the implicit or explicit betrayal in the patient's having secretly sought and seen a different therapist, as well as the threatening rivalrous feelings that it aroused. After the clinician has made himself extra-available to this type of patient and been at least symbolically spurned nonetheless, there is particular need for self-scrutiny. The therapist must be especially alert in anticipating potential retaliative responses.

AD HOC TRANSFERENTIAL CONFRONTATION: DEALING WITH NEGATIVE TRANSFERENCE MANIPULATIONS

Ad Hoc Confrontation of Manipulations for Secondary Gain

Strasburger (1986) has observed the curious attraction of patients with an "antisocial veneer" (p. 192). Frequently, such patients will attempt to charm or even intimidate the therapist. These behaviors by triadic deficit patients are intended to manipulate the clinician into doing something special, especially something ethically questionable. This may start as a seemingly simple favor, but more likely involve a white lie or some other form of finagling that is devious, if not outright dishonest (e. g., having him write an extra prescription, switch the session schedule for an unwarranted reason, complete insurance forms for unearned benefits, sign dubious official papers, or lend his name to letters of reference or recommendation). Any therapist who hopes to attain an alliance with the patient by complying with his manipulative requests will instead only end up losing the patient's confidence and feeding into his psychopathology, confirming the patient's view of the therapist as another manipulable person, not someone to respect or listen to.

The therapist should communicate frankly, if not bluntly, when he senses that he is being manipulated, and hopefully will not succumb to the patient's charm. The deliberate rejection of these manipulations, however, must carry no messages of repudiation of the patient qua patient. Simultaneously, the therapist should explore the patient's feelings and thoughts about the therapist's refusal to comply with the specific manipulative request, thereby refocusing the session on their relationship and on their mutual therapeutic task.

> *Patient:* [charmingly and casually] Would you please put the last four visits of December into my January form so that I can get reimbursed, because I used up all my current year's allowance.

The therapist may be intimidated, fearing that the patient will be angry if he refuses the request, or he may rationalize the situation by minimizing its countertherapeutic consequences (e. g., Why not do it— it just means rearranging the dates; after all, the patient is entitled to a total sum of two years anyway).

> *Therapist:* I would like to be helpful, but I can't tamper with the forms.
> *Patient:* Well, these sessions are becoming too expensive. I know my wife's internist even changes the procedure codes so that she can be reimbursed.

The patient may attempt to set up a competition for the therapist with other people or shame the therapist into complying with his request.

> *Therapist:* How do you understand these two different attitudes?
> *Patient:* [looks angry] I don't know, maybe you're playing holier than thou.
> *Therapist:* You mean maybe I'm pretending to be something I'm not?
> *Patient:* [speech pressured, angrier] Yeah, you do have this attitude of the only honest man; but who knows what skeletons you have in your closet.

The patient may provoke the therapist into defending himself, and the therapist in turn may be tempted to assert and document his honesty. However, the more the therapist tries to assert his integrity, the more it will be called into question.

> *Therapist:* My rejection of your request angered you.
> *Patient:* I'm not sure whether you're rejecting it to show off to me that you're a man of principles, or whether you're saying something else.

In the patient's narrative, vague statements are usually the most productive avenues to follow.

> *Therapist:* Something else?
> *Patient:* [looking angry] You tell me!
> *Therapist:* Was I accusing you of not being honest?

When the patient confronts the therapist, the therapist cannot hide behind the neutral attitude (i. e., simply returning or rephrasing the original question). That will only create a serious impasse and more anger.

> *Patient:* [furious] I don't care what you think! I'm as honest as the next guy; you show me a guy who one way or another doesn't cheat on his IRS forms.
> *Therapist:* I must at least be cheating the government?
> *Patient:* That's between you and the IRS.

If the patient easily dismisses the therapist's making himself a target for the patient's aggression, this is not necessarily a sign of dissolution of manipulation or negativity, but it is likely a wrong route. Therefore, the therapist goes back to the previously emotionally charged subject.

> *Therapist:* But to be accused of not being honest by . . .
> *Patient:* [interrupts the therapist] It's hypocrisy, man; everyone makes some concessions, plays a little flexibly.

Therapist: I'm behaving as holier than thou, implying that you're dishonest, all the while I'm cheating the government.

It is only after the therapist renders himself open to accusation and allows himself to be the direct target multiple times, that the patient may temporarily drop his hostility.

Patient: Eh, it *is* just the money. You may even be right; I wasn't sure whether I should ask you about the insurance form thing. I don't think you're accusing me of dishonesty either; it's just one of those things—some doctors do, some don't. I was going by my wife's experience.

After full expression of the patient's hostility, now that a temporary truce is obtained, the therapist may try to interpret the patient's anger in relation to the rejection of the request.

Therapist: If it's just money and there's no accusation of your dishonesty in it, would it be that you personally felt rejected by me—not just that the request was denied?
Patient: I knew that was coming. No, not really, maybe a touch. . . . [shifts the subject to the prior one] Maybe you don't cheat on your IRS either . . . but then you're an ass, what can I tell you?

As with the above case example, when working with patients who characterologically do not tell the truth, a common reaction of righteous indignation has been observed (Weinshel 1979). Kernberg (1975) agrees that patients who habitually lie or cheat need to see the clinician as comparably corrupt (while projecting their own immoral attitudes onto him or her) as a way of asserting their superiority over the therapist and deflecting his or her efforts. In the foregoing instance, the therapist first gives the triadic deficit patient a chance, waiting to see whether the patient would volunteer insight before actively making an interpretation. But, as the patient's change of subject suggests, the slow unfolding of interpretations (i. e., onion peeling) is not productive here, especially when such statements are transferentially loaded. In making therapeutic recommendations when working with habitual liars and other immoral individuals, therapists of triadic deficit patients must nonetheless vigorously confront dishonest behavior, even though each active attempt, at least temporarily, places the treatment in jeopardy.

Ad Hoc Confrontation of Manipulations for Primary Gain

At times the patient takes on subtler forms of manipulation, with communications that contain skillfully and, at times, charmingly masked rejections and devaluations of the therapist. Such manipulations would have no obvious tangible advantage or secondary gain (e. g., a lower therapist fee), but are purely psychological in motivation, for primary gains (e. g., for control, to satisfy sadomasochistic needs, to bolster self-esteem). The fact that the patient uses this highly successful disguise of his intentions means that the therapist must remain alert so as not to miss the subliminal messages in the midst of an even entertaining interchange. However, the recognition of these subtle manipulations is not as difficult as having to deal with them.

With the triadic deficit patient, the therapist seizes the opportunity to identify the patient's hidden sarcasm, put-downs, and other negative feelings toward the therapist. Without intensifying the transference and without heightening affect, the therapist can start to search genetic material. In this regard, devaluation of the therapist as a devaluation of father is geared toward validation of the patient's self-justification of his philosophy of life; it acts as an equalizer that permits him to continue his behavior.

> *Patient:* [as he enters] Hi, how are you? Oh, nice tie, hmmm, you look good today.

Under most other circumstances, the chit-chat of the patient may be a sign of anxiety, but commonly not with this type of patient. Instead it is usually a warning signal of the patient preparing the stage for something he wants from the therapist—a form of "set-up," in which the patient attempts to gain the therapist's favor through flattery or false expressions of their presumed "friendship."

> *Therapist:* Thank you.

The therapist is alerted to an oncoming manipulation.

> *Patient:* [extends his legs to use the therapist's ottoman, broadly smiling] So what would you like to talk about today?

Such maneuvering of the patient is designed to get the therapist to choose the subject for the session. It can be responded to by simply asking the patient why he is doing that. Such resistance may also be reduced via various ways of encouraging the patient to talk. All this, however, succeeds only temporarily.

> *Therapist:* Have you given any thought to it?

This is a typical, generic delaying technique when the therapist is confronted with an unanticipated encounter. Beginnings and endings of sessions tend to be untidy, requiring special attention and alertness of the therapist with regard to transferential intensification.

> *Patient:* Oh, gosh, no, I've been so busy. When I took a cab on the way up here, I said to myself, "What will I talk about?" Then the driver [laughter] tells me this joke, a psychiatrist joke. So I told him to speed up, otherwise I'm going to be late to see my shrink. [laughing so hard he can hardly tell the story] Well, this patient goes [laughter] to the psychiatrist and says, "Doctor, I think I'm a dog." [more laughter] The doctor asks, "How long have you been that way?" [laughing even harder] The patient says, "Since I was a puppy!" [still laughing]
>
> *Therapist:* Has that joke inspired you regarding what you may want to talk about?
>
> *Patient:* No, not really. I don't know; you're the expert—you tell me what we should talk about.

For the patient who is aggressively confrontative, the therapist may get intimidated and try to introduce a subject, or he may become defensively educative, turning the interaction into an object lesson, "It is important that *you* initiate the topic." With these responses, however, the therapist is only hardening the patient's defenses.

> *Therapist:* Let's start where we left off last time.
> *Patient:* Where we left off? What did we talk about last time?
> *Therapist:* You don't remember what we talked about?

The session is deteriorating.

> *Patient:* I swear I don't. I know it was important, but I have no idea what it was. Come on, you're a smart fellow; you'll remember, give me a clue.

Immediate confrontations may be anxiety-producing for the therapist, but not as painful as the longlasting avoidance of them.

> *Therapist:* How come I'm getting all these compliments of "expertise," "smartness," and so forth, trying so hard to get me to start the topic?
> *Patient:* Because I honestly don't remember what we talked about. In fact, I don't remember our sessions after I leave the office. I know that I talked a lot, but if someone asks me what we talked about, I have no idea. Sometimes this happens with other conversations also.
> *Therapist:* Especially you don't remember our sessions?
> *Patient:* Not only the sessions—everything. I've been a little forgetful.
> *Therapist:* How long have you been that way?

This mimicry of the doctor in the patient's joke was completely unconscious on the part of the therapist—but every parapraxis can be a successful discourse.

> *Patient:* [bursts out laughing] Since I was a puppy. Oh, that is really funny. Doc, you do have a sense of humor, I must say.

With a distrustful and disengaging patient, the therapist may consciously or unconsciously set the stage for the patient's banter or joke but, as discussed earlier, he himself does not initiate humorous comments because the patient will consider that a putdown.

> *Therapist:* Thanks, but the joke itself carried some sarcasm, obviously towards the psychiatrist, and maybe it reflects some of your feelings towards me?
> *Patient:* Well, occasionally you say certain kinds of prepared stuff, textbook stuff, you know, learned questions, you know, playing doctor.
> *Therapist:* Another crook!

The therapist may elaborate on the negative adjectives of the patient, but only slightly. Any excessiveness may be perceived by the patient as caricaturizing his feelings.

> *Patient:* No, no. I know you're not . . . [grins] at least I think not. Well . . . maybe it's me again, all sarcasm and condescension, as they say. That isn't what I want to do, but it comes out like that.
> *Therapist:* How confusing!

The therapist shows empathy when the patient's comments are self-directed.

> *Patient:* Yeah! Why don't I come out straight and say, "Look, how smart are you really" . . . ? Why do I hide behind this polite or even funny facade, when I'm really after blood? You know, I must be sicker than I think I am. [silence of 30 seconds] Now I remember what we talked about in the last session: we talked about my fear of being discovered as a really sick person who should be locked up. [The patient continues to talk about his fears of being found out as truly crazy.] [ten minutes later] I think my father also had some problems. He used to run out of the house early in the morning; I think he just couldn't stay

in the house. I wonder where he went so early in the morning. He never talked about it, always evaded or gave some cocka- mamie explanations, never straight . . . he never said anything straight. You never knew whether he was pleased or not, what he really wanted. He was a sarcastic and a bitter man. God, he was the last person I wanted to be like . . . yet I wanted his approval. . . .

The patient is now able to reveal his deep sadness, not just blame, of his father.

WORKING THROUGH PATERNAL DEFICIENCY: INDUCTION OF MICROINTERNALIZATION

Paternal Empathy

In the expression of paternal empathy toward the patient, the therapist does not tap dyadic stage-related feelings of dependency and affectional ties. Rather, he tunes into the patient's affiliative domain—he understands the implications of not having an internalized triadic structure. Here the therapist becomes not an emotional extension of the patient, but a cogni- tive one—as the route to underlying affect, such as the profound and hid- den sadness beneath an antisocial veneer (Reid 1978). Moreover, as the therapist provides a paternal model or *prosocial introject* for the patient by representing a value system, having expectations, establishing reward/ punishment feedback, and setting up structure and goals, the patient can gradually gain a sense of self that is developmentally more advanced than that of the dyadic deficit patient. There will be a maturational movement from maternal mirroring to paternal morality.

> *Patient* [male]: Why should I always be on top? Am I so insecure that I wouldn't accept someone else's superiority, let the other person have their say and set the standard? I really don't know. The very thought makes me feel bad. It took me a while, even here, to talk about things like that, and I still don't like it.

Therapist: Not totally comfortable to expose your vulnerabilities?
Patient: Yeah. I'd rather, you know, take care of my own problems, not let some other guy tell me what to do.
Therapist: How lonely—to always know better than the next guy!

The fact that the patient accepted the cognitive recognition of the therapist regarding his dilemma does not mean that the therapist can escalate the communion of cognition to a communion of feelings that are related to dyadic stages.

Patient: [turns and looks at the therapist for a while] I really don't feel lonely as much as I feel isolated . . . more alone than lonely.
Therapist: No self-pity in aloneness, in contrast to loneliness.
Patient: No self-pity. I'm alone up here because people are down there.
Therapist: Couldn't they be just elsewhere?
Patient: [little smile] People are either up or down . . . is our time up yet?
Therapist: Wondering about the time?

The therapist doesn't follow the "one down" issue between them, which was dealt with many times previously and has been relatively settled—although it will never be completely settled.

Patient: [looking at his watch] Do we have to have the full 50 minutes in each session?
Therapist: Especially this one!
Patient: I don't know what it is, I felt the same way last week. I don't know what it is.
Therapist: Not alone enough?
Patient: Not alone enough! Hmmm, I have to think about it. . . . I think I sense my aloneness and I don't necessarily like it, but it seems the alternative is even worse; being crowded, people coming at you all the time. You've got to be on your toes, plus why do I have to have it? Who needs it?

Therapist: Am I crowding you?

Patient: Well, not usually, but today I feel you are. You're talking more than you usually do. You seem to be challenging me, like who understands me better, you or I? How ridiculous! You're trying to say that I'm an emotionally lonely person, a loser. . . . My father used to make me feel that way. He was always cynical. If I was reading, it wasn't a good book, or he already had read it, but in reality he hadn't . . . he was just a liar. He also was kind of a skirtchaser in the neighborhood. He had several affairs, too. He used to nudge me to go after the girls. I was actually, if anything, turned off by all that, although I ended up doing the same things. But I despised him. He was certainly talented and all that, but something was missing, something was seriously wrong. Hard to like or understand him.

Therapist: Hard to respect!

Patient: Yes. In his earlier years he must have been a formidable man. But later on, I really didn't even appreciate him. I even know the day I lost my respect for him. That arm wrestling thing—one day I saw him, finally struggling. I beat him. He didn't accept this and wanted to try again and again, tried to cheat by holding onto the table with the other hand and all kinds of stuff. I just walked away.

Therapist: Not worth competing!

The therapist's emphasis is on the unworthiness of the father.

Patient: Not at all. He was a scared little man. He had this smirk on his face whenever he won anything. How petty! He had that face, sick face. I think I just shied away from engaging sports and did solo activities like skiing, hiking, biking, jogging.

Therapist: And thinking?

This expresses paternal empathy—the therapist's understanding of the emotional roots of the patient's behavior without emphasizing the emotion itself.

Patient: Thinking?

Therapist: Another solitary activity, rather than conversing.

Patient: Oh! That's interesting. Do you think I prefer not to converse with my wife or others because they aren't worth conversing with? . . . I don't think my wife has really anything to offer. I know, I have this attitude . . . but what can she tell me that I don't know? . . . I think that goes for all women. I mean, if they're beautiful, all I want is to fuck them. If not, for me they don't exist. She could be a Nobel prize winner, but I have no interest. To me, a woman is a female. Is this terrible? Am I like the animals? Do other men really listen to women for what they say?

Therapist: Your father certainly didn't.

A genetic connection is made without affect intensification, bypassing the transferential bridge and without expecting the patient's regression.

Patient: Yeah, I guess I learned from him. Is this correctable? I mean . . . I hated him on the one hand, and I'm behaving like him on the other.

Corrective Cognitive Inoculation

Insofar as the triadic deficit patient may maintain a picture of himself or herself as totally bad, it is considered useful to specify realistic versus unrealistic attributions, or to define particular problem areas that contribute to the patient's antisocial behaviors, underlying sense of badness, and lack of trust of others. It permits the patient to receive small, manageable doses of reality-based, nonpunitive feedback from the therapist (Strasburger 1986). Cognitive inoculations also purposely avoid emotional expressions by the therapist that can be misconstrued or misused as colluding against others. The clinician helps the triadic deficit patient to observe self and others, and to see his own responsibility instead of externalizing problems; he does not collusively cast blame or join in a vendetta against the ostensible aggressors.

Patient [female]: I never keep my contact with women friends. In my last job, I met Anna; I thought for a while that we were going to be good friends after all, but when I left the job I lost interest in her. This happened many times before. I don't know what that is; it seems easier for me to make friends with men, but then it gets sexualized and sooner or later ends. I just don't have faith in women; it's funny because I'm a woman and I don't think much of them. It's so bizarre. It's not that I believe in men that much either. Men all seem a little sociopathic and women are pathetic. I think I do have some sociopathic traits myself. So I thought I should just get married to a rich person and forget about the real thing, love, whatever; I wonder, does that really exist? I had some inclinations but never totally lost myself in a man. No way.

Therapist: The way that your father related to women!

A cognitive inoculation is an explanation of the patient's behavior that not only may offer a useful observation in and of itself, but is utilized here to set the stage for exploring a further therapeutic issue—disidentification with father.

Patient: He really totally screwed me up, didn't he! I used to dread seeing him. When he got drafted and went to the Far East somewhere, the whole family cried. I don't know why, but I was in great joy. He was a cruel and abusive man. He hit me frequently, not severely though. More important was his scolding. I wasn't the only one. I think he terrorized the whole family. When he came back from the service, he was even worse; he ran the household now as if it was an army base. I remember as a child I would go to their bed when I had a nightmare or something. He'd just yell and demand that my mother take me back to my room, that they couldn't sleep with three people in the bed. I used to spend as much time outside as I could, out of his sight. The last year he was in the hospital, I went to visit him; there he was, on his deathbed, cursing me because I couldn't get him a private room.

Therapist: How unreasonable!

The therapist does not say, "How awful!" (or painful, sad, etc.) Instead of empathy, which is not well received, the therapist offers a cognitive reframing—a cognitive corrective experience.

> *Patient:* I was hoping that we'd make up before he died. He was always unreasonable, I guess, but I felt it was my fault. He died angry and I don't know how I feel—just disconnected.
>
> *Therapist:* The way that you relate to the world.
>
> *Patient:* Yeah, until recently it was only to you that I've really opened up. How pitiful that I only related to my therapist. Can I really believe the world? I do want to do it and I know now that not everyone is no good. Samantha is another fucked-up woman. But there are good people out there, wonderful, smart, knowing people who have lots to offer, I presume. I just have to open myself to it, as you say.

Cognitive Insight: Generalized Disbelief and Disbelief in Father

The triadic deficit patient's insights into his or her deficiencies and disbelief in others progress from the general to the specific, from the cognitive to the affective. Such gradual understanding may start with general cynicism and distrust of everyone and everything, and eventually find its way to the more specific early target—the missing or unprincipled father.

> *Patient:* I was very interested in how well you predicted John's behavior. When we met, the whole conversation went exactly the way you said it would. It's as if you wrote the script.
>
> *Therapist:* Surprised also?

The therapist does not indulge in the patient's compliment, but instead explores the patient's disbelief.

Patient: Yeah, I guess it's my old attitude that no one knows a fucking thing. People tend to bullshit. Even the doctors, you know, so I tried to stay away from them. When I had this gall bladder operation, I must say it renewed, no, renewed is not the word, somehow I just started to have trust in my doctor. But mostly, I'm a cynic. . . .

Therapist: Hmmm.

Patient: It's like my father, you know, he'd talk about something that I would want to comment on, and he'd say, "Look, whatever you're going to say, I already know it." What bullshit! He knew nothing.

Therapist: Hmmm.

Patient: [silence of a few minutes] I had this dream last night. I was accused of killing someone. I was arrested in a boutique and I tried to explain that I didn't do it, but the person was suffocated under a huge pile of sweaters and skirts. I had a lawyer who was to defend me; he knew the case well, but I wanted to change the lawyer. So this is it, this is all I remember.

Therapist: Any associations?

Patient: The person, obviously, has to be a woman, in a boutique; I guess my wife. We talked about my hostility toward Liz. It's funny, of course, that I claim in the dream that she got suffocated under the clothing. Part of my anger, of course, is related to her excessive shopping. She can easily open a boutique with the unused outfits in her closets.

Therapist: And the lawyer?

Patient: I thought about it; that could be you. You know, I always want to change therapists. Here, the lawyer knew the case. But the one I had was going to trick me; I just couldn't trust him.

Therapist: Even though I know you well, it may be safer to go to another therapist, because I might trick you.

Patient: Yes, like going to a family therapist. Now, I know that's not going to solve my problem, and God knows how many family therapists we've already seen. You know, I'm not even truthful with them. So it's just the fact that they can't help, if for no other reason, because of me. But there's nothing to lose;

do you understand what I mean? With you, it's like there's some subtle possibility of change, but I don't really believe that it could happen. I don't even want it; I just don't believe it.

Therapist: Hmmm.

Patient: It's terrible. I just don't believe, but the fact that I can tell you that I don't believe you is some progress, because I wasn't able to say that to the other therapists.

Therapist: True. Yet you still think that I might trick you?

Patient: I don't know what that trick would be. In reality, I'm the one most likely to do the trick. At worst, I guess you'll keep me coming without, at the end, any result. I don't even know what result I have in my mind. I think, though, you do. Although I feel I already have made some change, you know, I don't even want to acknowledge that. I don't know why.

Therapist: Maybe because after such acknowledgement, you have to acknowledge my ability.

Patient: And to believe in you. I think that's the hardest. I can behave as if I believe in you, but I don't really. Why am I so cynical? I mean, I don't believe in God either. I think the whole idea is just a big con game. I mean, is it? I didn't believe the teachers.

Therapist: And the earliest such experience is with your father.

Patient: Yeah, my father, for sure. He was a selfish bastard. He was promiscuous and a drunkard. He was just a no-good SOB. I really despise him. I remember dinner time: he'd be there, he'd eat his food, then read his newspaper. When I was born he was 42 years old, so almost like one generation too old. He never played ball with me, anything like that. He was too old to have a child. He was always sickly, always popping pills. I had no good role model for a man. I don't think he believed anything himself. [silence of a few minutes] Believing issues aside, I really like coming here to talk to you and I like you. At times, I feel like you're my uncle or something. I never had an uncle, so I don't know what that's like, but if I were to design a nice uncle, it would be like you—interested and savvy.

Therapist: Hmmm.

Patient: Not a father. You see, a father is sort of an imprinted image I can't change. I don't know what I would become if I had a father like you. What a shame, what a shame! You know, I could have become someone. I could have really been, truly not what just looks right. I just went through life without—if I had a father, you know what I mean, maybe I could have been less cynical. Do you think so?

Corrective Cognitive/Affective Experience

After the development of some belief in the paternal qualities of the therapist, the treatment may move from a cognitive engagement to a genuine affective one as well. A certain degree of confidence in the therapist's value helps the patient to begin to explore his lifelong behavior patterns. Nonetheless, the triadic deficit patient's attempts to be truthful and to authentically engage the therapist remain tentative for a long period of time. The therapist must tolerate this "two steps forward, one step backward" progress.

Patient: [teasingly] You don't take off on Lincoln's birthday or Washington's birthday? What is this? Don't you believe in patriotism?
Therapist: Furthermore, they all fall on Mondays!
Patient: You mean, my sessions. Yeah, but these are national holidays. Do you hate holidays?
Therapist: I just hate shopping!

The therapist's bantering may be excessive.

Patient: [laughs] So do I.
Therapist: So we have that in common.
Patient: And nothing else! That's all we have in common. But let's not get too friendly here. I'm tall, you're short. I'm blond, you're not. I like sports, you, I'm not sure, most likely you like reading books. So that's it! Don't look for other commonalities!

Therapist: I want to engage and you want to run away!

Patient: I don't know. I thought my joke about the President's birthdays was very engaging. You're like Paula—when I give an inch, you want the whole yard. . . . She was complaining the other day that at the party I was very talkative and funny with other people, but when we came home I became silent. I tried to explain to her that with other people I put up this social face of friendliness, an interested attitude, you know; I make jokes, tell stories, but that's not real, not the real me. People consider me very charming and entertaining, but that's how I control these relationships, in order to maintain a certain distance. As long as I'm the one playing that I'm engaging, I can determine its nature.

Therapist: What do you make of your President's birthday joke in that light?

Patient: You mean not being real with you either. Well, I guess it's true to some extent. But I'm much more real here than anywhere else, mind you. . . . Life seems a sort of zero-sum game for me. If you have more, then I'll have less, whatever that is. If I entertain you and you laugh, then I have an edge on you. I don't really want to relate. I just behave as if I'm relating, but in fact, I always have my own agenda—whether to get someone to like me, or get some deal worked out, or create a certain image.

Therapist: And with me?

Patient: I guess I want you to think of me as one of your healthiest patients.

Therapist: So that you'll maintain your distance?

Patient: You mean by pretending to be healthier than I am? Yeah, that's true. But everyone pretends a little. If you ask people, they'll say it's easy to relate to me. Others, including Paula and you, have a mission to have me relate better. I don't ask people to relate differently to me. So I end up pretending and people seem to like it. Maybe they all pretend—how do I know?

Therapist: Do you wonder whether I pretend too?

Patient: No, I think a lot about you, actually. You seem genuinely who you are. At least that's how I feel. I have to ask your wife what you really are like . . . just a joke, just a joke . . . I see you're getting ready for some of your "I wonder" kind of heavy statements. So let's drop that. I think you're real. You say things straightforward, which amazes me. It seems so natural . . . your being tough, but also very considerate and respectful. I try to be like you, in my mind. I say to myself, "Okay, now if you were Dr. K, how would you behave?" At times, it works . . . at times, it doesn't. The other day I was in bed with Paula. You know, we haven't slept together for over six months, ever since I had that affair. So for Valentine's Day, she prepared a real gourmet dinner, bought an expensive wine, you name it. This was also a celebration of her 90-day abstinence from alcohol. So we end up making passionate love. Afterwards, she asked me whether I slept with Nancy only once, as I told her before. I wanted to be truthful this time and I said, "No, many times." She went crazy. Oh, God, what have I done! She called me every name in the book. I felt terrible that I hurt her again. She began to cry. I didn't know what to do, so I held her for a while. I felt so wretched and for the first time, as far as I remember, I cried with her. Then she wiped her tears and asked whether I gave her oral sex. Now, that was some tricky moment. "Okay," I said to myself, "If it were Dr. K, what would he do?" This was in the middle of my crying, so I said, "Yes, only once." Boy! She went totally berserk this time. She packed my clothes and put them outside the door. What is it that I'm doing so wrong? If I'm not real, it's not good. If I am, it certainly isn't. . . . Maybe you know. I'm not suitable for this kind of stuff, you know, the real relationship. I'm now so shaky, I feel like crying now. I can't live my life like this. You know, I was much better off shielding myself from everyone. Now that you got me to be truthful to myself, to express my emotions, I'm totally messing things up. Maybe, Doc, I'm not capable of relating. Why should I disturb my stable life for something that I'm not sure I can achieve.

Therapist: And I got you into this. . . .

Patient: Well, I wonder. Are you sure we're doing the right thing? You know, I'm putting all my eggs in your basket. . . . I think I believe you. I think I have to choose to be real, but I'm scared. It's like the first time of any experience. You need to believe that the one who's helping you really knows what he's doing.

Therapist: Hmmm.

Patient: I remember my first bicycle ride. No one taught me how to ride. All the other kids were helped by their fathers or older brothers. I had to do it all by myself. It would have never occurred to me to ask my father to help me. It was so strange, as if he was not my father. He was never able to hold a job, so he never gave me money or bought me something. I don't believe we ever went shopping together. If anything, he used to ask me to give him the money I made mowing the lawns in the neighborhood. He said that he would save it for me. But I knew that he would spend it on his cigarettes or something. It didn't bother me then. He wasn't my father . . . it was almost like I was his father and he was the kid.

Therapist: How sad!

The therapist recognizes that the patient is accessible to empathy.

Patient: [eyes tearing] Yeah. . . . [trying to wipe his eyes casually] yeah.

Therapist: You want to stop the tears.

Patient: Yeah, I hate this.

Therapist: Yeah . . . ohhh. [makes some empathic sounds]

Patient: Oh shit! This is so embarrassing. God . . . I pretended, in all my childhood . . . that [intercepted with little choked feelings] I had a wonderful father. I used to make up stories about him. The money that I earned I would show to the kids and say that he gave it to me. When he got imprisoned for some crooked deal, I was so ashamed I didn't go to school for a few months. Then my mother transferred me to another school. Of course, my father was never around, and I had to make up all kinds of stories to explain his absence . . . he had a business in Europe, he was in the CIA, all kinds of fantasies. I became so good at it that at times even I believed my own stories. The truth became almost irrelevant. The truth became what was believable, and that all depended on how well I told the story. Occasionally I would be caught in a lie or accused of lying. I was not a liar, I just wanted my father to be that way like in my stories, different from what he really was. You talk about sadness? One of my stories about my father is so pitiful for a child to invent.

In a mixture of embarrassment and pretense, the underlying fantasies and sadness finally emerge.

In the totality of the triadic deficit patient, the therapist needs to engage the disengaging person by emerging in their encounters as an honest, believable person with certain uncompromised principles and values. Beyond this, the nontransferential interpretations are targeted to explore these patients' nonbelief or pseudobelief in a social structure, discredited father, and frequently all authority, as well as the devaluation of mother and other loving figures.

However, in the transferential sphere, the therapist does *not* interpret these patients' disengagement as a latent homo/heterosexual panic or as a fear of intimacy and dependency. This will only alienate them by making them feel misunderstood, even though some or all of these characteristics may be present. If genetic interpretations are made, they are done so through bypassing the affective pathway of transference, making a direct connection between present affect/content and genetic content. The genetic material, incidentally, may be received first as cognitively understood rather than affectively felt. When such patients begin to experience themselves as being not trustworthy or reliable, and as nonrelating, nonbelievable persons, and also allow themselves to get depressed, then they may be genuinely amenable to genetic affect as "felt experience."

The working through of triadic deficiency is accomplished through induction of socially sanctioned microinternalizatons, which require the steady presence of the therapist as a paternal self-object and prosocial introject. As one who receives paternal empathy as well as repeated corrective cognitive inoculations, the triadic deficit patient can work towards cognitive learning as well as moral development. Eventually, the integration of affect, cognition, and behavior is facilitated by other affiliations that the patient is encouraged to belong to and to believe in, to supply the continued supply and structuring of affiliative needs that cannot come from psychotherapy alone.

The final point must be made that clinicians often treat antisocial patients superficially, as if they really had no inner dynamics. This is because their pain from intolerable feelings, such as sadness (Reid 1978), can be so deeply buried beneath a slick or unsavory surface. Since their overt behavior may be manipulative or dismissive, the important opportunity to understand the underlying psychopathology (Protter and Travin 1983) can easily be lost. Insofar as many qualities of the triadic deficit patient are received as alien or aversive to the moral therapist, it is incumbent upon the clinician to reverse the stigma, to go beyond the temptation for a superficial approach that presumably matches that of the patient. This means to find the universal qualities beneath the antisocial veneer—the depression, anxiety, and helplessness (Strasburger 1986, Vaillant 1975), and ultimately, to see "sociopathy as a human process" (Vaillant 1975).

As with other deficit patients, it is the clinician's task to regard such persons with respect for their developmental delay or deficiency. With these particular patients, he has to be willing to look for "the child behind the mask" (Kegan 1986, p. 45). In conclusion, in order to be therapeutic it is necessary to seek the vulnerable child who hides behind the invulnerable or unprincipled patient, and the feeling human being who becomes buried beneath an antisocial surface. Despite seemingly insurmountable obstacles, it is the therapist who will search for—and share—the triadic deficit patient's inner world. He is the one who will eventually uncover the profound sadness that resides underneath the facade of the false self. Ultimately, it is that new paternal object who gets internalized as a prosocial introject to replace the missing, or perhaps worse, sorely remiss father figure.

7

The Triadic Conflict Patient and the Reflective Object

PSYCHOTHERAPY SCENARIO

Treatment of *triadic conflict* patients entails working with individuals whose reality is intact, who have a relatively advanced level of adaptive functioning and sense of self, but who feel unduly anxious and/or guilty in dealing with the unresolved residues of their deepest desires. These conflictual feelings are largely attributed to unconscious intrapsychic events, especially repressed and ungratified libidinal longings, wishes, and fantasies—and the defenses against them—that disruptively impact upon current adult adaptation. Such frustrated or inhibited individuals are nonetheless developmentally capable of intimacy, which refers to the fact that they have the internal structures necessary for forming potentially positive and enduring interpersonal bonds with others, including the therapist.

However, unlike the dyadic conflict patient, who needs to split antithetical affects of love from hate or good from bad objects, the triadic conflict patient easily merges the two into a fused form of ambivalence; this refers to the less pathological and more compatible coexistence of opposite emotions and attitudes toward another person, thing, or situation. And unlike the triadic deficit patient, whose primary primitive defensive maneuver is projection or projective identification, a major, more mature mechanism manifested by the triadic conflict patient is *displacement*, as distortions from the earlier father–mother–child configuration are unwittingly repeated and transferred (i. e., displaced) onto significant others as well as the clinician. In particular, the therapist is a largely libidinalized figure, the predominant object of the patient's reawakened oedipal cravings.

An important implication is that, during psychotherapy, triadic conflict patients can become preoccupied with a need to please—and be pleased by—the therapist, frequently forming a positive transference that is its motivating force and allows the patient to proceed with therapy, even survive regression, within an intentionally frustrating therapeutic relationship. This means that, amidst a sexualized scenario of unrequited love, the therapist deliberately does not gratify the desires of the patient nor reciprocate his or her conscious or unconscious seductions. It also requires that the clinician remain a *reflective object*, a dispassionate observer who takes a professional position equidistant from the patient's warring "three harsh masters" of id, ego, and superego.

This particular posture has two major rationales: first, it facilitates transference formation and access to lost memories by promoting regression; second, it allows the triadic conflict patient to utilize the therapist's impartial interpretations to explore his or her own hidden erotic and rivalrous feelings, in order to gain understanding of repressed yearnings and unresolved internal struggles. Importantly, the reflective listening (i. e., neutrality) of the therapist does not preclude the expression of empathy, as the two elements are deemed necessary for both cognitive and emotional insight to occur. Ultimately, within this accepting atmosphere, these patients are helped to delve beneath the surface of their lives and to carefully work through their current conflicts as the endproducts of their psychosexual past.

Like therapeutic work with other types of patients, the therapist of the triadic conflict patient is not exempt from a host of countertransferential reactions. Major countertransference problems, paralleling those of the patient, primarily pivot upon intimacy issues. While sexual feelings and temptations may be a natural consequence of the libidinal content or of classic seductive behavior on the part of the patient, acting out of the clinician's own amorous responses as well as other forms of personal reciprocation as a real object are considered to be anathema to the therapeutic process and are among its prototypic perils. Comparable to the transference of triadic conflict patients to their therapists, which is intricately examined as an integral part of the psychotherapy process, the clinician must also become acutely aware of his or her own countertransferential feelings and their potential impact on each patient.

OUTLINE OF INTERVENTIONS
FOR TRIADIC CONFLICT PATIENTS

CASE EXCERPTS WITH THERAPIST COMMENTARY

Despite unconscious ambivalence, triadic conflict patients are relatively compliant and cooperative in their general engagement with the therapist. These patients usually can conduct themselves in a socially acceptable manner, with interpersonal behaviors and attitudes appropriate to a professional relationship. Within the basically benign ambience that offers the promise of help, such patients are usually attentive and appreciative of the therapist, eager to establish a working rapport and to negotiate the terms of treatment. The triadic conflict patient—though appropriately anxious—nonetheless may be able to converse quite comfortably, even encourage friendly or personal interplay; indeed, he or she is often only too willing to sustain a cordial, if not casual, interchange. Regardless of the specific clinical picture or presenting complaint, these individuals generally tend to be reasonable and responsible, overtly pleasant and ready to please, for the most part sufficiently self-motivated to seek needed assistance for their symptoms and suffering.

This positive presentation acts as a prelude to the mutual establishment of a therapeutic or *working alliance* (Greenson 1967), the task-
oriented collaboration between therapist and patient. Here the clinician metaphorically forms a connection with the conscious adult ego
of the triadic conflict patient and encourages that individual to be a
scientific partner in the joint exploration of his or her problems. The
formation of this realistic, trusting alliance is the first task of treatment, before any deeper affective relationship can be facilitated (or
forestalled). With triadic conflict patients, who are at the most mature
end of the developmental spectrum, such an alliance is fairly easily
formed.

Yet somewhere close behind this ostensibly sane and structured
scenario is the start of a sometimes subtle shift of decreasing interest
away from one's problems per se; the earlier focus becomes progressively
preempted by a different purpose—the triadic conflict patient's unwitting wish to gain the unrivaled love of the therapist. Of special psychosexual significance, such compelling personal feelings eventually form
the foundation of an essentially erotic transference that occurs regardless of gender[1] or other real characteristics of the clinician. This means
that as the two begin to bond, these patients will also explicitly or implicitly show signs of desire (or flight) as a signal of their conscious or
unconscious striving for (or fear of) increasing intimacy.

Typically, however, in conjunction with the expression of generally good and rational feelings toward the therapist, of love in its many
forms—trust, concern, admiration, affection, and desire for closeness—
are exaggerated responses of overvaluation and adoration of an ideal-

---

1. Although the phenomenon of transference transcends gender, Person (1985)
has clinically compared its form in opposite-sex therapist–patient dyads. She found that
with women treated by men, the expression of an erotic transference was more often
overt, consciously experienced, intense, long-lived, and discernibly directed toward the
male therapist. By contrast, in men treated by women, transference feelings were muted,
relatively short-lived, appeared more in dreams than in conscious experience, and were
frequently displaced away from the therapist and transposed to a female figure outside
of the therapeutic relationship.

ized and sexualized image. Here, triadic conflict patients will endow the therapist with some of the same magical powers attributed during infancy to these patients' parents, as they also eventually display (across a spectrum of relative repression) reawakened oedipal feelings toward the therapist qua significant triadic figure. This in turn may reveal itself across a libidinized range of amatory actions and affects, whether seductively presenting as a coquettishly coy or flagrantly lustful yearning for the clinician, in fantasy if not in fact.

In particular, as manifestations of the underlying infantile wish to win the therapist's favor, the immediacy of interest, enthusiastic involvement, and/or preoccupation with the therapist can be excessive. At the same time, the intrusion of strong sentiments at the other end of the affective spectrum, including hate, anger, envy, hostility, mistrust, and rebelliousness, are equally irrational and likewise repeat comparable negative feelings toward former significant others. At bottom is the triadic conflict patient's repeated attempts to maintain a defensively unexamined status quo, in which the unhealthy part of the psyche still needs its psychopathology. In spite of the pain of the presenting symptomatology and the presumed purpose of relief or cure, he or she is simultaneously resistant to change and, usually unconsciously, will fend off the clinician's exploratory efforts as well as sabotage his or her own therapeutic progress.

More specific in its implications for intervention is the patient's distorted and displaced desire (albeit ambivalent) for the therapist's love and, in return, the latter's requirement that it remain unrequited, that is, explored rather than reciprocated or acted out. This necessitates that, in general response to this roster of mixed emotions, the therapist here is nonreciprocative, remaining a deliberately dispassionate and reflective object. It is a special stance that is professionally assumed, while scrupulously searching the patient's subtle (or not so subtle) conflicted affect in the midst of sometimes seemingly nonconflicted content. The overall therapeutic question thus becomes: How does the therapist deal with the same basic frustration–gratification equation that is differentially delivered to deficit and conflict patients; and of particular pertinence here, how does the caring clinician continue to tread the threatened thin line of untempted neutrality, in light of implicit (if not explicit) invitations to intimacy?

BEING WITH THE TRIADIC CONFLICT PATIENT:
MAINTAINING DISTANCE IN VIEW
OF THE INVITATION TO INTIMACY

Identifying and Exploring the Patient's Problems and
Disappointments—Without Soothing

Typically, the triadic conflict patient neither needs—nor receives—the same degree of protection and nurture offered to very fragile, traumatized, deprived, and deficient individuals. In contrast to deficit patients, for whom not only the actual methods but the environmental atmosphere and nature of communication can be characterized by the purposeful supply of succor, support, and/or safety, triadic conflict patients are least served by soothing, or by specific direction, counsel, or control. Nor do they need the therapist as a buttress or bridge to support a weak ego or insufficient self structure. Therefore, although an empathic and caring context is always appropriate for facilitating compliance and for easing the receipt of explanations, interpretations, clarifications and confrontations, it is considered countertherapeutic to actively advise, persuade, reassure, or otherwise comfort these particular patients.

Failing to provide the latter activities is not an arbitrary act or, worse, a sadistic decision; it has technical motive and merit. As an integral part of the uncovering process, these patients are required to reach into the deepest recesses of their buried memories, whose remnants must gradually emerge from the depths of repression. In order for this to occur, such individuals must be able, at least temporarily, to delay gratification and to risk regression—taken together, to venture into and bear the pain of the past. By virtue of one's psychopathology, all patients feel unfulfilled to greater or lesser degrees. Yet, in the interests of introspection and eventually of insight, this type of patient is especially expected to tolerate tension, frustration, and disappointment on the intrepid road to conflict resolution. This requires that the therapist neither soothe pain nor assuage fear as the sole or primary interventive thrust. Even when making preliminary, reality-based contractual arrangements with the patient as the foundation of the working alliance that must be established before any deeper delving can be done, the meaning of the triadic conflict patient's verbalizations, as well as the feelings beneath the words, are considered significant. Early in the therapeutic process, these initial reactions, however overtly trite, can begin to be explored.

> *Therapist:* The sessions will be 45 minutes long, so we'll begin at 7:00 P.M. and end at 7:45.

The triadic conflict patient will usually respect the therapist's schedule and at least overtly obey the prescribed guidelines of treatment. Nonetheless, it is always worth being very specific about such procedural matters, even with the most sophisticated individuals. In the beginning it will establish structure and diminish misunderstanding, while at the same time allowing the person to express his or her conscious concerns. These in turn may begin to reveal the nature of more hidden, unconscious feelings or conflicts.

> *Patient:* Not 50 minutes?
> *Therapist:* No, 45.
> *Patient:* Okay. So it's from 7:00 to 7:45. Very good.
> *Therapist:* You had some concern because it isn't 50 minutes?

The fact that the patient agrees quickly with the treatment rules does not mean that the therapist should drop the subject. With this type of patient every utterance is worth elaborating in order to discover its unconscious meaning. The patient's possessive need for exclusivity, the accompanying rivalrous feeling, and the intense curiosity about how she is or is not different from the therapist's other patients may reflect some of the wishes, fears, or disappointments that reside behind her questions.

> *Patient:* Well, no, but I have this friend who's in therapy and she spends 50 minutes. I guess each therapist is somewhat different. I think hers is Jungian or something like that.
> *Therapist:* Are you disappointed that our hour here isn't 50 minutes? Would you like the session to be longer?

If the therapist "understands" too quickly, the patient will likely feel preempted. It would have been better to say, "How do you feel about that?" rather than "Are you disappointed or angry?" There is no need to be ahead of this patient, nor does the patient need to be educated in naming emotions. It is certainly preferable that any feelings be spontaneously identified by the patient herself.

> *Patient:* No, what's the difference between 45 and 50 minutes? I'm glad that you told me, though, otherwise I would have expected 50 minutes, that's all.

Since the patient dismisses the difference, the therapist does not belabor the subject further. He simply raises some questions, giving the issue time to incubate in the patient's mind. In order for the therapy to realistically proceed without introducing impediments, he then moves on to other necessary negotiations of the therapeutic task.

> *Therapist:* Also, I'll give you the bill for the month in our last session.
> *Patient:* [interrupts the therapist] And I can bring my checkbook and pay you in the last session.
> *Therapist:* That'll be fine. Also, I'll be taking one week off during Christmas and the last two weeks in August for my vacation.
> *Patient:* No problem. I usually take the Christmas week off anyway. I didn't think about my yearly vacation. I haven't been taking it with any regularity. I tend to take one week here, one week there, but I'll coordinate them now with yours. I wouldn't want too many interruptions. If I take a few days here and there, I'll certainly pay for the missed sessions. I gather that's the rule. I checked a few things out with my friends. I shouldn't come early to the session to sit in the waiting room, and I. . . .

With her religious recital of therapy rules, the patient expresses her eagerness to be a good and compliant patient in order to please the therapist, despite tacit disappointment. She has willingly offered to synchronize her schedule to conform with his and, as if that does not suffice, has dutifully promised to pay for missed sessions without having been asked! The downside of this positive transference, however, has yet to come. The greater the undue devotion to the dicta and desires of the therapist, the greater the likelihood that unrealistic perceptions and expectations will lead to later, deeper disappointments and, inevitably, to an equally irrational reversion to resistance in the form of negative transference and/or acting out.

Identifying and Exploring the Patient's Negativity
Underneath Even Overwhelmingly Positive Feelings

In psychotherapy with triadic conflict patients, the presenting symptom soon loses its valence as the focal point of treatment. Instead, the therapeutic target becomes the therapist as transferential recipient of affect and attitudes toward earlier significant figures. As reiterated in the therapist–patient relationship, transference is never all positive or all negative, although it might be primarily one or the other in a particular developmental prototype. (In general, triadic conflict patients usually present with the former disposition.) Overtly at least, such patients will view treatment as a very helpful process, willingly cooperate and comply with structural procedures or rules, elaborate without great difficulty on their reasons to be in therapy, accept and even praise the therapist's personal and professional qualities, and, however idealized, may explicitly express their trust and belief in the therapist's good faith and intention.

Nonetheless, even with these patients, there will always be negative elements that the therapist must be tuned into. As with all other patients, it is usually negative transference that becomes problematic and requires immediate attention if treatment is to proceed. Although negative transference can manifest in ways that naturally interrupt or sabotage therapeutic progress, either through direct or indirect attacks on the therapist, or by acting out of malevolent feelings instead of exploring them, the forms it takes are usually less extreme and primitive than in deficit or dyadic conflict patients. (Likewise, the types of interventions are different, being exploratory and nondirective rather than supportive and directive.)

More subtle in its intrusion into the therapeutic process, however, is the fact that triadic conflict patients often overtly appear receptive to psychotherapy and even express with optimism the wish to be free of their symptoms or problems, yet unconsciously would also rather remain unchanged. This requires that the therapist be especially alert to suppressed and masked negative feelings. In fact, presumed positive feelings can be equally perilous, whether real or transferential; no matter how explicitly complacent or even exuberant the patient's presentation, manifold forms of resistance can nonetheless surreptitiously make their appearance.

In triadic conflict patients especially, negativity may be buried beneath their need to seem benign. Greenson (1967), for one, has warned that persistent positive transference virtually guarantees that negative transference is lurking close behind; under such circumstances, it is merely hidden, not absent. He has particularly observed a phenomenon of frequent cheerful hours during which "great enthusiasm and prolonged elation indicate that something is being warded off—usually something of the opposite nature" (p. 69). It has been further pointed out that resistance in the ironic form of extreme benevolent or beatific affect can make its duplicitous appearance at any phase of treatment.

There may even be stage-specific risks of positive transference across the entire therapeutic course. For example, at the beginning of the psychotherapy process, there is a danger of premature termination or flight, as the rise of intense affection and yearning for the therapist evokes unleashed wishes for—and fears of—increasing intimacy; in the middle of treatment, excessive erotic feelings and sexual acting out can occur, as tabooed emotions are avoided in therapy, thus played out elsewhere; and, in the final phase, there is the threat of perpetuated or prolonged dependency, as regressive reactivations of entrenched attachment and blissful feelings of communion increase the inability to separate, precisely when the patient is preparing to terminate treatment (Karasu 1992).

Indeed it is the very intense positive transference, with overt expressions of appreciation and adoration or excessive passionate desires and demands on the therapist, that can be the most misleading. Deceptive in its apparent ardor, this type of transference constitutes a paradoxical product of resistance, as the overly admiring patient also wards off further probing into repressed feelings and unresolved conflicts. Under these circumstances, obstacles to treatment occur with a generally less offensive—but equally defensive—form of affect. This can be compounded by countertransference tendencies: by feeding unfulfilled fantasies through flattery or otherwise meeting some personal needs of the susceptible therapist, the latter may in turn countertransferentially contribute unconscious collusion. Consequently, it too can serve, perhaps more insidiously, to distract and derail both parties from their mutual therapeutic task. In short, the subtle nuances of negative feelings should never be glossed over, even if the material in which the emotion is embedded seems trite, occurs infrequently, or is easy to overlook because it is pleasantly presented in positive disguise, as the following case excerpt exemplifies.

> *Patient:* I am so lucky to have you as my therapist. I hear all kinds of stories about therapists, ranging from incompetence to not caring, coming late to sessions, and making frequent cancellations without much notice, but you haven't ever been late to our sessions. A couple of times I called you on the phone, and you've always spent a few minutes with me. Joseph's therapist, if he ever gets him on the phone, always says, "I'm sorry I can't talk to you right now; why don't we talk about this in our next session?" What if the patient calls because he really needs to? If the patient exploits the therapist, that I can understand . . . but there are times that one could be a little bit human, not tell you to wait for a scheduled time. I know that you have excellent credentials and so forth, but also personally that you care; I feel it. Even when I don't agree fully with some of your ideas, I still believe that you're rooting for me. It's nice.
>
> *Therapist:* Do you think that "niceness," at times, is a little too much and gets in your way, especially when you don't agree with some of my ideas?

The therapist needs to be alert to and access covert feelings. Thus, in spite of the patient's explicit compliments, the clinician is always on the lookout for the potential problems that lurk beneath the surface of their seemingly compatible relationship.

> *Patient:* Oh, God! No, please no. I couldn't stand that cold, "What do you think?" kind of therapist for a minute. No, I was telling you all that to express my appreciation of you, because one, at times, takes all that for granted. It's just my lucky strike that I found you. . . .
>
> *Therapist:* Doesn't all that appreciation interfere with your disagreeing with some of my ideas?

The therapist believes that this patient, in Shakespeare's words, "doth protest too much." Thus he continues to elicit latent material— the patient's negative feelings and disagreement with the therapist— despite avid praise. In fact, any such adulation should not so satisfy the therapist as to prevent him from pursuing the subject further, because behind the clinician's unanswered question resides the still unconscious and unexpressed negative transference.

> *Patient:* [struggling to get the words out] Well . . . I guess, occasionally [pause] like the other day when you implied that there was another reason for my being late than the one I told you. I wondered if you thought I had some secret motive that I wasn't admitting. I felt like you doubted my word, and it wasn't like you to be suspicious. Usually you're so accepting . . . much more so than anyone else I know.

As the triadic conflict patient is able to allow more negative content to come through, the therapist can further explore the underlying ambivalence that would otherwise remain repressed. However, here the nature of the negativity may be much more muted and inhibited than that expressed by the dyadic conflict patient. For the most part it is the subtle rather than explosive expression of hostility, as well as a less turbulent therapeutic course, which tends to characterize the triadic conflict patient's interaction with the therapist. Nonetheless, both positive and negative transference, as inappropriate and anachronistic attitudes and affects primarily meant for oedipal persons of the past, must be equally unearthed and examined.

Identifying and Exploring the Patient's (Conscious or Unconscious) Wishes and Desires—Without Reciprocation

The patient's expression of feelings, wishes, and desires toward others as well as the therapist—and even especially toward the therapist—are fitting grist for the clinician's mill. At the same time, the therapist's reciprocation of these feelings, wishes, and desires needs to remain unexpressed, that is, not acted upon (or acted out). This, of course, does not mean that the therapist fails to have emotions evoked by the patient in the natural course of treatment; indeed, sensitive and responsive individuals may make the best therapists. It is desirable, for example, that the good therapist resonates with the patient's emotional state. It is also inevitable that the human clinician will not only feel what the patient feels (to greater or lesser degrees) but have reasonable reactions to a particular patient's presentation. It would be unrealistic to expect that a therapist will never feel frightened by an aggressive patient, burdened by a demanding patient, bored by a detached patient, protective of a traumatized patient, envious of a successful patient, depressed by a dying patient, or, as in the following example, aroused by a seductive patient.

Under such circumstances, however, he should function professionally as a relatively anonymous and abstaining observer who neither reveals himself nor reciprocates as a real object (i. e., by supplying personal information, opinions, or answers, or satisfying the drives and desires of the patient). In essence, here the committed, concerned and caring clinician of the triadic conflict patient remains primarily a dispassionate and nonjudgmental reflective object. Pine (1990) has referred to this therapeutic posture as a "triad of neutrality, relative anonymity, and nongratification of drive aims" (p. 50). Having originated in Freudian orthodoxy, this particular stance incorporates three traditional analytic dicta: the principle of "evenly suspended attention"(Freud 1912), the analyst as a "mirror" (Freud 1915a) and the rule of "abstinence" (Freud 1915b)—which have since become the source of considerable discussion and controversy.[2] Despite deviations (i. e., parameters) (Eissler 1953) that characterize the widening scope of contemporary psychoanalytically oriented or dynamic practice, they have largely retained their relative roles and rationales in the treatment of triadic conflict patients. How strictly or flexibly the therapist applies these three guiding postures has important implications for the interventions that follow.

> *Patient:* I see that the patient before me must have been lying on the couch. It looks like that. I can't believe that people could do that. I understand the rationale is to help the analysis along, making it easier to recall my memories and dreams . . . to tell you more. But I also read somewhere that Freud invented the couch because he couldn't stand to look at his patients all day long.
>
> *Therapist:* Do you wonder whether *you* should also be lying on the couch, to help the analysis and tell me more?

By reframing the patient's narration to focus on this patient instead of the prior one she has referred to, the therapist explores her implicit

---

2. The principle of evenly suspended attention (Freud 1912) requires that the analyst suspend judgment and give impartial attention to every detail equally. However, it has often been misconstrued, or misapplied, as an intellectual or scientifically objective orientation that detrimentally distances the therapist from the patient. In contemporary thinking, the neutral listener has been supplanted or replaced by a more emotional "empathic listener" (Jackson 1992).

The analyst as mirror (Freud 1915a) requires that the analyst be impenetrable to the patient and, like a mirror, reflect only what is shown (i. e., remain a blank screen). Although this means not bringing in his or her own personal reactions, attitudes, or values, contemporary thinking regards the concept of the therapist as an empty organism who is value-free as a fallacy (Strupp 1974).

The rule of abstinence (Freud 1915b) requires that the analyst conduct treatment in a state of renunciation. This means not merely corporal or sexual abstinence, but denial of the patient's emotional needs and wishes. Contemporary thinking, especially when working with deprived and traumatized patients, has placed in bold relief the need for an optimal balance between deliberate frustration and gratification (Bacal 1985).

wish to be more revealing and, ultimately, her desire for (versus fear of) greater intimacy.

> *Patient:* Well, at times, but I feel I'm in analysis, anyway. The whole process of self-exploration in one way or another is a form of analysis. The frequency of contact, I think, determines the degree of involvement, the intensity of transference, if you will. In my own practice, I see some patients 3 or 4 times a week, sitting face to face; I don't believe that they could get more out of treatment if they lie on the couch.
>
> *Therapist:* But you have some doubts as to whether the same would be true for *you.*

Here the therapist does not express an opinion, thus retains a non-preferential position of impartial equidistance from the "three harsh masters" of the psyche (A. Freud 1936). Thus the clinician does not act against or for any of the the patient's conflictual wishes and feelings.

> *Patient:* Yes, but on the other hand, I have to judge the gains and losses. I do like looking at you. I enjoy watching your face, your eyes, reading your reactions to my statements. Being with you gives me a therapeutic boost, and the talk is sort of an added dimension. If I lie on the couch, I may lose that touch. Will I be more in touch with myself? Well, maybe, but is it worth it? My feeling is no, but if you said, "I want you to lie down on the couch," I certainly would . . . [smiling] or if you want to be on the couch yourself while I'm sitting, that's okay with me too. [teasingly smiling] Or shall we both lie on the couch?
>
> *Therapist:* Hmmm.

The clinician continues to listen with free-floating attention and does not directly answer, or return, her increasingly seductive suggestions. His trained vigilance allows him to restrain himself from being reciprocally reactive as in a "real" personal relationship. He thus maintains the needed professional distance, as the uninnocent patient both raises arousal and salaciously lowers the threshold of intimacy by obviously offering forbidden fruit, inviting the therapist to lie on the couch with her.

Thus the clinician must meet an unsubtle test of his neutral and abstinent stance. As noted earlier, a classic vulnerability relates to the respective genders of therapist and patient, here a male therapist and a female patient (see footnote 7–1). Regardless of gender, however, a technical and personal question prototypically presents itself on such occasions: To what extent can the therapist resist temptation versus countertransferentially succumb to the patient's charms by seeking to satisfy the latter's conscious or unconscious wishes? As the therapist is advised to remain neutral and nonreciprocating, the thrust of treatment is on the meaning of the particular patient's verbal and nonverbal behaviors.

For example, there are several real as well as symbolic functions of the couch. It is well known clinically that fear of the use of the couch as well as overeagerness to lie down (i.e., "couch-diving") *both* reflect resistance on the part of the patient. Whereas the reclining position can realistically be relaxing because it is associated with sleep and eases the conscious control of one's thoughts, this prone position may also generate threat and discomfort during treatment, as it echos anxieties derived from the earlier parent–child configuration that it physically resembles. Moreover, it naturally has an assortment of subsequent real or fantasied sexual associations. For some patients in therapy, it may mean wishful submission to an authority (i. e., father figure) and/or become a portent of dangerous impulses that must be kept at bay.

Yet for others (such as this patient), the focus on the couch may offer relief from a presumably worse fate—the greater fear of direct confrontation and pursuit of the therapeutic task by the therapist. Ultimately, the patient's (as well as the therapist's) survival depends on their not being drawn into a mutual seductive scenario. Whether choosing to be on the couch or not, in therapy the triadic conflict patient ideally learns that his or her sexual wishes and desires, however aroused and delved into, will *not* be reciprocated by the therapist, but nonetheless can be safely expressed verbally and explored within the walls of treatment.

BEYOND TRANSFERENCE FORMATION BY THE PATIENT: FACILITATION OR DILUTION OF TRANSFERENCE BY THE THERAPIST

The formation vs. facilitation of transference refers to two different phenomena, which may be occurring at the same time. The former generally reflects the unconscious reiteration of feelings of the patient toward the therapist (or any other figure) that belong to another person in the past. It is a spontaneous arousal of intense affect that unwittingly presents itself as a revival of the early triadic bond. Simultaneously, the latter reflects the part that the therapist plays in the facilitation or dilution of transference—not countertransferentially, but interventively, in which the type and depth of the transference may be clinically encouraged or discouraged, intensified or weakened.

The nature of the triadic conflict psychopathology itself can unconsciously contribute to the extent of the repetition compulsion and to the amount of regression the patient has already undergone in the development of symptom formation. Superimposed on the illness, however, the treatment situation also influences the degree of transferential dependency and desire, including the following elements: the amount of frustration (i. e., intentional withholding of wish fulfillment and of any information about the therapist, in order to increase drive tension), the absence of reality information (i. e., the paucity of cues or feedback that is provided to validate the patient's perceptions), and the therapist's technical stance and activity (i. e., the greater the neutrality, anonymity, and silence, the deeper the transference regression). In general, the more extensive the use of analytic, interpretive, and uncovering techniques, the greater the facilitation of transference. Conversely, the greater the application of nonanalytic, supportive, and directive interventions—whether by design or by mistake—the greater the dilution or undoing of transference.

Responding to Personal Questions, Not with Direct Answers but with Inquiry while Maintaining Dialectical Neutrality

As an expression of the emergence of transference, the triadic conflict patient will invariably express intense curiosity about the therapist and actively search out personal information about his or her life, both from the therapist directly and elsewhere. The patient may also show extreme interest in knowing what the therapist thinks about everything or anything, especially his or her opinion of the patient and of the patient's progress. Despite the pressing nature of these questions and the easy expedience of their answers, providing closure is not the preferred manner of dealing with these inquiries. Rather, in order to maintain the transference and to sustain the pressure that is needed for therapeutic exploration, it is technically recommended that the clinician not "strangle the patient's questions by answering them" (Karasu 1992, p. 84). On the face of it, not meeting direct requests for concrete information, opinion, or advice may seem inconsiderate, but it is advisable from a therapeutic point of view. Instead, the clinician should be alert to the underlying pattern or purpose of the triadic conflict patient's questions. He should not be sidetracked by the compelling nature of the content or the enticing manner in which the queries may be made.

> *Patient:* Do you live here too, or is it just your office?
> *Therapist:* Curious about me?

The therapist does not respond to specific questions, although he need not remain silent either. One therapeutic approach is to respond to the patient in question form, which facilitates exploration of the patient's inner and deeper motivations.

> *Patient:* I just wondered, because I hear some noises in the apartment. I'm curious whether it's coming from your family, like little steps running around. I was just wondering.
> *Therapist:* Whether I have a family, kids.
> *Patient:* A couple of times while I was coming in, I ran into a young woman, nice, she said "Hello" to me; she might be your wife. I almost asked her, but then I thought it may not be right. I asked a fellow who lives around here; he says he sees you a lot on the street with her and if I wanted to, I should come around 8:00 P.M. and most likely would run into you.

Therapist: Gathering information here and there, hoping to run into me.

Patient: I wasn't going to try to run into you on purpose. I thought sooner or later that would happen anyway. I looked at a directory in the library, though. I know where you were born, trained, and so forth. The directory also says that you're interested in psychotherapy. It says your major interest is in psychosomatic medicine . . . but I don't really have hypochondriacal complaints.

Therapist: Concerned whether that's a requirement of mine.

Patient: I was wondering whether I might have some psychosomatic problems that I've never paid attention to. I think I get headaches quite often, right here; they don't last too long. I don't even get around to taking aspirin or anything like that. . . . I also have cramps when I menstruate, very painful. I've never checked that out. Especially the first day, I'm more or less in agony.

Therapist: You want to make sure that you fit into my expertise.

The therapist makes careful note of these symptoms that he is hearing about for the first time. Often patients' symptoms are not immediately apparent, just as the leak in the roof is never in the same location as the drip.

Patient: I'm not trying to make up illnesses. I do have them. I also wonder whether you have some psychosomatic illnesses yourself. You know, people do get interested in a subject that usually bothers them.

Therapist: Curious about me?

The therapist gives no information about himself to the patient, because it would dilute the transference; rather, he remarks on and interprets her curiosity.

Patient: Yeah, I guess so, but you don't answer my questions. Am I not supposed to ask questions? I know so little about your life . . . gosh. . . .

Tarachow (1963), for example, has explored the multiple motives that reside behind the patient's quest for answers, such as "When am I going to get well?" or "Am I your worst patient?" He has suggested that this type of interrogation (here, regarding patienthood status) can have many psychological functions: a rivalrous effort to be measured against other patients; an aggressive attempt to provoke the therapist or to make him defensive; a disguised way of requesting reassurance or favor; or a test of the clinician's expertise or commitment. These and other questions may also represent a maneuver for gaining control of the session; an act of dependency (by setting up a situation in which neediness is satisfied through another's answers); or, most often overlooked, may merely serve to gratify a basic desire to hear the therapist's voice. Moreover, simple requests for information invariably reflect some kind of solicitation for *something* (even *anything*), not necessarily a direct answer (Strean 1985).

Although all questions in and of themselves are revealing and should not be squelched, to answer a question as a form of need gratification, emotional comfort, or diversion from therapeutic investigation should be avoided. As Strean (1985) has suggested: "If requests are gratified by the therapist rather than understood by both clinician and patient, the anxiety that provoked them is not confronted, the conflict that is being expressed is not mastered . . . and the resistance that is demonstrated is not resolved" (p. 132).

Deliberate Nongratification of the Patient's Yearnings

The triadic conflict patient not only tends to perceive the therapist as an ideal and will make every attempt to be liked and respected by him, but is also quite jealous and possessive of their relationship. At times this may be revealed by expressing some need for the therapist that is not sufficiently met, by wanting the therapist more to oneself, or by comparing how the therapist treats him to some other patient who he is simultaneously treating (see also prior query about another patient). Whereas the clinician's neutral posture deliberately does not reciprocate and gratify the patient's desires, wishes, or fantasies, such nonfulfillment of these yearnings does not mean that the therapist is wantonly rejecting the patient, nor does it predicate, contrary to frequent belief, that the therapeutic environment will become more threatening to the patient.

In his research on the impact of the therapist's neutrality, Weiss (1990) has in fact come up with some illuminating findings with implications for the therapeutic process. He has presented empirical evidence that the therapist's neutrality was, as expected, significantly related to an increase in the patient's verbal expression of warded-off forbidden material. However, this came about not because repressed impulses had become intensified by frustration (as the dynamic hypothesis would suggest), but because the therapeutic setting made expression seem safe (the control hypothesis). "Because patients will feel safer, they are likely to become emboldened—free to express themselves more directly" (p. 107).

The research also found that while patients made unconscious demands on therapists as a way of assuring themselves that they could safely confront the thoughts, feelings, and memories that were blocked by repression, they were *undisturbed* by the lack of gratification received. Instead, when the patient tried to get the therapist to satisfy certain infantile wishes and the therapist did not do so, the patient became more relaxed rather than more anxious. Weiss (1990) suggests that this response may be explained by the thesis that most patients want to "master, rather than gratify" unconscious urges, keeping at bay the infantile ideas and desires that caused their conflicts. What most patients apparently needed was the reassurance that the therapist would *not* be drawn into their infantile or irrational demands. They want to be reassured that the therapist will not be seduced by their sexual wishes or destroyed by their aggressive wishes.

In these ways, the traditional therapist's neutral (unconditional) acceptance and affective equanimity can foster a feeling of safety in triadic conflict patients. The clinical evidence presented by Weiss (1990) indicated, more specifically, that only when a patient learned that she was not actually hurting the therapist did she feel safe enough to express omnipotent fantasies and wishes. Similarly, only when another patient felt completely assured that the same-sex therapist would not be aroused by him could he express his homosexual fantasies and fears. Pine (1990) more recently suggested that what may be facilitating and mutative about this particular stance is the *absence of condemnation* that it affords the patient, as well as the reassurance that no matter how enticing or threatening the thoughts and feelings expressed, the therapist is neither drawn in nor destroyed—that is, the therapist "survives" (p. 252). And ultimately, so does the patient.

As Basch (1980) has pointed out,

> there is nothing inhuman or inhumane about abstaining from gratifying a patient's immediate needs if the abstention is in the interest of the therapeutic goal; and if the therapist believes not only that the patient can tolerate the resulting tension, but that the treatment will benefit because optimal anxiety thus generated may enable the patient to mobilize pertinent material. The needs of the treatment—rather than the therapist's consideration of what kind of person he will seem to be to the patient at the moment—should determine what he says or does not say. [p. 81]

Patient: I just couldn't believe that you stopped the session the last time while I was in the middle of a very important matter. You've done that before. To you it seems like the moment the time is up, the time is up. Does it make any difference whether I'm into something extremely revelatory?

Therapist: Hmmm.

The anger of the positively engaging patient should not be diluted; instead it needs to be intensified by the therapist's silences and, later, to be interpreted.

Patient: I was close to tears when you said, "I'm sorry, we have to stop." I can't remember now what the issue was, but I know I was about to cry. It had something to do, I think, with being alone, the last date I had, a rigid guy who just would not go to this restaurant or that neighborhood.

Therapist: You would like me to be more flexible with you?

When the patient stops complaining about the therapist and begins to bring up separate unrelated content, the therapist returns to the original complaint about himself by using a specific connection from the earlier narrative.

> *Patient:* I'm not sure whether you're a flexible person, though that's not how you are with me. I always see the patient before me coming out of the session 4 or 5 minutes late. She seems to stand by the door and talk on the way out, too. You don't seem to be rigid with her, throwing her out in the middle of *her* sentence.

This previous patient actually starts 5 minutes after the hour, but the therapist does not explain this and provides no excuse to stop the complaint. Regardless of whether it is true or false, accurate or mistaken, it is the patient's perception—with its distortion—that matters. Such material can be used to further intensify the transference, in order to more deeply explore the patient's feelings of rejection and rivalry, whether realistically justified or not.

> *Patient:* Well, I can't say that I'm favorably treated if someone can get an extra few minutes, even if they need to and I don't. I'm not sure what else I should feel.
> *Therapist:* Hmmm.

The therapist's silence deprives the patient of any reassurance of love, and adds to her frustration by failing to negate her jealous feelings.

> *Patient:* Not getting it seems to be my fate. I felt the same way at home. My brother somehow always got the most attention, the most love. There's no question in my mind about that. Although my parents would vehemently deny it, I know it. He even got more expensive gifts . . . and . . . [gives numerous examples to make her point].

Although Basch's (1980) point about the humane abstention of patient gratification is well taken, *what* the therapist responds to and *how much* he or she gratifies is always an issue. Tarachow (1963) has emphasized the need to regulate the nature and degree of gratification that the therapist provides the patient. He notes that every contact has its own reality, based on the degree of psychopathology and distortion of the patient, and that the therapist has to bear in mind that he is more real to the patient than he may realize. For example, every gesture, intonation, or verbalization can have special meaning (i. e., potential gratification or nongratification) to particular patients with particular problems. As he broadly put it, "When you shake hands with an obsessional neurotic it is a challenge. With a paranoic, it is an assault. . . . with a hysteric, it is a sexual overture" (p. 96).

Similarly, what the therapist must recognize is that there are all sorts of real or perceived satisfactions, however small or subtle, to be given and gotten at specific moments in treatment, such as offering one patient a tissue or telling another the time. Ultimately, it is the therapist's task to decide how he will deal with each individual instance as well as to gauge its implications for both parties. Despite the fact that triadic conflict patients typically can tolerate the paucity of gratification by the therapist, the danger of excessive regression always lurks in the background.Therefore the therapist must continually titrate the extent and timing of frustrated desires or demands.

Frustrating—and Interpreting—the Patient's Seeking a Special Relationship with the Therapist

Most triadic conflict patients eventually try to have a special relationship with the therapist, either by increasing the number of possible connections to him or otherwise extending beyond strict impersonal boundaries of therapy (e. g., recommending additional family members or friends for treatment, requesting referrals to other medical specialists, bringing in personally created writing or artwork for the therapist to see). These personal efforts, whether wanting something special from him or offering something special to him, should not be ignored—or indulged. Rather, they are to be acknowledged *and* interpreted. Like other nongratification, the interpretation per se can be a form of frustration of the patient's wishes, which also acts as a motive force towards further exploration.

> *Patient:* I brought this short novel that I wrote a few years ago. I thought it would give you some idea about . . . oh, uh . . . about, you know. It isn't really a Nobel prizewinner for literature but [extends the manuscript toward the therapist]. No, you don't have to read it right now; it's for later, whenever you have some leisure time; no urgency.
>
> *Therapist:* Tell me about it.

Such a request need not be rejected. However, the therapist may ask the patient first to talk about it; in this way, he can wait until he finds a relevant and congruent moment to explore the patient's motivations for bringing in the book for the therapist to read.

> *Patient:* Oh, no, you read it at your leisure. It's a little biographical, but not completely. You don't have to read the whole thing, just glance through it and get a sense of it. I know it's a long manuscript. Actually, I brought the short version of it. I didn't want to overburden you with the longer version, which is more like a novel.
>
> *Therapist:* You didn't finish your sentence. You said if I read the manuscript, I'd get a good sense of . . . ?

The therapist explores the patient's reason for the request, without talking about the content of the novel.

> *Patient:* Well, it's just, you know, how I think, my thoughts, you know, my fantasies. I'm a reasonably good writer; but I don't know. I guess it's for you to see it too, that maybe I want to impress you that I'm a writer, give myself a kind of sense of importance.
>
> *Therapist:* So that I would have special appreciation of you?
>
> *Patient:* Appreciation! Ooh, I'm blushing! Do you think it's more than that? I feel foolish all of a sudden. I want to take the

manuscript back. I guess I do want to show off . . . again, I guess, my insecurity. . . . I remember when I started training. Whatever the teacher wanted to be done, I would volunteer, just to get close to him; then I would want him to get to know me even better. . . . Oh, no . . . it's so embarrassing. . . . [picks up the manuscript from the table and puts it back into her bag] You've got to wait until it's punished.

Therapist: Punished?

Patient: Did I say "punished"? No, I mean *published.*

Therapist: What do you think of the slip?

Patient: Well, I guess it's a little frustrating that I can't just have a normal relationship with you. Of course, I understand, but still, you know . . . I wish. Punished? Maybe I'm a glutton for punishment, wanting your opinion of my work. I guess it depends what you think of it. . . .

As a classic example of parapraxis (Freud 1901), this unwitting slip of the tongue represents a compromise formation between forbidden impulses or ideas and the censorship imposed upon them. As conflictual energy is shifted between id and ego functions, it is the apparent product of the mutual interference of two different intentions. Like all other symptomatic manifestations, it blends drives and defenses of the psyche in an adaptational effort. Here the patient wants the therapist to share an intimate creative expression of herself (i. e., what she has written), but also defends against her fear that he will reject her (i. e., her work as a measure of her worth).

Parapraxes can arrive as a sudden "gift" to the therapist, unconsciously offering him an immediate, succinct, and perhaps transparent expression of ambivalence and conflict in the patient's transference. Since this classic type of error is never a matter of chance, it provides direct access to repressed affect that can be most amenable to joint investigation. As such, it is a momentary window of opportunity for interpretation by the clinician—and for insight by the patient—that is probably unparalleled in its parsimony.

The Therapist's Need to Maintain Countertransferential Vigilance to Prevent Transference Dilution

There are many common ways that the transference is diluted (whether intentionally or unintentionally), in large part because most therapists would find it very difficult to deprive and frustrate such "nice" patients. In fact, it seems almost cruel. Therefore, the therapist may end up unwittingly diluting the transference, usually bringing it to a positive impasse, with the patient feeling good in the therapist's presence—and vice versa— while at the same time neither one talking about it. Unfortunately, such noncontrolled weakening of the transference, by mutually sabotaging the route to insight, can quickly unravel the therapeutic process. This unintended transferential dilution is not unusual, however; it may take various forms, ranging from the very obvious unethical behaviors, like becoming involved with the patient outside of treatment, to subtle countertransferential communications disguised as technical mistakes. In the following clinical excerpt, the latter type occurs through the therapist's straying from the topic at hand (instead of delving into it further), and in his inadvertently turning the emotional tenor of their interaction towards a more casual one than would be technically warranted.

> *Patient:* The question of whether I should leave the marriage seems to baffle me. I know that it's the right decision, but somehow I'm reluctant to make the last move. Now, I went through the same problems when I was thinking about leaving my job. But, ultimately I left and I'm quite happy about it. It was the right decision but, boy, did I procrastinate about it! I'm really not by nature a procrastinator, but whatever the problem was, I just couldn't leave the job. Just bringing myself to submit my resignation baffled me.
>
> *Therapist:* Do you think the difficulty might have been related to the issue of separation?

The therapist, unnecessarily if not countertransferentially, is diluting the transference even though on the surface the content seems congruent. The dilution here takes the form of introducing a new topic.

Patient: Yes, separation is an issue. But more important is my own assertion that I'm making that decision . . . that I'm asserting myself. It was an important decision for me. Here I was leaving a stable, comfortable job and venturing out, you know, to an unknown world. Gosh, as I remember those days two years ago, I feel it right now, even by just talking about it.

Therapist: It must have been frightening.

This sympathetic recognition of the affect of the past is an example of the right technique with the wrong patient. Even the best supportive statements dilute the transference by their gratification of the patient. An even worse response would be an explicit empathic expression of the patient's feeling state, for example, "How frightening!"

Patient: It was sort of frightening, but what was upsetting to me the most was that I was confused. Here I was making a crucial decision in my life. I was a little dazed. I didn't even discuss the subject with my husband or with my close friends. Of course, going to see someone didn't even occur to me.

The patient has generously accepted the therapist's two content suggestions (i. e., that separation is an issue and that venturing out is frightening), while offering alternatives (i. e., it was not really a matter of separation, but assertion; she was not as much frightened as confused). At the same time, she has charitably forgiven the therapist's process mistake by politely shifting to a new topic introduced by the therapist.

Therapist: We should have met two years ago.

Again the therapist makes a technical mistake. In hindsight, this was not the best statement to have made. For one thing, the use of "we" to help bond is unnecessary, if not seductive, with this type of patient. And the word "met" rather than "treatment should have started" is still too chummy. For a patient who has a tendency to equalize treatment through attempts at friendship, such an error by the therapist will only dilute the transference further through gratification instead of frustration, compounding the patient's repeated efforts toward a more casual or too intimate direction as a defense against therapeutic exploration.

> *Patient:* Two years ago? We should have met 20 years ago! Are you kidding?

This patient is no doubt being gratified by their interaction, even though she does not really agree with the therapist. Meanwhile, here the therapist, by having failed to be vigilant, keeps doing everything to dilute and undo rather than facilitate and intensify the transference. Some other ways to dilute the transference include:

1. Using undifferentiating language. This type of behavior serves to foster a real bond between therapist and patient by emphasizing their unity. At the same time, it can erroneously equalize their relationship in a way that reduces the transference, for example, through gratification rather than frustration of the patient's desires and wishes.

   Example

   > *Therapist:* From what you said about your marriage last time, we'll have to look into your relationship to your husband further, because we're getting closer to understanding what is going wrong.

2. Making centrifugal interpretations (i.e., attributing the patient's feelings toward the therapist to his/her relationship with present and past others, instead of exploring the feelings toward the therapist per se).

   Example

   > *Therapist:* From the way you just reacted to me, I wonder whether I'm standing in for your mother.

3. Providing specific information, especially about the therapist. This serves to decrease the transference intensity by focusing on realistic events or facts, rather than on transferential fantasies and feelings about the therapist. Such responses not only take time away from the therapeutic task, but avoid attention to, and affect aroused by, the therapist as a transferential object.

   Example

   > *Therapist:* I can't see you on Thursday evenings because I attend a special conference with Dr. A. at the medical school at that time.

4. Making circumverate interpretations that bypass the transference (i. e., attributing the patient's present life behavior and feelings outside the therapy to his or her relationship with past figures). This moves the focus away from the therapist and onto others outside of treatment, again avoiding the transference.

   Example

   > *Therapist:* Do you think your attraction to Joseph has something to do with your father?

5. Subtle reciprocating of the patient's wishes to equalize the relationship. This turns the sessions into conversations, discussions, playful bantering, or the like.

   Example

   > *Therapist:* I just saw the same movie and had a very similar reaction to yours.

Any behaviors or verbalizations that alter the boundaries or roles of the formal professional relationship between therapist and patient, and extend their contact outside of treatment, are antithetical to transference development. Blurring or removal of these boundaries through increased informality, friendship, or intimacy, or other reciprocal relations threaten the integrity of the therapeutic process, thereby precluding, or at least temporarily preventing, the achievement of insight.

Facing Up to, and Fast Recovery from, Countertransferential Mistakes

Countertransference of the clinician, like transference of the patient, may be largely unconscious, chronic, out of the person's control, and so ingrained that the therapist remains blind to it without external intervention. With vigilant therapists who are actively aware of their own behavior and feelings, however, countertransference can be acute, temporary, superficial, easily recognized, and expediently managed. Some countertransference invariably occurs in response to very specific content or in identification with a concrete aspect of the patient's personality. Classic countertransferences may manifest as eagerly making an unavailable hour available for an attractive patient, or failing to remember the changed appointment of an uninteresting patient. Common warning signs can include being preoccupied or dreaming about a particular patient or wishing to help him or her outside of the session. In collusion with the patient's wish for gratification rather than exploration is the therapist who simply finds himself unwilling or unable to examine certain material. For example, the clinician may experience himself behaving in an especially lively manner with a particular patient. This can be a clue that he may be enjoying this patient as well as his own performance as therapist too much, at the expense of treatment.

At such times, the therapist must deliberately maintain an attitude of formal seriousness, in view of the patient's enthusiastic engagement and his own urge to reciprocate. Ideally, the therapist needs to reflect a dispassionate presence, responding to the patient's seduction with quiet affection, to his or her aggression with neutral receptivity, and to his or her submission with inquiry. Any reciprocation of the patient's excessive friendliness will result in a deterioration of treatment in the direction of a less than strictly professional relationship; this in turn can increase the patient's resistance, forcing difficult topics underground. Therefore, the therapist has to be alert to his own countertransferential tendencies, and when a countertransference intrusion occurs must quickly move to recover before a pattern of nontherapeutic communication or countertherapeutic action takes hold.

Patient: I may be practicing psychiatry without a license, but I told my husband that he shouldn't be so enmeshed with our son's temper tantrums. Every adolescent boy must go through this separation-related battle with his parents. How else does one ever leave home? Our job should be just listening to him, not being indifferent, mind you, but being understanding and certainly not being pulled into his craziness. God! They fight every day over the smallest matters. Clearly the kid provokes him, but he so easily gets sucked into this push-and-pull scenario that it's pathetic. Again, I don't want to practice psychiatry without a license, but that's how I feel. Am I right, or should my husband be fighting it out with my son?

Therapist: You may be ready to receive your license.

The therapist's surface intention was to compliment the patient's progress, as well as to encourage her healthy attitude toward their son, along with her good mediator role between son and husband. However, bantering is a treacherous technique, especially because it can come so easily with these patients; the clinician should have chosen a more serious manner of communication. Under such circumstances, the question of what else is going on in therapist's mind must be searched.

Patient: Thanks. I'll write a paper and deliver it at the next APA convention on the separation of young adolescent boys from the family.

This patient's reciprocative banterings has escalated to a degree of informality that is leading to role confusion.

Therapist: You wanted my approval!

This constitutes a weak try on the part of the therapist to recover, to get back on a more professional track.

Patient: Well, you are my supervisor, aren't you? Of course I have to check it out with you. I'm just the disciple, for the moment.

> *Therapist:* Is there an attempt here to change our relationship from a therapist–patient to a supervisor–supervisee relationship?
> *Patient:* You could be co-author of the paper!

The dialectical relation between the therapist and patient is not linear, but progressively and cumulatively spiral, mediated by both directions (Lacan 1957); this is best demonstrated by susceptibility to countertransferential mistakes. Once having erred, the therapist's chance for recovery will depend on his ability to prevent the relationship from spiralling further towards any nontherapeutic direction. This can best be accomplished by returning to and remaining in an interpretive mode.

> *Therapist:* Making our relationship even closer.
> *Patient:* The paper by Jackson and Karasu.
> *Therapist:* Not Karasu and Karasu?
> *Patient:* [Laughing loudly] No, even when we marry, I'll keep my last name. Okay, now we're back to my seducing you or again reducing you. Why do I do that? Although this time you started. I don't know, maybe you were innocently praising my judgment when you said, "Okay, now you have the license," and that I was good in my thinking. Or maybe not; maybe you were poking fun.
> *Therapist:* And I gave you the license to reciprocate.

The therapist's recognition of his mistake is now expressed within the semantic context.

> *Patient:* Yeah, I think your comment was an aggressive one. Now I understand my response even better. I understand my responses. . . .

The therapist's final response is loaded with countertransferential, or just transferential problems, that is, the discomfort of the therapist in closeness to this patient. This in turn reflects the *therapist's* developmental disposition and his own conflicts. One might think that given such cooperative and eager patients, all you have to do is just collect the daisies. Well, not exactly. For one thing, these patients have the second largest premature dropout rate—not because of a quick "transference cure" (loss of symptoms without insight), but because of transference panic and flight if treatment is mismanaged. In order to prevent this and maintain the patient in psychotherapy, the therapist has to be alert to this early danger. He should be prepared to interpret the fear of closeness *before* the patient acts on it.

> *Patient:* During the week I often think of you. I'm sort of preoccupied with you, the things we talked about and things you said, how close I feel to you at times.
>
> *Therapist:* How do you feel about your being so preoccupied with me?

The therapist explores the fear of closeness.

> *Patient:* It's frightening. In fact, to be so intimate and close to someone, and also not knowing that person well.
>
> *Therapist:* Is it frightening enough, this sense of closeness, that at times you feel like running away from me?

Here the therapist attempts an interpretation of the fear; he does not deal with the patient's wishes to get to know the therapist better and wanting to get closer.

> *Patient:* [laughs] Well, like right now! No, I'm kidding, but last week and this week, many times I thought about calling and canceling and I didn't know why, because part of me wanted to come. I guess I do want to feel that closeness, but also am somewhat scared and want to run away.

In the foregoing instance, both therapist and patient appear to have at least temporarily recovered from the clinician's countertransferential tendencies and, with closer examination and revelation of the patient's fears, can get back on track.

INTENSIFICATION OF TRANSFERENCE: CENTRIPETAL INTERPRETATIONS

Just as a centripetal force impels an object inward toward an axis or center of rotation, so a *centripetal interpretation* by the therapist moves the central focus from an event or person outside of the therapeutic relationship onto the therapist per se. Similarly, just as a centrifugal force impels an object outward from an axis or center or rotation, so a *centrifugal interpretation* shifts the central focus from the therapist to a person or event outside of the therapeutic relationship per se. Moreover, although both past and present figures in the patient's life may be involved in both centripetal and centrifugal interpretations, the former type of interpretation more often relates to a horizontal relationship (that is, from a contemporary outside figure to the current therapist), the latter type more often relates to a vertical relationship (that is, from the current therapist to an outside figure from the past) (see also Centrifugal Interpretations, p. 288).

From Current Content to Focus on the Therapist

In order to intensify transference, the triadic conflict patient's interactions in the contemporary external world need to be brought into the interaction between therapist and patient. Here, their own interplay can be carefully examined by both parties as a way of making their relationship central to treatment. Every conflict has to be fought out in the sphere of transference, and one of the clinician's major tasks is to translate the patient's verbal content into transferential meaning (i. e., from others to the therapist) via centripetal interpretations. The basic working assumption is that the therapist is really the contemporaneous target of the patient's conflict-laden thoughts and feelings that are brought into the therapeutic hour.

> *Patient:* At the end of the workshop, this middle-aged, unattractive man approached me and asked what I thought of the conference. I said, "I really enjoyed it," but I was wondering why

he was asking. Was he trying to pick me up or something? Then
he began to give a lengthy critique of the workshop. It was truly
impressive. He picked up subtle issues that had completely
escaped me. We sat in the lobby and had some coffee and talked
about ourselves. He's a psychologist in private practice, divorced, three kids, a very attentive man. He listened to me in
a very interested way. Also he was very friendly to others.
People kept saying hello to him, his friends, I guess. He was a
very warm and affectionate man. Rarely had I been so well
understood by any man in my life. I ended up telling him my
whole story. I felt so comfortable with him, it was uncanny. I
was falling in love with this man I just met. First, I even thought
he was an ugly man, well, not exactly ugly, but not attractive
at all. I couldn't believe that my feelings changed so quickly
toward him. Anyhow, we spent the whole afternoon together
and, to make a long story short, ended up in his hotel room.
You know, that's most unusual for me. While we were making love, he kept telling me that he loved me. I felt the same
way, but so quick? I just met the guy, but I felt as though I
knew him all my life.

Therapist: At least a year and a half!

Patient: [seemingly startled] You mean us? Well, first of all, it's a
year and 10 months. [long pause] I can't believe this. Are you
saying that the whole thing is really about my feelings towards
you?

Therapist: Hmmm.

Patient: Now that you mention it, it's beginning to click. I mean,
his manners were somewhat similar to yours and he was clearly
very helpful in his interactions with me. Since I came back
we've been on the phone with each other at least once every
day [laughs] lasting 50–60 minutes! He always seems to remember in detail what I said in the previous session [laughs]
I mean previous *call*, and always comes back with some new
ideas and perspectives on it . . . as if he's constantly thinking
of me, that I'm his only preoccupation. It's such a wonderful
feeling, so special. This man thinks about me all day, replays

> every minute of our conversation in his mind and comes up with new insights, like giving some kind of gifts.
>
> *Therapist:* You wish I were equally preoccupied with you and gave you such a special place in my life.
>
> *Patient:* I suppose so—it's so similar. So I wonder whether you think about me between sessions, not only what I say here, but what I'm doing when I'm not with you.

Although transferential thoughts and feelings are presumed to be spontaneous, like dreams they may sometimes be subject to the therapist's suggestion, especially in susceptible individuals. Calestro (1972), for example, made the remarkable clinical observation that patients in Freudian analysis produced oedipal dreams with themes of sexuality and rivalry, whereas those in Jungian analysis dreamt of primordial archetypes, legendary spirits, and demons. Similarly, sometimes it is a clinician's stance or comment that, intentionally or unintentionally, can prematurely place the focus upon himself or be too directive in obliging the patient to examine attachments to others as a replica of the therapist in order to see similarities between them. Of course, how much attention is to be given to going from outside content to the therapeutic relationship is a matter of intersubjective timing, which reflects where both therapist and patient are in the developmental process of treatment. On a more practical level, content as well as affect matter in any interpretive intervention: the sessions are not content free, and excessive focus on transference would be like punctuation without the text, just as no focus on transference is like a text without punctuation (Frank and Frank 1991).

When to place emphasis on the transferential versus real here-and-now relationship has important therapeutic implications. If the patient is not ready to make connections between the therapist and others in his or her current life, or to see the link between the therapist and prior significant others, resistance will certainly arise. Worse perhaps is a facile acceptance of the therapist's suggestion, which may have in part occurred in the prior example. Under such misleading circumstances, the clinician cannot tell on the basis of one instance alone whether this was an intellectualization on the intrigued patient's part, without true affective understanding. It may have been artificially or superficially confirmed in apparent compliance, just to please the therapist—a kind of copycat reaction. It will take future spontaneous connections on the part of the patient about transferential feelings for the therapist, as well as other centripetal interpretations, in order to reflect real insight as an emotional expression that endures.

From Current Affect to Focus on the Therapist

In contrast to centripetal interpretations that are derived from current content, going from current feelings to centripetal interpretations requires a preparatory step: affective attunement. Here the emotional pain of the patient that is related to present life situations requires the empathic (not distant or dispassionate) presence of the therapist. The patient's positive transference would be interrupted should the therapist fail to empathize with a patient who is struggling with current affectively loaded issues. If the therapist assumes that this is a developmentally mature patient who does not need an empathic response, and therefore jumps to make an interpretation, he will probably evoke a negative reaction regardless how incisive his interpretive comment may be.

> *Patient:* Yesterday it was the second anniversary of my son John's death. If he had lived, he would have been 11 now. We went to the cemetery; it was just a stone—he is gone. I cried a little, but not the same way as it was two years ago. As time goes by, the pain is becoming more remote; all is distant now. Yet somehow that doesn't feel good, even though the pain is not there. Do you understand what I mean? The other day I went into a panic—I couldn't remember his face, just couldn't visualize him. Oh my God! I felt like I lost him completely. Is that what's supposed to happen when one is cured from depression?
>
> *Therapist:* [makes empathic sounds]
>
> *Patient:* [crying] I want my baby back. I can't bear this. . . . I know he's dead; I know I can't have him back, but I want to keep him in my head all the time. I can't bear to lose his image!

Therapist: Hmmm.

Patient: And the pain, that was my last connection with him. I would rather have the pain; its absence is worse. Now what I have is emptiness. And I've been really irritable and angry. A little provocation throws me into full-scale anger. George says, "Why are you angry at me; what have I done?" I myself am not sure. Everyone gets it. Am I just angry because I lost my child and they still have their own? . . . I don't even know whether you have children.

Therapist: What about anger at me?

The therapist dismisses the important content "whether you have children" and instead works towards a centripetal interpretation.

Patient: At you? You know, you helped me, but you also took my pain away.

Therapist: And caused you to lose your last connection with him?

Patient: [Crying] Yeah . . . I'm not sure which is worse. . . .

Here the expression of empathy, which can increase the patient's sense of safety as well as assure that the therapist understands and accepts the other's feelings, allows him or her to release emotions that might otherwise be held back. It also has helped to facilitate acceptance of the centripetal interpretation to come, by explicitly sharing the patient's anguish.

INDUCTION OF REGRESSION: CENTRIFUGAL INTERPRETATIONS

In those patients whose psyche is very fragile, or whose behaviors are developmentally immature, primitive, and/or out of control, inducing greater regression could be a grave mistake. With triadic conflict patients, however, the induction of regression is usually temporary and does not lead to permanent deterioration or arrested development. Rather, it may be useful, without undue damage, to access repressed memories and facilitate the uncovering process. It should be noted, nonetheless, that many patients may naturally fear regression and loss of control; even the therapist may have difficulty in keeping under wraps his or her own regressive tendencies, as the child in the therapist can likewise be evoked in the course of treatment. No matter how mature either or both parties, early ungratified wishes, fantasies, and fears accompanied by their regressive pulls can occur at any time or with any patient.

From Transferential Affect to Genetic Reconstruction

Centrifugal interpretations, which trace current patient verbalizations, behaviors, and feelings about the therapist back to their earliest origins in infancy and childhood, are based on genetic reconstructions that maintain an essentially cause–effect framework. They seek the meaning of highly disguised and distorted events in old unresolved conflicts or traumas (for example, tracing current affect of the triadic conflict patient to prior sexual or rivalrous feelings as expressions of unfulfilled and forgotten oedipal wishes). These interpretations are comparable in their potential depth to transference interpretations as compared to nontransference ones, insofar as the former, which focus on the therapist as substitute or fantasy figure, require a degree of patient regression not necessary in the latter type. Since the uncovering of genetic material and making centrifugal interpretations are more penetrating— and threatening—than interpretative comments based on the here and now, the clinician must be especially careful that these are introduced gradually, that is, preceded by more conscious or preconscious clarifications that have been already accepted by the patient.

In the following instance, regression as a preparatory step to genetic reconstruction is facilitated by focusing on a newly introduced affect of the patient towards the therapist. It thereby uses the transference as if it were an affective memory to explore past content.

> *Patient:* The other day I was in the cafeteria with other employees. This newlywed guy was telling his story, how he had to divorce his first wife, in spite of the psychiatrist's advice. The psychiatrist

was telling him that marriage was a compromise, that the decline of their sexual desire for each other was quite natural, etc. He was furious at the psychiatrist for encouraging him to stay in the marriage. Then he says that if he had listened to "Dr. Karasu's bad advice" . . . I almost fell off my chair . . . that if he had listened to your advice, he would have remained in that marriage and never have what he now has. I was stunned, blanked out. I don't think he really noticed my reaction. Then the subject changed. . . . You know . . . I wasn't going to tell you this.

Therapist: But you're wondering whether you should stay in treatment with a therapist who gives such bad advice.

First, the therapist brings the material from the patient's current life outside of treatment into the psychotherapy situation between therapist and patient.

Patient: Yes, I thought of dropping out. If you noticed, I wasn't really talking much in the last few sessions.

Therapist: Hmmm.

Patient: I don't think you noticed, but I was sort of withdrawn.

Therapist: Here I was not even astute enough to notice your withdrawal!

When some negative material emerges, the therapist remains with the material until the affect is expressed. Then, the therapist gives up on focusing on their relationship and uses the affect to explore the past connection—a centrifugal exploration.

Patient: I wasn't really referring to the question of your being or not being astute. Quite the contrary, you were innocently carrying on in your usual way without knowing what I was harboring underneath.

Therapist: Innocently!

The patient presents negative affect that is increasingly veiled—the possible threat of leaving based on overheard criticism, then challenging the therapist's comment while proposing his "innocence." When the negative feelings and disappointment in the therapist seem to have dissipated, a new affect begins to develop (i. e., guilt).

> *Patient:* Yeah, as if I was plotting against you, tacitly agreeing with this man. I didn't say to him, "Yes, you're right; he's a terrible therapist." Nor did I say, "I'm also in treatment with him; he's good," or something positive like that. I just turned against you, meanwhile feeling awful for not discussing it with you.
>
> *Therapist:* Awful?

The therapist identifies a new affect of the patient in relation to the therapist.

> *Patient:* As if I've committed a major crime, an unforgettable . . . no! . . . I mean an unforgivable one. I was dreading today all day. It's like a situation where I felt I was betraying you by not telling you about the incident.
>
> *Therapist:* Unforgettable!
>
> *Patient:* You mean the slip? I don't know what that was all about. Unforgettable? Maybe it's the guilt . . . but when I think of it, it's not such a bad thing that I didn't tell you. For one thing, maybe I was even trying to save you from some pain, and secondly, what if I told you, what would you do that could be so terrible? Really, it makes no sense. Nevertheless the guilt is there.
>
> *Therapist:* The guilt?

By focusing and refocusing on the affect, the therapist facilitates regressive memories of the patient.

> *Patient:* [silence of 30 seconds] My father used to tell me that my mother was ill and not to make noise, not to talk, not to make demands; he said she was crazy. So I used to leave her alone, withdraw from her completely. She was always trying, in her own way, to relate to me. I knew that I could have tried to relate

to her, but that would have meant betraying my father. He seemed to convey the message that he would love me if I were in his camp. . . . He used to give me baths and I used to look forward to them; I was a little embarrassed too. I must have been 5 or 6 years old. It seemed like I was a little too old for that. Dr. Brown used to focus on that. We'd spend a number of sessions on the subject of my sexual attraction to my father and his availability. I think he may have used me to replace my mother. Now I remember that I used to look forward to bathing but not necessarily enjoying it. It was a bizarre combination of excitement and guilt. Somehow I knew that there was something wrong with it. All that time he would talk against my mother.

Only from a positive transference can the therapist move toward exploration of the past. Centrifugal explorations require a launching pad of intensified positive transference, and thereby constructive regression. At the same time, negative material must remain centripetal until it is dissipated.

From Transferential Content to Genetic Reconstruction

The following excerpt is similar to the prior one, but here it is not transferential affect but transferential content that is utilized as a regressive bridge to genetic reconstruction and centrifugal interpretation.

Patient: It's beautiful outside, one of the most delightful days of the whole spring, warm and dry. I love this weather. I love spring, anyway. I feel like falling in love again. All this anticipation of a new life; the trees and birds, they all say, "Come out." . . . Come on, let's take a walk; we can still talk. Why sit here on such a wonderful day? You see, I'm no longer afraid of your getting to know me.

Therapist: You want to get to know me.

The therapist focuses his interpretation on the patient's wishes and simultaneously deprives the patient of gratification of those wishes.

> *Patient:* Just a walk. It would do you some good. It looks like you haven't been out all day. You'll get some fresh air, feel good. Who says that psychotherapy can't go on in the park? But, if you don't want to chat, that's okay with me too. We'll walk side by side and just meditate.
> *Therapist:* Side by side.

The therapist picks up all the enticing metaphors and highlights them for the patient to focus on.

> *Patient:* Well, what else could it be? I can't follow you, or vice versa.
> *Therapist:* Hmmm.
> *Patient:* You're making this more complicated than it is. You thought I meant side by side, like sitting on a couch.
> *Therapist:* On a love seat!

This response is a little too fast, especially since the patient has not yet accepted the earlier one. The therapist needs to be reminded that "psychotherapy is . . . a slow-cooking process that has no microwave substitute" (Karasu 1992, p. 282). The only rationale for such an accelerated pace may be that the therapist seizes the opportunity to accentuate the sexuality of the patient's comments in order to help bring it into consciousness for further exploration, especially when it seems so close to the surface. This can hopefully prevent the deterioration of the session into one of continued eroticized teasing and undue informality without increasing insight.

> *Patient:* [laughing] You mean to say that I'm trying to seduce you by asking you to take a walk with me in the park? If I am, I swear I'm not conscious of it. Furthermore, why would I want to do that? I do have a lover, and I'm not really interested in you that way anymore. Didn't we go through this before? I

THE PSYCHOTHERAPIST'S INTERVENTIONS

thought at the beginning that I was in love with you, but it just dissipated. I still like you a lot, but I wouldn't want us to be lovers. This was, this asking you to take a walk with me, a friendly gesture.

Therapist: If not a lover, at least to make a friend out of me!

Patient: (Laughs) Just for one hour, so we can talk like two people. You'll tell me a little bit about yourself if you want to, and I'll look at you with understanding eyes. You may complain to me how you don't have a lover in your life, and I'd say, "I wonder whether you want me as a lover?"

Therapist: We'll reverse the relationship.

Patient: Just temporarily, to find out a few things, what kind of problems you have. You know I have lots of good sense. People usually tell me about their problems. I do have this uncanny sense of understanding people's problems and also have a very sophisticated, complicated way of looking at things.

Therapist: Hmmm.

Patient: I wasn't really selling, was I? All this for a walk, at such a reduced price.

Therapist: Do you think, besides the price, some other reducing is going on?

Patient: Reducing you, you mean, to make a patient out of you? I wasn't really intending to do that, but let's say maybe leveling a little bit.

Therapist: Hmmm.

Patient: At one level, I would like us to be friends; at another, I'm glad we're not. We can't talk about problems all the time. What would we do if we were together a lot? Also, it would no longer be the same. I think, in spite of my insistence to go for a walk, I was hoping secretly that you would refuse.

Therapist: Also afraid that I might accept!

Patient: Yeah . . . and I don't know exactly why I was afraid that you'd accept. Like it would have rubbed me off or something. You know what I mean! But the temptation and curiosity was there, in spite of my inner better judgment.

Therapist: Temptation and curiosity!

Patient: [silent] . . . Like entering the forbidden world. . . . My father had a girlfriend when I was growing up and I always was curious about her. I would ask questions about her and he'd show me her picture, read her letters to me, like we were two friends. I was sort of enjoying it, but at the same time I hated it. I lost all my respect for him. I felt as if I no longer had a father. This grownup, older man who was not a bit ashamed of having a girlfriend and telling his own daughter, bragging. A grownup, but a child, basically an insensitive and selfish man. He was behaving as if he were out to please me by giving in to my request to know about his girlfriend, but in fact he was getting something out of it. I felt short-changed, like I lost something permanently. He was no longer my father. When people talk about being friends with their parents, they have no idea how costly such a proposition is.

From Antagonistic Resistance to Genetic Reconstruction

Since the patient invariably resists the treatment despite overall cooperation, another route to genetic material is in the uncovering of antagonistic resistance (whether transferential or nontransferential). The therapist actively interprets this combative alliance until the patient makes some content-congruent association to the past. Then the therapist shifts to a more sustained evenly hovering attention, listening and relating in the way that he does with any genetic material, as a slow-paced unfolding. To some degree regression requires that the patient be left alone; this is because the unconscious needs extra time to reveal itself. This does not mean, however, that the patient is left *unprotected*. Rather, the therapist must remain especially close at hand, always alert to ensure safety of the patient from his or her unleashed regressive needs or actions, as well as from the therapist's susceptibility to reciprocally regress.

Patient: [sounding irritated] Next Monday is a holiday, so I suppose I'm going to lose the hour. I'd really like you to schedule another time for my session, so I don't have to miss it.

This is obviously a reasonable request, but before giving an alternative time the therapist uses the opportunity to explore the patient's thoughts and fantasies about the request. Making requests is a vulnerable act for the patient, thus potentially lending itself to regressive associations.

Therapist: Any thoughts about the request?

Patient: I've been thinking about it the last couple of days, whether I should ask or not. I wasn't sure whether you'd think that I couldn't afford to skip one session, that I may be sicker than you thought I was.

Therapist: Hmmm.

Patient: Of course it's strange, the whole thing. How could I present myself in a good light and still be a patient to please you? But I could be a good patient, never missing a session, paying my bills on time, accepting your interpretations, working hard in the sessions, trying to remember my dreams. . . . Oh, I just remembered, I bought a dream calendar. It has a little booklet, a pen, and a night light attached to it. So you put it next to your bed and when you wake up from the dream, it's all there for you to jot down immediately before you forget what you just dreamt. So hopefully I'll be bringing lots of dreams. So far, though, just zero.

Therapist: Whether to please me or not!

The therapist makes a transferential resistance interpretation, rather than presenting the patient's intrapsychic conflict (e. g., "You seem to be in a struggle as to whether you should remember or repress your dreams"). Incidentally, when the patient is going all out to be a good patient, obviously trying to please the therapist, it is difficult to be "ungracious" and nonreciprocating in return.

Patient: I guess so. You know all the dream stuff, I'm not sure whether it really gives me any clues to my unconscious or whatever. Even if so, so what? What good does that do me? I'm not sure anyway that there are some dark secrets in my mind that would be revealed by my dreams.

Therapist: Nevertheless, you bought a dream calendar, in spite of your not believing the dream analyses.

Patient: I guess the idea that I want to please you or just go along with your ideas . . . well, you are the therapist after all. You know more than I know. I have to accept your direction.

Therapist: Have to accept?

The therapist picks up the critical words in the patient's narration to punctuate the transference.

Patient: Well, do I have a choice? I'm the patient, and you tell me that I should try to remember my dreams and bring them in, to talk about my fantasies. And for a long time I couldn't remember my dreams. I felt terrible, as if I were a bad patient. Even when I wrote down the notes, I couldn't read what I wrote the following morning. It was as if I was fighting you on this. On the one hand, I wanted to bring the material to talk about, and on the other, I'm doing my best to undermine it.

Therapist: As much as you submit, part of you is rebelling!

The therapist interprets the patient's needing to be an antagonistic ally in the therapeutic partnership.

Patient: [with escalating anger] Yeah, but why shouldn't I rebel? I asked a simple question, whether you could give me a substitute hour, and now I'm just supposed to do what you want me to do . . . remember my dreams and all that. I guess I'm mad because you want me to do things I don't really want to do, expect things from me . . . just like everyone else.

Therapist: Everyone else?

Patient: Well, I battled with my father the same way. He wanted me to go directly to work instead of college and I did what he wanted. It didn't do me a bit of good, but I did it just to please him. It's always been that way, ever since I was a kid. He was forever expecting me to do what *he* wanted . . . but I got nothing in return. When I was little, it was like that too. I wanted so much to please him, but it was never enough. . . .

The exposure of the transferential resistance serves to generate earlier genetic material as well as increased expressions of uncovered anger and longing.

Therapist: [a few minutes before the end of the session] We have a few minutes left. Is Tuesday morning at 7:00 A.M. convenient for you as an alternative session?

After the elaborations and explorations of the patient's requests, the therapist concretely deals with the subject.

Patient: Let me see. [opens her calendar] Yeah, it looks like I can make it. . . . [long pause] Thanks. See you then on Tuesday.

From Complacent Resistance to Genetic Reconstruction

The triadic conflict patient may respond to the therapist's questions with eager attention, even to his interpretations with elaborate self-searching responses. However, such explicit compliance at times is used as resistance to the elaboration of current material of one's life or, with greater resistance, to the investigation of in-depth genetic material, as if the patient, by his complacency, would like to appease the therapist in order not to confront the particular subject. Under such circumstances, straightforward confrontation of resistances as they occur can prevent the sessions from deteriorating into chronically resistant scenarios. Moreover, even complacent resistance, when immediately met with confrontation or interpretation, can lead to the greater recall, reconstruction, and acceptance of conflict-laden material from the past.

Patient: Yes, we had a wonderful vacation. My aunt has a small condo down in Florida, so my wife Jennifer and I checked in with her for a whole week. I missed our sessions though; I thought a great deal about it. I can see how the interruptions aren't good for treatment. I feel a little rusty. Okay, before I left you said something like, "Isn't it interesting that you haven't talked about your aunt who more or less raised you?" So I kind of prepared myself for it. May I just talk about her?

Therapist: May you?

Statements of excessive compliance by the patient are confronted with a stark inquiry, even though it seems rather unappreciative on the part of the therapist.

Patient: I wasn't sure whether I should talk about the vacation first, or go back to where we left off. Of course, I don't need your permission to talk; I shouldn't ask for permission; it's so silly that I should ask for permission. This is contrary to the very idea of psychotherapy. How stupid can one be? Anyway, I'm going to talk about her . . . but, first let me give you a little flavor of the vacation itself. I love Florida; it's my kind of place; I can spend all my day at the beach. I don't swim much but just walk, sunbathe, you know. There were some problems, though. My wife is a couch potato who wanted to stay in the apartment and basically watch TV. I don't understand why one goes to Florida to do that. She chastised me and our daughter Josie for being in the sun a lot, not spending time with her. She has a way of making you feel guilty. You've got to be on time for lunch and dinner; she made sure that I did the grocery shopping with her and other shopping—clothes and jewelry, shoes, you name it—which is so ridiculous; she could do much better in New York. She just wanted me not to be on the beach and used every excuse, including stomach sickness, to keep me in.

Therapist: Hmmm.

Patient: I have quite a high frustration tolerance. Furthermore, she was right; I mean, I should spend more time with her. Here we were on vacation together and I was just selfishly doing my thing.

Therapist: Is it hard to indulge in the resentment you might have towards her controlling you?

Any search for the patient's feelings toward family members must be done carefully. In spite of justifiable negative feelings, the patient will invariably have strong positive feelings toward the members of the family as well; it is highly probable that he will resent the therapist and become defensive. Thus, the patient's feelings can be explored, not towards the individual totally, but with regard to a specific attitude towards that particular person.

Patient: Maybe, but she's such a good woman. I am, Doc, believe me, one of the luckiest men in the world. So she has certain peculiarities I've got to accept. I don't know, maybe I don't have to accept them; maybe I should indulge in my resentment towards her. She keeps controlling me. Why do I have to be so grateful that she's my wife? Furthermore, I'm a good husband, if I say so myself. She's also lucky to have *me*. I don't need to praise her all the time or do whatever she wants me to do. We, in fact as a family, accept her wishes about most anything. I obviously felt controlled over the weekend, but I couldn't bring myself to feel the resentment until you mentioned it. Of course, I resented it because this was my vacation too . . . though I did feel compelled to follow her rules, let her dictate my days.

Therapist: Do you feel compelled to follow my rules?

The therapist weaves in a centripetal exploration.

Patient: Well, about my aunt, you know, that I should talk about her. I felt like you were dictating the subject. Usually you don't, so that's the only exception.

Therapist: What about encouraging your resentment towards your wife?

Patient: Oh, yes, that maybe, too. But you were right about it; in fact, you were right about my aunt too. Incidentally, when we were in Florida, I dreamt about her. She cooked every day for us and I love her cooking, but in the dream she was very upset that I wasn't eating what she cooked. There was this vague sexual sensation in the dream. I mean, no kissing, intercourse, anything like that; just a sense of sexual excitement. That was it, not much of a dream.

Therapist: Any associations?

Patient: I don't know. She isn't someone I could be attracted to. She's quite a masculine woman; in fact, she has this dark mustache, a little gross. But about the control issue, she must stand in for my wife. I was, I guess, rejecting my wife's controlling my vacation. I must be taking my opposition toward my wife and expressing it to my aunt.

Therapist: What about the sexual excitement?

The therapist actively explores the material only when the patient is overly compliant.

Patient: I guess I couldn't hold back my sexual desire towards my wife and express it to my ugly aunt! Could I? So I don't know what to make of it. Control, yes, resentment, yes. You were obviously right in asking that I should talk about my aunt; there is lots of stuff there; is it possible that I was once attracted to my aunt, I mean as a child? I think she was very tactile. She still is, mind you; hugs and kisses, you know.

Therapist: Hmmm.

Patient: Anything else I should talk about?

Therapist: Have you noticed that you safely complied with every subject that I introduced?

Patient: I guess. Is that unusual? I mean, shall I pick and choose? Well, why do I do that? We talked about my trying to please you before, but you mean something else now, as if you're providing me with a safe subject to latch onto and I grab it.

Therapist: Hmmm.

Patient: I thought expressing resentment towards my wife was damn dangerous and frightening; so is there possible sexual interest in my aunt? So all this is hiding some real frightening subject behind it? What could that be—that vague sexual sensation—if not belonging to my wife or my aunt? The beach was full of beautiful young women.

Therapist: One beautiful young woman, somehow, is absent in this consideration.

The therapist actively introduces a potentially conflicted subject. Again, this is only appropriate with the complacent patient.

Patient: Oh, you mean Josie? [blushes] Well, she's certainly stunningly beautiful. Oh gosh, this is so embarrassing. But I have no attraction to her . . . I mean it. Believe me, you're on the wrong track. It may be that way in the books, but not in real life, not in my life anyhow. . . . I had a bad dream about her, though. She and I were watching this tall building and there was a scaffold around it. We thought it might be dangerous to go near it. We were holding hands, alternately urging each other to cross the street, each one meanwhile resisting it—I guess cautious, I don't know, don't ask my association with it . . . it makes no sense at all.

Therapist: Unless you dropped the scaffold.

Patient: Dropped the scaffold? God, am I hiding something behind? Strangely, my association to the scaffold was a condom that you can sort of see through. I don't know where all this is taking us to. What if I'm still following your lead and this is another convenient subject? No! Damn, this is so embarrassing. . . .

Therapist: What would I think of you?

The therapist makes the material a transferential matter.

Patient: Yeah . . . I don't want you to think of me, this, you know, having some kind of incestuous father.

Therapist: And, lose my . . .

Patient: [interrupts] Yeah, your respect. I don't know, I guess the shame that the . . . you know . . . I spend all my life trying to receive my father's love and approval, you know. He was just too good, I guess, in everything. He was smart, handsome, competent, you name it, decent. He also expected a lot from us. I always felt inferior to him. I mean, I was, objectively. He was also a righteous man. . . . One day, I must have been 9 or 10, I pulled out my handkerchief from my pocket; guess what falls out! . . . I took it from his drawer. . . .

WORKING THROUGH TRIADIC CONFLICTS: OVERCOMING RESISTANCES TOWARD ACHIEVEMENT AND ASSIMILATION OF INSIGHT

The working-through process for the triadic conflict patient can be characterized as a continual battle within the psyche, as expressed between patient and therapist. Here infantile triangular problems of childhood are played out, with the therapist as both displaced object and reflective observer of the patient's repressed strivings. In this context, sexuality, aggressiveness, submissiveness, competitiveness, fear, and guilt are constantly removed from repression and explored. This is the marrow of the work—to be repeated, revisited, and intertwined with daily life occurrences, transference, and recollections of the past.

It constitutes a protracted and painstaking process, in which recall, repetition, and synthesis of early interpersonal patterns vis-à-vis both parental figures, as a fusion of fact and fantasy, are relived and reconstructed over and over until the patient develops new modes of reacting and interacting that are more mature and realistic, that is, can better separate reverie from reality. Through this process of working through, the patient's ego is confronted with the same material, or variations of it, many times over until the warded-off material is sufficiently neutralized and integrated into the psyche.

The length of this phase of treatment (sometimes considered interminable) is a function of the resilience of infantile behavior patterns and a manifestation of the fact that it takes numerous, repeated confrontations, clarifications, and interpretations to alter the psychic structure in order to effect permanent change. Put in other terms, neither solely abreactive experiences, however intense, nor particular interpretations, however incisive, are sufficient for the ego to achieve mastery over deep and long-repressed wishes and feelings.

Therapist: Hi. I'm sorry I'm a few minutes late.

Patient (male): I wasn't sure whether I should knock on the door or not. I listened from the door; there was no noise, no one on the phone kind of stuff. So I thought maybe you were ill or something.

Therapist: Something!

Patient: [laughs] Maybe dead. Then I said, what would I do if you were dead? Do I call an ambulance, take you to the hospital? The police would come and what if . . .

Therapist: And accuse you of . . . ?

Patient: No, no, the previous patient killed you. You see! I just found you dead, you remember.

Therapist: Any thoughts about the wish?

Patient: I don't know, why should I wish that you were dead? I mean, I like you; I need you. You've been very helpful to me, so it makes no sense that I should have such thoughts.

Therapist: Hmmm.

Patient: Really, I'm drawing a blank on this. Maybe if you were dead, then I wouldn't have to come here. The treatment may end . . . so I don't have to worry about changing, growing up, you know, going through all this struggle.

Therapist: Hmmm.

Patient: In a strange way, as long as you exist, I guess, I feel I'll be a patient. I could never be your equal. We'll never be real friends. If I see you at a party or something, I would most likely shy away.

Therapist: Hmmm.

Patient: I feel the same way with Carol. When we go to a dinner party or meet some people, she quickly becomes the center of the conversation. She's so comfortable, witty, and verbal. I told her. She says I'm exaggerating. No, but I really believed that as long as we're together I'll be the less social one. Do I wish her death, too? . . . I used to have this fantasy as a child: in the middle of the night, a burglar would break in and get into a fistfight with my father; they would kill each other off. Again, he was a good father, mind you, but I had these thoughts all the time when growing up. I used to hope that his plane would crash, things like that. Isn't that awful? It wasn't a kind of anger or hate for him. I just wanted him out of my way. So bizarre, because we needed him to survive and he was a good provider.

Therapist: We?

Patient: Well, the whole family; me, my mother, my sister.

Therapist: Did you think that your mother also shared your secret thoughts in regard to your father?

Patient: I don't think so. I mean, I have no way of knowing. They were quite loving towards each other. So there's no reason to think that. Do you think I presumed that? She used to stay up, wait for his comings, out-of-town trips. God! I remember strong jealousy feelings. I used to even get into fights with her about that.

Therapist: As long as he was alive, you were . . .

Patient: Yes, I was going to remain a kid. One night, again she wouldn't take us to the movies because he was coming home.

Patient (female): I had this dream last night. I was in a big house, half built, you know, all that construction seems to be going on. But there were no workers around, like that, except my older brother, Andrew. He was behaving as if he were in charge of the construction; I'm not sure, but I think the house was going to be mine. And I was putting things in order, and so forth. But clearly he was more skillful or something, doing the right things. There were two small cottages on the side, also being built. I can't remember anything else. I woke up; it must have been just before my alarm clock went off.

Therapist: Hmmm.

Patient: So you would want me to associate with the dream. Let's see, the half-built house, that could be my school, or it might be the treatment; we are sort of halfway, would you say? I don't know why my incompetent brother Andrew seems to be capable in the dream, unless of course it represents someone else. Let's see, who do we know is such a competent builder? Certainly that professor of mine with bedroom eyes, or could it be you? I guess I am sort of jealous of him and also of you. I want to be as competent as both of you.

Therapist: What do you make of the fact that you want to be as competent as I am, at the same time an incompetent figure stands in for me in the dream?

Patient: Do I perceive any incompetency in you as a therapist? Not really, but I wish you could build the rest of the house a little faster. Maybe that's it; I don't know. Although I can't complain so far. But I guess even if I had some questions about your competence, what I want is still to be as competent as you are, or more competent. That's it. That's all I want, eventually.

Therapist: Nothing else?

Patient: Well . . . you think so? . . . Yeah . . . I guess I want that house for us. On the one hand, I'm competing with you as to who is the better housebuilder; on the other, I want you as my husband. You know the sexual stuff still is too guilt provoking. The marriage, on the other hand, sounds a little better. So what else can I tell you? It was a very short dream.

Therapist: And those two cottages?

Patient: Oh yeah! They were for our guests, I guess, or for our children. But why would the kids sleep outside the main house? . . . My father had built a big doll house for me in the backyard when I was 4 or 5 years old. I used to spend lots of time there. I loved that house. Andrew and I used to play Mommy and Daddy in there. I used to ask him to lay on me so that we'll have babies. He was two years older, but still quite awkward. My parents didn't object to our little sexual games at all. In fact, they were a kind of "supermodern" family. My father used to walk around naked in the house. He

used to explain that everything was natural—this was a penis, this was a vagina—I can't believe that he did that. Anyway, I used to sit on my dad's lap. I think I felt his penis a
couple of times. It was exciting and scary and I felt like I
betrayed my mother, but she seemed not so disturbed. She
was beautiful and I guess secure. I could listen to their laughs
from their bedroom; I knew that I just couldn't compete with
her. . . . I am still competing with her and still attracted to
older men. So will I ever get over this?

Therapist: Hmmm.

Patient: Let's hurry. God, I can't wait; I know it's coming, I know.
I feel it within me. The second half will be built faster. I have
better tools. Damn, I wasted so much time at the beginning.
Anyway, I got this nice offer for the summer. . . .

Despite this patient's personal sense of urgency, working through
is marked by the gradual dissolution of the therapeutic bond, including
a termination phase, as the patient makes his final emotional preparation for leaving. The irrational transferential attachment to the therapist has subsided and more rational aspects of the psyche preside. Greater
mastery of psychological problems may be seen as well as more mature
adaptation. However, termination is never an unambivalent experience
because it inevitably revives separation anxiety around old conflictual
issues of dependence versus independence from significant persons of
the past (along with transient recurrences of original symptoms and
accompanying defenses).

As in all patients, termination has also been likened to a mourning
process, in which the triadic conflict patient grieves over the impending loss of the therapist as well as the loss of his or her former self. The
latter is less recognizable because it no longer needs the old familiar
symptomatology and self-protective scenarios. In addition, by incorpo-
rating the insights received with the assistance of the therapist as a reflective observer as well as internalizing the therapist as a real model of
identification (Offenkrantz and Tobin 1974), the patient can better use
his or her self-knowledge to separate the reality of the therapist from
the fantasy, and the present from the past.

Most critical, neither termination nor working through are hard-and-fast events; they need time to be consolidated. Despite developmental gains made and insights achieved, triadic conflict patients will invariably have to continue to internally integrate partially resolved problems outside of the therapy situation, without the actual aid of their therapists; or in times of subsequent stress and renewed conflict, they may naturally need intermittent assistance after treatment has technically terminated.

8

Conclusion: Practice for the Future

It has been observed that an integrative movement is gaining momentum throughout the psychotherapeutic field and is likely to be the *zeitgeist* of the future (Beitman et al. 1989, Pine 1990). This embrace of many conceptual and clinical viewpoints derives from an understanding of the inherent limitations of theory in general, as well as the special constraints of a single theoretical position or perspective over all others. In this behalf, it should be borne in mind that at best each theory represents "an ideal or hypothetical set of facts, principles, or circumstances" (Webster's 1989, p. 1223). As my recent book on deconstruction of psychotherapy suggests (Karasu 1996), theories necessarily sustain an unsettled status that resides somewhere between myth and truth.

Every theoretical postulate or premise nonetheless functions to form a framework for the organization of data and explanation of events, which operates both to guide one's thinking initially and to continually shape and reshape it thereafter. Theories thus steer one's observations by providing direction and focus, while creating (sometimes arbitrary) boundaries for what is included—and thereby implicitly or even explicitly excluded. Because a theory naturally confers constraints it can force closure upon what one looks at and sees and, in a more extreme sense, consciously or unconsciously distort data by eliminating whatever appears inconsistent or competitive with preferred preexisting beliefs. In this way, ardent attachment to a single preferred theory may reify that which is favored or familiar and, wittingly or unwittingly, obliterate those that are presumed to be unfavored or unfamiliar. A theory can thus be overendowed and professionally become a kind of transitional object that links the believer to idealized teachers or mentors, thereby providing, in Mitchell's (1988) thesis, "partially illusory safety and reassurance" (p. 11). One's treasured theory can even subjectively serve as a refuge from reality and personally form an intimate connection to the particular theorist as a "dwelling for the self" (Wright 1991, p. 329).

However, it has also been pointed out that even entrenched theories will never really prevent the occurrence, and possible acceptance, of new observations and hypotheses. All theoretical constructs are by their very nature hypothetical and open, to be used or discarded, in whole or in part. In the above sense, all theory is, according to Rangell (1985), "conjectural, not closed" (p. 60). At bottom, theoretical frameworks can therefore be viewed as forever fluid. This means that there is increasing acknowledgment that many psychological perspectives may potentially participate—and can be complementary—in understanding and treating a broad range of psychopathology (Pine 1990). Indeed the state of the art of psychotherapy suggests that new paradigms are necessary to combine or transcend diverse schemas of theory and therapy (Beitman et al. 1989, Pine 1990). In the psychodynamic realm, this refers to the integration of drive, ego, object relations, and self approaches (Pine 1990), and to the more global synthesis of conflict and deficit models that reside at the contemporary core of major clinical controversy (Eagle 1984). In tandem with this conceptual schism has been the dual nature of the psychological healer as scientific versus humanistic, and the current call for complementarity of these two contrasting modes in the modern role of the psychotherapist as an empathic listener (Jackson 1992).

In answer to these contemporary needs, the purpose of this book is to propose a model of psychotherapy practice for the future that is both integrative and experience-near. It has applied two predominant paradigms—conflict and deficit—in the treatment of a wide range of patients, which bridge theoretical constructs with pragmatic experiences of the practitioner. An enduring history of clinical teachings on empirical techniques and modes of healing, drawn from early psychoanalysis to contemporary dynamic therapy, have thereby been adapted to a broad diagnostic and maturational spectrum. The foundation is a developmental model, which forms the particular framework here that combines and transcends multiple models of psychopathology and treatment. Major preoedipal and oedipal events, interfaced with significant two-person (mother–child) and three-person (father–mother–child) influences, are together viewed as instrumental in the formation of different relationship patterns that are reiterated in psychotherapy. These clinical interactions between therapist and patient thus serve to provide a template for designing and modifying therapeutic practices. In this way, both classic and modern models of psychotherapy, which aim to resolve intrapsychic conflicts and to supply deficient self-objects of early life, may be utilized together by shifting and sharing different stances and strategies in today's—and tomorrow's—treatment.

This developmental model of psychotherapeutic practice acknowledges the joint impact on psychic structure formation of unresolved conflictual urges and wishes interfaced with early environmental deficiencies and traumas in the real object world of the patient (Eagle 1984). In terms of treatment, the therapist must thus address and deal with conflictual concomitants as well as developmental derailments. Because the patient is a product of both, the clinician is necessarily placed in a dual position of being, according to Settlage (1994), "both a transference object and a developmental object" (p. 39), a fantasied and a real object. It also recognizes the pivotal roles of both erotic and narcissistic transferences in the nature of the therapist–patient relationship (Stolorow and Lachmann 1980). Moreover, by bridging theoretical concepts and actual applications, an experience-near working model aims to address the pressing problem of lack of synchrony between theory and practice (Pulver 1993, Sundland 1977).

It has also been acknowledged that both pathology (and practice) reside on a continuum. Conflict theory neither applies solely to the neuroses, nor object relations to borderline disorders, and self theory need not be reserved for narcissistic disturbances. The prototypical hysterical patient can have ego defects as well as sexual conflicts (Rangell 1985); similarly, the depressive patient can show self deficiencies as well as unresolved conflictual problems derived from drive frustration (Deitz 1991). Moreover, conflicts are not necessarily restricted to oedipal phases nor deficits to preoedipal ones (Karasu 1992). Rather, these conflictual phenomena and their resolution are naturally influenced by preceding maturational and environmental events. Although the precise nature of prior impact upon present disturbance varies, old entrenched and enduring wounds that represent structural defects (from deficiencies at a prestage of defensive formation) can camouflage the recognition of more recently acquired symptomatology and defense mechanisms against anxiety (from current painful and incompatible intrapsychic forces) (Stolorow and Lachmann 1980). Thus, the susceptibility of some deprived or developmentally arrested individuals to disorders based on dyadic deficits or conflicts may preempt, but in no way precludes, the emergence and exacerbation of triadic conflicts. As Westen (1989) points out, "The vulnerability of patients with serious character pathology to feelings of loss, abandonment, and rejection renders them more likely . . . to focus on these issues; but such people do have genitals as well as competitive feelings" (p. 342).

In a similar vein, conflicts themselves can interface with deficits or defects, compounding their deleterious effects. Eagle (1984) has aptly concluded that these two phenomena are integrally connected regardless of origin. "[w]hatever defects one has, whether constitutionally given or the result of early traumas, what further weakens the personality is the existence of excessively intense and pervasive conflicts and other incompatibilities which, through their failure to be resolved, threaten one's sense of self-coherence and self-integrity" (pp. 142–143).

Greater understanding and challenge of this presumed polarity is now occurring in conjunction with increased efforts at their theoretic and technical reconciliation (Adler 1986, Eagle 1984, Glassman 1988). Recent works represent attempts to close the erroneous schism between oedipal and preoedipal object relations (Westen 1989) and to more broadly synthesize several psychodynamic or psychoanalytic perspectives in theory or practice (Pine 1990, Tyson and Tyson 1990). The increasing convergence of these dialectical divisions highlights the natural tensions between patients' internal fantasy life and external environmental events as well as between objective and subjective standpoints of attentive and empathic clinicians.

On the basis of the above prevailing views, this book embodies the following fundamental formulation with regard to the complex interactional template upon which the individual relates to the therapist and others: that the clinical state of the patient is reflective of his or her respective deficiencies and/or conflicts—what is lacking (e. g., sense of self, formation of prosocial values) as well as what is wished for or feared (e. g., intimacy/engulfment, success/failure). Developmental manifestations (i. e., interference with proper attachment, individuation, conscience formation, or sexual identity formation) as well as types of disposition (i. e., depressive, hostile, acting-out, or anxious) are also direct extensions of this model. This combined orientation toward psychopathology delineates a clinical paradigm by which psychotherapy can be geared towards remedying both the underlying psychological deficits (lacks) as well as conflicts (wishes/fears) in the progressive maturation and adaptation of an individual. Moreover, at a minimum it would expand and incorporate the two preeminent conflict versus self models of therapeutic cure, in Kohut's (1977) words:

> And no satisfactory definition of the concept of a cure, and thus of a concept of a proper termination of [treatment], can be given if we fail to determine the patient's greatest terror—whether castration anxiety or disintegration anxiety—and his most compelling objective—whether conflict solution or the establishment of self-cohesion, or, stated in different terms, if we disregard the question whether the [therapy] has enabled him to perform those central psychological tasks through which he can establish the conditions that will guarantee his psychological survival. [pp. 280–281]

In light of the critical currents of psychotherapeutic treatment, it is becoming increasingly evident that no single school can meet the needs of the practitioner in interaction with, and change or cure of, all patients. A transtheoretical approach is warranted as a first step towards addressing this goal and acts as the embracing construct that binds both developmental theory and practice. It is believed to cut across assorted approaches to children and adults as well as to act as a bridge between different disciplines and sources of data, including child analysis, longitudinal studies of psychopathology, cognitive psychology, and direct observation and research on infant interaction (Tyson and Tyson 1990). Representing nearly a century of investigation of child development since Freud's (1905) original theory, it offers renewed conceptual and practical promise as a guiding framework for the future (Remschmidt 1993).

A developmental view of psychopathology and normality along with its understanding of the individual's childhood impact on the adult are not new. Yet specific descriptions of the developmental spectrum are highly varied. Familar phase-related continuums, of course, include Freud's (1905) classic drive development from the oral phase of early sexuality to mature genitality; or Erikson's (1963) eight stages of man that extend from the child's development of trust vs. mistrust to the integrity vs. despair of old age. In a recent overview of self development across illness and health, Wolf (1994) referred to three successive stages and their consequences: an undeveloped self stage that manifests as a *deformed* self, which can give rise to "preemergence disorders"; a partially developed self stage that manifests as a *fragile* self, which can give rise to "consolidation disorders"; and a fully developed self stage that may nonetheless be weakened by life events and manifest as an *unfulfilled* self, which can give rise to "life curve disorders." Each, of course, has direct implications for treatment. Although various developmental theorists have differed in their views of the precise nature of maturational unfolding and the sequence of events in the differentiation and integration of self, Kavaler-Adler (1993) has concluded that "there is one common denominator, and that is the common denominator of an internal dialogue of proposed psychic structure personas that generally *rearticulates a child–parent interaction*" (p. 29; italics mine).

It is further suggested that, without such internal dialogue, externalized reenactments result that forevermore preclude the prospects for internal integration. It is this rearticulation upon which the future of practice is pivoted. As such, this orientation supports a transformational model, which asserts that experiences at each successive developmental phase are continually created and recreated by both past and present events; such a model "recognizes both the continuous construction and potential reorganization of experience at various stages as well as the repetition of ways of organizing experience shaped by early interactive patterns . . . " (Lachmann and Beebe 1992, p. 143).

More specifically, psychotherapy practice for the future would be directed toward titrating treatment across the entire maturational spectrum. This would be based upon the individual patient's developmental pathology and problems, deficits and conflicts, defenses and compromise formations, unfulfilled needs and unfinished tasks, as well as on the level of adaptation and new mastery of affective and interpersonal life. At the same time, the ongoing goals would reach towards the restructuring, strengthening, and/or fulfillment of the self. For the therapist it means carefully shaping the therapeutic relationship in the same way that any other interventions are designed by the clinician. At a minimum it relates to the dual roles in the history of the psychological healer—a scientific or listening versus a humanistic or empathic stance. Although the former is most associated with a conflict model and the latter with a deficit model, they are increasingly combined in today's practice in the expressed embodiment of the "empathic listener" (Jackson 1992). In a similar vein, Stolorow and Lachmann's (1980) exploration of the psychotherapy of developmental arrests—which distinguishes between patients with deficits (i. e., defects or voids in the self at a prestage of defensive development) and conflicts (i. e., expressions of drives and defenses within a more consolidated self structure)—demonstrates the respective effects of different maturational levels upon the changing nature of therapist–patient interaction:

> The therapeutic relationship may shift back and forth between the more advanced and more primitive positions throughout. . . . The two levels of object relationship can coexist. A communication by the [therapist] may at one point in the treatment require that he respond from the position of an archaic selfobject and at another point . . . from the position of a separate whole object. [p. 174]

The idea must be stressed that the therapist becomes a developmental self-object, object or introject, who invariably bears symbolic resemblance to the early parental figures, whether via displacement, projection, or wishful thinking. However, he hopefully transcends them by being a new person in the patient's life—the clinican does not function as a replica of the parent per se. It is this individually designed difference between the past and the future that is built by the therapeutic relationship, which allows each patient to get beyond mere reinforcement of old patterns and pathology.

In fact, several clinicians have increasingly indicated the need for an integration of relational concepts in theory and practice (Eagle and Wolitsky 1982, Karasu 1992, Mitchell 1988). Of special salience are the complex and sometimes contradictory roles of the transference relationship, therapeutic or working alliance, and real relationship (Karasu 1992) as they play their particular parts on the route to therapeutic cure. In a current article on tailoring the therapeutic relationship, Lazarus (1993) has articulated the need for a flexible repertoire of relationship styles in addition to a wide range of pertinent techniques in order to enhance treatment outcomes. "For effective psychotherapy, 'relationships of choice' are no less important than 'techniques of choice' " (p. 404). He and his colleagues have gone further to suggest that while genuineness, accurate empathy, and warmth have long been therapist qualities associated with facilitating therapeutic progress (Lazarus 1971, Rogers 1957), there may be exceptions even to these esteemed and time-honored characteristics; they too may require modifications in therapist technique to best meet the needs of different diagnostic types. Kernberg (1982), for example, has pointed out the danger that an excess of support, warmth, and empathy in certain patients (i. e., borderline personality disorder) will lead to a primitive idealization of the "good therapist," thereby preventing the needed expression of aggression. In this way, the so-called relationships of choice interface here with particular clinical characteristics that issue from stage-related deficits and/or conflicts. In like fashion, the dyadic deficit patient and the empathic self-object, the dyadic conflict patient and the projective container, the triadic deficit patient and the prosocial introject, and the triadic conflict patient and the reflective object—separately or together, in whole or in part—reflect different relationship roles that attempt to answer particular patient needs.

The final point must be made that there must be a conscious differentiation of interventions and types of relationship, which are mutually formed within the proposed perspective. More specifically, all psychotherapists become—to greater or lesser degrees—empathic self-objects, projective containers, prosocial introjects, and reflective objects for their patients; these therapeutic functions invariably present themselves in combination and permutation with every form of psychopathology. Although Mahoney (1991) has warned that there are real limits to how much change can occur by both clients and clinicians, and that some developmental trajectories and interpersonal styles may have greater "maturational pull" than others, Mahoney and Norcross (1993) also take a more positive position by noting that "These real limitiations on the extent of relational match-making should help us guard against grandiose expectations and capricious posturing on the therapist's part" (p. 424). In fact, Schacht's (1991) recent research on the nature of expertise has affirmed that experienced therapists are both more disciplined as well as more improvisational in their therapeutic repertoires; they show greater innovation as well as finer attention to the subtle nuances of the individual patient. For Wolf (1994) this refers to the observation that the skilled clinician has to have a high tolerance of uncertainty along with a willingness to discard what does not work, a special openness to look again and try something different (even if it does not precisely fit with that therapist's preordained theoretical stance).

Such flexibility in the embrace of new forms and functions, however, does not mean that the therapist loses his own identity in the process. Nor does it mean that the therapist is not genuine in his responses to each individual. Rather, all clinicians and patients form complex bonds that are unwittingly distorted (i. e., transference relationship), deliberately realistic (i. e., therapeutic alliance), and spontaneously natural (i. e., real relationship) (Karasu 1995); yet all of them must be equally experienced as faithful to the past, the present, and the moment. In order for such fidelity to be fulfilled, it is best to become, in Lazarus's (1993) term, an "authentic chameleon" (p. 404)—a psychotherapist who, befitting the fine nuances of interpersonal relatedness and interventive diversity, all the more must remain true to the patient as well as oneself.

References

Abelin, E. L. (1975). Some further observations and comments on the earliest role of the father. *International Journal of Psychoanalysis* 56:293–302.

——— (1980). Triangulation, the role of the father, and the origins of core gender identity during the rapprochement subphase. In *Rapprochement: The Critical Subphase of Separation-Individuation*, ed. R. Lax, S. Bach, and J. A. Burland, pp. 151–169. New York: Jason Aronson.

Adler, G. (1986). Psychotherapy of the narcissistic disorder patient: two contrasting approaches. *American Journal of Psychiatry* 143:430–436.

——— (1993). The psychotherapy of core borderline psychopathology. *American Journal of Psychotherapy* 47:194–205.

Ainsworth, M. D. S. (1979). Object relations, dependency, and attachment: a theoretical review of the infant–mother relationship. *Child Development* 40:969–1025.

Appelbaum, S. (1976). The dangerous edge of insight. *Psychotherapy: Theory, Research and Practice* 13:202–206.

Atwood, G. E., and Stolorow, R. E. (1984). *Structures of Subjectivity: Explorations in Psychoanalytic Phenomenology.* Hillsdale, NJ: Analytic Press.

Bacal, H. (1985). Optimal responsiveness and the therapeutic process. In *Progress in Self Psychology,* vol. 1, ed. A. Goldberg, pp. 222–226. Hillsdale, NJ: Analytic Press.

Baker, H. S., and Baker, M. N. (1987). Heinz Kohut's self psychology: an overview. *American Journal of Psychiatry* 144:1–9.

Basch, M. F. (1980). *Doing Psychotherapy.* New York: Basic Books.

———— (1983). Empathic understanding: a review of the concept and some theoretical considerations. *Journal of the American Psychoanalytic Association* 31:101–126.

———— (1994). Selfobjects and the selfobject transference: theoretical implications. In *Kohut's Legacy,* ed. P. Stepansky and A. Goldberg, pp. 21–41. Hillsdale, NJ: Analytic Press.

Bateson, G. (1972). *Steps to an Ecology of Mind.* New York: Ballantine.

Beck, A. T., Rush, A. H., Shaw, B. F., et al. (1979). *Cognitive Therapy of Depression.* New York: Guilford.

Beitman, B. D., Goldfried, M. R., and Norcross, J. C. (1989). The movement toward integrating the psychotherapies: An overview. *American Journal of Psychiatry* 146:138–147.

Bion, W. (1962). *Seven Servants.* New York: Jason Aronson, 1972.

———— (1967). *Second Thoughts: Selected Papers on Psychoanalysis.* London: Heinemann.

Bleuler, E. (1930). *Textbook of Psychiatry.* New York: Macmillan.

Bollas, C. (1987). *The Shadow of the Object.* New York: Columbia University Press.

Bowlby, J. (1969). *Attachment and Loss, Vol. 1. Attachment.* New York: Basic Books.

———— (1973). *Attachment and Loss, Vol. 2. Separation: Anxiety and Anger.* New York: Basic Books.

———— (1980). *Attachment and Loss, Vol. 3. Loss: Sadness and Depression.* New York: Basic Books.

———— (1988). *A Secure Base: Clinical Applications of Attachment Theory.* London: Routledge.

Brenner, C. (1976). *Psychoanalytic Technique and Psychic Conflict*. New York: International Universities Press.

Bretherton, I. (1985). Attachment theory: retrospect and prospect. In *Growing Points of Attachment: Theory and Research*, ed. I. Bretherton and E. Waters, pp. 3–35. Monograph of the Society for Research in Child Development, Serial no. 209, vol. 50.

Bridges, L. J., Connell, J. P., and Belsky, J. (1988). Similarities and differences in infant–mother and infant–father interaction in the strange situation: a component process analysis. *Developmental Psychology* 24:92–100.

Buie, D., and Adler, G. (1982). The definitive treatment of the borderline patient. *International Journal of Psychoanalytic Psychotherapy* 9:51–87.

Calestro, K. (1972). Psychotherapy, faith healing and suggestion. *International Journal of Psychiatry* 10:83–114.

Campbell, R. J. (1989). *Psychiatric Dictionary*, 6th ed. New York: Oxford University Press.

———— (1996). *Psychiatric Dictionary*, 7th ed. New York: Oxford University Press.

Chessick, R. D. (1977). *Intensive Psychotherapy of the Borderline Patient*. New York: Jason Aronson.

———— (1980). *Freud Teaches Psychotherapy*. Indianapolis, IN: Hackett.

———— (1993). *A Dictionary for Psychotherapists: Dynamic Concepts in Psychotherapy*. Northvale, NJ: Jason Aronson.

Connors, M. E. (1997). A relational obstacle on need and responsiveness with a severely traumatized patient. *American Journal of Psychotherapy* 50: winter (in press).

Cooper, A. M. (1987). Changes in psychoanalytic ideas: transference interpretation. *Journal of the American Psychiatric Association* 35: 77–98.

Cooper, J., and Maxwell, N., eds. (1995). *Narcissistic Wounds*. Northvale, NJ: Jason Aronson.

Crumley, F. E., and Blumenthal, R. S. (1973). Children's reactions to temporary loss of the father. *American Journal of Psychiatry* 130: 778–782.

Deitz, J. (1991). The psychodynamics and psychotherapy of depression: contrasting the self-psychological and the classical psychoanalytic approaches. *American Journal of Psychoanalysis* 51:61–70.

Demos, V. (1984). Empathy and affect: reflections on infant experience. In *Empathy*, ed. J. Lichtenberg, M. Bernstein, and D. Silver, pp. 9–34. Hillsdale, NJ: Erlbaum.

Dorpat, T. L. (1976). Structural conflict and object relations conflict. *Journal of the American Psychiatric Association* 24:855–874.

Eagle, M. (1984). *Recent Developments in Psychoanalysis*. Cambridge: Harvard University Press.

Eagle, M., and Wolitsky, D. L. (1982). Therapeutic influences in dynamic psychotherapy: a review and synthesis. In *Curative Factors in Dynamic Psychotherapy*, ed. S. Slipp, pp. 349–378. New York: McGraw-Hill.

Earls, F., and Yogman, M. (1979). The father–infant relationship. In *Modern Perspectives in the Psychiatry of Infancy*, ed. J. G. Howells, pp. 213–239. New York: Brunner/Mazel.

Ehrenberg, D. B. (1992). *The Intimate Edge*. New York: Norton.

Eigen, M. (1996). *Psychic Deadness*. Northvale, NJ: Jason Aronson.

Eissler, K. (1953). The effect of the structure of the ego on psychoanalytic technique. *Journal of the American Psychoanalytic Association* 1:104–143.

Erikson, E. (1963). *Childhood and Society*. New York: Norton.

Fairbairn, W. R. D. (1952). *Psychoanalytic Studies of the Personality*. London: Routledge and Kegan Paul.

———— (1954). *An Object Relations Theory of Personality*. New York: Basic Books.

Fogel, G. I. (1994). The seductions of the deficit model. Unpublished manuscript.

Forrest, T. (1967). The paternal roots of male character development. *Psychoanalytic Review* 54:277–295.

Forster, E. M. (1954). *Howard's End*. New York: Anchor.

Frances, A., and Cooper, A. M. (1981). Descriptive and dynamic psychiatry: a perspective on *DSM-III*. *American Journal of Psychiatry* 138:1198–1202.

Frank, J. D., and Frank, J. B. (1991). *Persuasion and Healing: A Comparative Study of Psychotherapy*, 3rd ed. Baltimore: Johns Hopkins University Press.

Freud, A. (1936). *The Ego and Mechanisms of Defense*. New York: International Universities Press.

———— (1963). The concept of developmental lines. *Psychoanalytic Study of the Child* 18:245–265. New York: International Universities Press.

———— (1965). *Normality and Pathology in Childhood: Assessments of Development*. New York: International Universities Press.

Freud, S. (1901). Slips of the tongue. *Standard Edition* 6:53–105.

———— (1905). Three essays on the theory of sexuality. *Standard Edition* 7:125–246.

———— (1912). Recommendations to physicians practicing psychoanalysis. *Standard Edition* 12:111–120.

———— (1914). On narcissism: an introduction. Part III. Ego-ideal, inheritor of narcissism. *Standard Edition* 14:92–104.

———— (1915a). The unconscious. *Standard Edition* 14:159–204.

———— (1915b). Observations on transference love. *Standard Edition* 12:157–171.

———— (1918). From the history of an infantile neurosis. *Standard Edition* 17:3–124.

———— (1923). The infantile genital organization: an interpolation into the theory of sexuality. *Standard Edition* 19:41–148.

———— (1933). New introductory lectures on psycho-analysis. *Standard Edition* 22:1–192.

Gabbard, G. (1982). The exit line: heightened transference–countertransference manifestations at the end of the hour. *Journal of the American Psychoanalytic Association* 30:579–598.

———— (1991). Psychodynamics of sexual boundary violations. *Psychiatric Annals* 21:651–655.

Gediman, H. K., and Lieberman, J. S. (1996). *The Many Faces of Deceit: Omissions, Lies, and Disguise in Psychotherapy*. Northvale, NJ: Jason Aronson.

Giovacchini, P. L. (1990). Erotism and chaos. *Journal of the Academy of Psychoanalysis* 18:23–39.

——— (1993). Treatment issues with borderline patients and the psychosomatic focus. *American Journal of Psychotherapy* 47:228–244.

Glassman, M. B. (1988). Intrapsychic conflicts versus developmental deficit: a causal modeling approach to examining psychoanalytic theories of narcissism. *Psychoanalytic Psychology* 5:23–46.

Glover, E. (1955). *The Technique of Psycho-analysis.* New York: International Universities Press.

Goffman, E. (1974). *Frame Analysis: An Essay on the Organization of Experience.* Boston: Northeastern University Press.

Goldberg, A. (1973). Psychotherapy of narcissistic injuries. *Archives of General Psychiatry* 28:722–726.

Good, L. (1995). Addiction as a narcissistic defence: the importance of control over the object. In *Narcissistic Wounds,* ed. J. Cooper and N. Maxwell, pp. 148–158. Northvale, NJ: Jason Aronson.

Gottdiener, A. (1982). The impostor: an interpersonal point of view. *Contemporary Psychoanalysis* 18:438–454.

Greenson, R. R. (1960). Empathy and its vicissitudes. *International Journal of Psycho-analysis* 41:418–424.

——— (1967). *The Technique and Practice of Psychoanalysis,* vol. 1. New York: International Universities Press.

Guntrip, H. (1961). *Personality Structure and Human Interaction.* New York: International Universities Press.

Hansen, D. B. (1985). The influence of early deficits on later development. *Journal of the American Psychiatric Association* 33:631–644.

Harlow, H. F. (1958). The nature of love. *American Psychologist* 13: 675–685.

Harpur, T., Hare, R., and Hakstian, R. (1989). Two-factor conceptualization of psychopathy: construct validity and assessment implications. *Journal of Consulting and Clinical Psychology* 1:6–17.

Havens, L. (1986). *Making Contact.* Cambridge, MA: Harvard University Press.

——— (1989). *A Safe Place.* Cambridge, MA: Harvard University Press.

Henderson, J. (1982). The role of the father in separation–individuation. *Bulletin of the Menninger Clinic* 46:231–254.

Ivey, G. (1995). Interactional obstacles to empathic relating in the psychotherapy of narcissistic disorders. *American Journal of Psychotherapy* 49:350–370.

Jackson, S. W. (1992). The listening healer in the history of psychological healing. *American Journal of Psychiatry* 149:1623–1632.

Jacobson, E. (1964). *The Self and the Object World.* New York: International Universities Press.

Jenkins, R. L., and Boyer, A. (1969/1970). Effects of inadequate mothering and inadequate fathering on children. *International Journal of Social Psychiatry* 16:72–78.

Jong, E. (1973). *Fear of Flying.* New York: Holt, Rinehart and Winston.

Josephs, L. (1994). Empathic character analysis. *American Journal of Psychoanalysis* 54:41–54.

Karasu, T. B. (1992a). *Wisdom in the Practice of Psychotherapy.* New York: Basic Books.

——— (1992b). Developmentalist metatheory of depression and psychotherapy. *American Journal of Psychotherapy* 46:1–13.

——— (1994). A developmental metatheory of psychopathology. *American Journal of Psychotherapy* 46:581–599.

——— (1995). Psychoanalysis and psychoanalytic psychotherapy. In *Comprehensive Textbook of Psychiatry VI,* vol. 2, ed. H. I. Kaplan and B. J. Sadock, pp. 1767–1788. Baltimore, MD: Williams & Wilkins.

——— (1996). *Deconstruction of Psychotherapy.* Northvale, NJ: Jason Aronson.

Karasu, S., and Oberfeld, R. (1989). Table 6.1-2. A synthesis of developmental theorists. In *Comprehensive Textbook of Psychiatry/V,* vol. 2, ed. A. M. Freedman and H. I. Kaplan, Baltimore: Williams & Wilkins.

Kavaler-Adler, S. (1993). Object relations issues in the treatment of the preoedipal character. *American Journal of Psychoanalysis* 53:19–34.

Kegan, R. G. (1986). The child behind the mask: sociopathy as developmental delay. In *Unmasking the Psychopath,* ed. W. H. Reid, D. Dorr, J. I. Walker, and J. W. Bonner III, pp. 45–77. New York: Norton.

Kernberg, O. (1975). *Borderline Conditions and Pathological Narcissism.* New York: Jason Aronson.

———— (1982). The theory of psychoanalytic psychotherapy. In *Curative Factors in Dynamic Psychotherapy*, ed. S. Slipp, pp. 21–43. New York: McGraw-Hill.

———— (1984). *Severe Personality Disorders*. New Haven: Yale University Press.

———— (1992). *Aggression in Personality Disorders and Perversions*. New Haven: Yale University Press.

Klein, M. (1946). *Envy and Gratitude and Other Works, 1946–1963*. London: Hogarth, 1952.

Kohut, H. (1971). *The Analysis of the Self*. New York: International Universities Press.

———— (1977). *The Restoration of the Self*. New York: International Universities Press.

———— (1984). *How Does Analysis Cure?* Chicago: University of Chicago Press.

Kohut, H., and Wolf, E. S. (1982). The disorders of the self and their treatment. In *Curative Factors in Dynamic Psychotherapy*, ed. S. Slipp, pp. 44–59. New York: McGraw-Hill.

Lachmann, F. M., and Beebe, B. (1992). Reformulations of early development and transference: implications for psychic structure formation. In *Interface of Psychoanalysis and Psychology*, ed. J. W. Barron, M. N. Eagle, and D. Wolitsky, pp. 133–153. Washington, DC: American Psychological Association.

Lacan, J. (1957). *Ecrits*. London: Tavistock, 1977.

Langs, R. (1975). Therapeutic misalliances. *International Journal of Psychoanalysis and Psychotherapy* 4:77–105.

Laplanche, J., and Pontalis, J-B. (1973). *The Language of Psycho-Analysis*. New York: Norton.

Lazarus, A. A. (1971). *Behavior Therapy and Beyond*. New York: McGraw-Hill.

———— (1993). Tailoring the therapeutic relationship, or being an authentic chameleon. *Psychotherapy* 30:404–407.

Lemaire, A. (1977). *Jacques Lacan*. London: Routledge and Kegan Paul.

Levi-Strauss, C. (1969). *The Elementary Structures of Kinship*. Boston: Beacon.

Lewin, R. A., and Schulz, C. (1992). *Losing and Fusing: Borderline Transitional Object and Self Relations*. Northvale, NJ: Jason Aronson.

Lichtenberg, J. (1989). *Psychoanalysis and Motivation*. Hillsdale, NJ: Analytic Press.

Lidz, T., and Lidz, R. W. (1982). Curative factors in the psychotherapy of schizophrenic patients. In *Curative Factors in Dynamic Psychotherapy*, ed. S. Slipp, pp. 298–320. New York: McGraw-Hill.

Mahler, M. S., Pine, F., and Bergman, A. (1975). *The Psychological Birth of the Human Infant: Symbiosis and Individuation*. New York: Basic Books.

Mahoney, M. J. (1991). *Human Change Processes: The Scientific Foundations of Psychotherapy*. New York: Basic Books.

Mahoney, M. J. and Craine, M. H. (1991). The changing beliefs of psychotherapy experts. *Journal of Psychotherapy Integration* 1:207–221.

Mahoney, M. J., and Norcross, J. C. (1993). Relationship styles and therapeutic choices: a commentary on the preceding four articles. *Psychotherapy* 30:423–426.

Main, M., Cassidy, J., and Kaplan, N. (1985). Security in infancy: a move to the level of representation. In *Growing Points of Attachment Theory and Research*, ed. I. Bretherton and E. Waters. Monograph of the Society for Research in Child Development, vol. 50.

Maslow, A. (1970). Neurosis as a failure of human growth. In *Psychopathology Today: Experimentation, Theory and Research*, ed. W. S. Sahakian, pp. 122–130. Itasca, IL: F. E. Peacock.

Masterson, J. (1976). *Psychotherapy of the Borderline Adult*. New York: Brunner/Mazel.

——— (1981). *The Narcissistic and Borderline Disorders*. New York: Brunner/Mazel.

——— (1983). *Countertransference and Psychotherapeutic Technique: Teaching Seminars on Psychotherapy of the Borderline Adult*. New York: Brunner/ Mazel.

Meissner, W. W. (1993). Treatment of patients in the borderline spectrum: an overview. *American Journal of Psychotherapy* 47:184–193.

Mitchell, S. A. (1988). *Relational Concepts in Psychoanalysis: An Integration*. Cambridge, MA.: Harvard University Press.

Mollon, P. (1993). *The Fragile Self*. Northvale, NJ: Jason Aronson.

Moore, B. E., and Fine, B. D., eds. (1990). *Psychoanalytic Terms and Concepts.* New Haven: American Psychoanalytic Association and Yale University Press.

Morgan, D. (1995). Destroying the knowledge of the need for love: narcissism and perversions. In *Narcissistic Wounds*, ed. J. Cooper and N. Maxwell, pp. 137–147. Northvale, NJ: Jason Aronson.

Nunberg, H. (1955). *Principles of Psychoanalysis.* New York: International Universities Press.

Offenkrantz, W., and Tobin, A. (1974). Psychoanalytic psychotherapy. *Archives of General Psychiatry* 30:593–606.

Ogden, T. (1979). On projective identification. *International Journal of Psycho-analysis* 60:357–363.

Ornstein, A. (1992). The curative fantasy and psychic recovery. *Journal of Psychotherapy Practice and Research* 1:16–28.

Orwell, G. (1945). *Animal Farm.* New York: Knopf.

Person, E. (1985). The erotic transference in women and in men: differences and consequences. *Journal of the American Academy of Psychoanalysis* 13:159–179.

——— (1986). Manipulativeness in entrepreneurs and psychopaths. In *Unmasking the Psychopath*, ed. W. H. Reid, D. Dorr, and J. Walker, pp. 256–273. New York: Norton.

Pine, F. (1990). *Drive, Ego, Object, and Self.* New York: Basic Books.

Plakun, E. M. (1993). Psychotherapy with the self-destructive borderline patient. In *Clinical Challenges in Psychiatry*, ed. W. H. Sledge and A. Tasman, pp. 129–155. Washington, DC: American Psychiatric Press.

Prall, R. C. (1978). The role of the father in the preoedipal years. *Journal of the American Psychoanalytic Association* 26:143–161.

Protter, B., and Travin, S. (1983). The significance of countertransference and related issues in a multiservice court clinic. *Bulletin of the American Academy of Psychiatry and Law* 11:223–230.

Psychotherapy Book News. (1996). An interview with Dr. Michael Eigen, vol. 30, July 25, pp. 6–10.

Pulver, S. (1993). The eclectic analyst, or the many roads to insight and change. *Journal of the American Medical Association* 41:339–357.

Rangell, L. (1985). On the theory of theory in psychoanalysis and the relation of theory to psychoanalytic therapy. *Journal of the American Psychoanalytic Association* 33:59–92.

Reid, W. H. (1978). The sadness of the psychopath. *American Journal of Psychotherapy* 32:496–509.

——— (1983). The antisocial personality: a review. *Hospital and Community Psychiatry* 36:831–837.

Remschmidt, H. (1993). Developmental psychopathology—an integrative approach. *Psychiatric Times* 10:15–16, 18.

Rogers, C. (1957). The necessary and sufficient conditions for therapeutic personality change. *Journal of Consulting Psychology* 21:95–103.

Ronningstam, E., and Gunderson, J. (1989). Descriptive studies on narcissistic personality disorder. *Psychiatric Clinics of North America* 12:585–602.

Rosenfeld, H. (1987). *Impasse and Interpretation*. London: Routledge.

Russell, P. (1993). The essential invisibility of trauma and the need for repetition. *Psychoanalytic Dialogues* 3:495–507.

Sandler, J. (1960).The background of safety. *International Journal of Psycho-Analysis* 41:325–356.

Schacht, T. E. (1991). Can psychotherapy education advance psychotherapy integration? *Journal of Psychotherapy Integration* 1:305–319.

Schafer, R. (1968). Generative empathy in the treatment situation. *Psychoanalytic Quarterly* 28:342–373.

Schonbar, R. A. (1964). Interpretation and insight in psychotherapy. *Psychotherapy: Theory, Research and Practice* 4:78–83.

Sechehaye, M. A. (1951). *Symbolic Realization*. New York: International Universities Press.

Seinfeld, J. (1991). *The Empty Core: An Object Relations Approach to Psychotherapy of the Schizoid Personality*. Northvale, NJ: Jason Aronson.

Settlage, C. F. (1990). Childhood to adulthood: Structural change in development toward independence and autonomy. In *New Dimensions in Adult Development*, ed. R. Nemiroff and C. Colarusso, pp. 26–42. New York: Basic Books.

——— (1994). On the contribution of separation–individuation theory to psychoanalysis: developmental process, pathogenesis, therapeutic process, and technique. In *Mahler and Kohut: Perspectives on Development, Psychopathology and Technique*, ed. S. Kramer and S. Akhtar, pp. 16–52. Northvale, NJ: Jason Aronson.

Shengold, L. (1989). *Soul Murder: The Effects of Childhood Abuse and Deprivation*. New Haven: Yale University Press.

Siegman, A. W. (1966). Father absence during early childhood and antisocial behavior. *Journal of Abnormal Psychology* 71:71–74.

Sledge, W. H., and Tasman, A., eds. (1993). *Clinical Challenges in Psychiatry*. Washington, DC: American Psychiatric Press.

Sperling, M. B., and Lyons, L. S. (1994). Representations of attachment and therapeutic change. In *Attachment in Adults: Clinical and Developmental Perspectives*, ed. M. B. Sperling and W. H. Berman, pp. 331–348. New York: Guilford Press.

Spieler, S. (1984). Preoedipal girls need fathers. *Psychoanalytic Review* 71:63–80.

Spitz, R. (1946). Anaclitic depression: an inquiry into the genesis of psychiatric conditions in early childhood. In *Psychoanalytic Study of the Child* 2:313–342. New York: International Universities Press.

Starcevic, V., and Piontek, C. M. (1997). Empathic understanding revisited: Conceptualization, controversies and limitations. *American Journal of Psychotherapy* 51 (in press).

Steiner, J. (1993). *Psychic Retreats*. London and New York: Routledge.

Stern, D. (1983). The early development of schemas of self, of other, and of various experiences of "self with other." In *Reflections in Self Psychology*, ed. J. D. Lichtenberg and S. Kaplan, pp. 49–84. Hillsdale, NJ: Analytic Press.

Stern, D. N. (1985). *The Interpersonal World of the Infant: A View from Psychoanalysis and Developmental Psychology*. New York: Basic Books.

——— (1990). *Diary of a Baby*. New York: Basic Books.

Stolorow, R. D., Atwood, G., and Brandchaft, B., eds. (1994). *The Intersubjective Perspective*. Northvale, NJ: Jason Aronson.

Stolorow, R. D., and Lachmann, F. M. (1980). *Psychoanalysis of Developmental Arrests: Theory and Treatment*. New York: International Universities Press.

———— (1984/1985). Transference: the future of an illusion. *Annual of Psychoanalysis* 12/13:19–37.

Stone, M. (1989). Long-term follow-up of narcissistic borderline patients. *Psychiatric Clinics of North America* 12:621–642.

———— (1993). Paradoxes in the management of suicidality in borderline patients. *American Journal of Psychotherapy* 47:255–272.

Strasburger, L. H. (1986). The treatment of antisocial syndromes: the therapist's feelings. In *Unmasking the Psychopath*, ed. W. H. Reid, D. Dorr, J. I. Walker, and J. W. Bonner III, pp. 191–207. New York: Norton.

Strean, H. (1985). *Resolving Resistances in Psychotherapy*. New York: Wiley.

Strupp, H. H. (1974). Some observations on the fallacy of value-free psychotherapy and the empty organism: comments on a case study. *Journal of Abnormal Psychology* 83:199–207.

Strupp, H. H., and Hadley, S. W. (1979). Specific vs. nonspecific factors in psychotherapy. *Archives of General Psychiatry* 36:1125–1136.

Sundland, D. M. (1977). Theoretical orientations of psychotherapies. In *Effective Psychotherapy: A Handbook of Research*, ed. A. S. Gurman and A. M Razin, pp. 189–219. New York: Pergamon.

Svravik, D. M., McCallum, K., and Milan, P. (1991). Developmental, structural, and clinical approach to narcissism and antisocial personalities. *American Journal of Psychoanalysis* 51:423–431.

Tarachow, S. (1963). *An Introduction to Psychotherapy*. New York: International Universities Press.

Truax, C. B. (1967). A scale for the rating of accurate empathy. In *The Therapeutic Relationship and Its Impact*, ed. C. R. Rogers, pp. 555–568. Madison, WI: University of Wisconsin Press.

Twomey, D. (1995). "I am glad I am late." In *Narcissistic Wounds*, ed. J. Cooper and N. Maxwell, pp. 127–136. Northvale, NJ: Jason Aronson.

Tyson, P., and Tyson, R. L. (1990). *Psychoanalytic Theories of Development: An Integration*. New Haven: Yale University Press.

Vaillant, G. E. (1975). Sociopathy as a human process: a viewpoint. *Archives of General Psychiatry* 32:178–183.

———— (1985). An empirically derived hierarchy of adaptive mechanisms and its usefulness as a potential diagnostic axis. *Acta Psychiatrica Scandinavica* 319:171–180.

Vaillant, G. E., and Perry, J. C. (1985). Personality disorders. In *Comprehensive Textbook of Psychiatry/III*, 3rd ed., vol. 2. ed. H. I. Kaplan, A. M. Freedman, and B. J. Sadock, pp. 1562–1590. Baltimore, MD: Williams & Wilkins.

Walant, K. B. (1995). *Creating the Capacity for Attachment*. Northvale, NJ: Jason Aronson.

Waldinger, R. J. (1987). Intensive psychodynamic therapy with borderline patients: an overview. *American Journal of Psychiatry* 144: 267–274.

Waldinger, R. J., and Gunderson, J. G. (1984). Completed psychotherapies with borderline patients. *American Journal of Psychotherapy* 38:190–202.

Webster's Ninth New Collegiate Dictionary (1989). Springfield, MA: Merriam-Webster.

Weinshel, E. M. (1979). Some observations on not telling the truth. *Journal of the American Psychoanalytic Association* 27:503–532.

Weiss, J. (1990). Unconscious mental functioning. *Scientific American* March, pp. 103–109.

West, M., and Keller, A. (1994). Psychotherapy strategies for insecure attachment in personality disorders. In *Attachment in Adults: Clinical and Developmental Perspectives*, ed. M. B. Sperling and W. H. Berman, pp. 313–330. New York: Guilford.

Westen, D. (1989). Are "primitive" object relations really preoedipal? *American Journal of Orthopsychiatry* 59:331–345.

White, M., and Epston, D. (1990). *Narrative Means to Therapeutic Ends*. New York: Norton.

Winnicott, D. W. (1958). *Collected Papers: Through Paediatrics to Psychoanalysis*. New York: Basic Books.

———— (1965). *The Maturational Processes and the Facilitating Environment*. New York: International Universities Press.

———— (1968). *The Family and Individual Development*. London: Tavistock.

Wolf, E. S. (1994). Selfobject experiences: development, psychopathology, treatment. In *Mahler and Kohut: Perspectives on Development*,

Psychopathology and Technique, ed. S. Kramer and S. Akhtar, pp. 65–116. Northvale, NJ: Jason Aronson.

Wright, K. (1991). *Vision and Separation Between Mother and Baby.* Northvale, NJ: Jason Aronson.

Zetzel, E. R. (1971). A developmental approach to the borderline patient. *American Journal of Psychiatry* 127:867–871.

Index